Move Beyond 5

STUDENT'S BOOK

macmillan education

Robert Campbell
Rob Metcalf
Rebecca Robb Benne

	LISTENING & VOCABULARY	GRAMMAR (2)	LANGUAGE & BEYOND	SPEAKING	WRITING
	Leaving home ***Recognize informal speech*** **Vocabulary (2):** Adjectives for describing objects	Past tenses review ***Talk about past actions***	Get organized ***Collaborate to organize a group activity***	Invitations ***Make and react to invitations***	A special object (description) ***Make a writing plan***
	Around the world ***Listen for the information you need*** **Vocabulary (2):** Travel	The future ***Talk about events in the future***	Respect others ***Respect other people's personal space***	At the airport ***Check in at the airport***	Wish you were here (postcard) ***Use correct verb tenses***
	Talking music ***Transfer spoken information to a table*** **Vocabulary (2):** Adverbs of degree	Comparison of adverbs ***Compare how people do things***	Get organized ***Stay on task and avoid distractions***	My sister thinks … ***Present other people's opinions***	My music profile (profile) ***Link contrasting ideas***
	Back from the future ***Use stress and intonation to help you understand*** **Vocabulary (2):** Extreme adjectives	Second conditional ***Talk about imaginary situations in the present and future*** PRONOUNCE Stressed words and phrases	Know yourself ***Decide what's important to you***	Do you mind? ***Make and react to requests***	A poem about true friends (poem) ***Use a dictionary***
	The power of color ***Follow a conversation*** **Vocabulary (2):** Color idioms	*(In order) to … , so (that) …* ***Talk about the purpose of doing things***	Communicate & cooperate ***Recognize nonverbal communication***	At the pharmacy ***Ask for help with words at the pharmacy***	A place I really like (description) ***Link similar ideas***

UNIT 1 LIFE STAGES

IN THE PICTURE Special days

>>> Talk about special days in your life

WORK WITH WORDS

1 RECALL **Work in pairs. Do the tasks. You have three minutes.**

a Match the stages of life to the photos (1–10). Some photos match more than one word or phrase.

___ baby ___ child ___ teenager ___ college student
___ young adult ___ adult ___ parent

b Complete the sentences with the words or phrases in the box. Then match them to the photos.

middle-aged person senior

1 A ______________ is old enough to stop working and receive money from the government. Photo ___
2 A ______________ is about 40 to 60 years old. Photo ___

2 Match the photos (1–10) to the actions in the box.

Go on a first date – 4

get a driver's license get a job get married go on a first date go to college have children leave home retire start school vote

3 01 **Listen and check your answers.**

4 a 02 PRONOUNCE **Listen and repeat the words. Pay attention to the /e/ and /eɪ/ sounds.**

/e/ get /eɪ/ stage

b 03 **Listen and circle the words with the /e/ sound. Underline the words with the /eɪ/ sound. Then listen and repeat.**

age baby date friend Net

5 a Complete sentences 1–6 with verbs from Exercise 2. Then guess the ends of the sentences.

b 04 **Listen and check your answers.**

1. The average age to ______________ married in the USA is ***18–21 / 26–28 / 29–31***.
2. Children in Finland don't ______________ school until they're ***7 / 8 / 9***.
3. In Brazil and Austria, you can ______________ in an election when you're ***14 / 16 / 17***.
4. In Venezuela, you can't ______________ a driver's license until you're ***16 / 18 / 20***.
5. In Latin America, young people often ______________ on a date with ***groups of friends / their parents / their grandmothers***.
6. The average family in Colombia ______________ ***3.9 / 4.5 / 6.7*** people.

SPECIAL DAYS
because every day is special

1

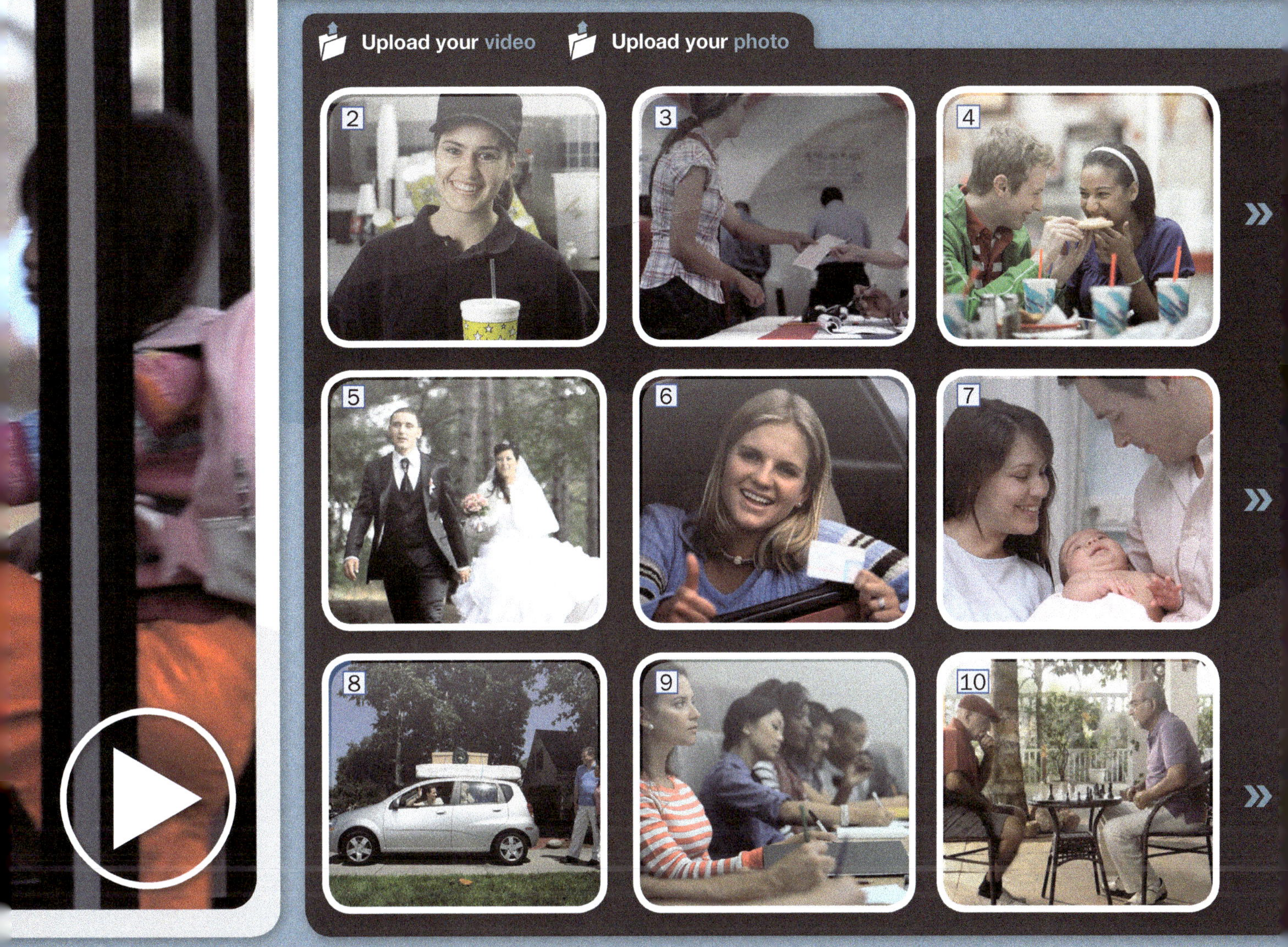

6 **THE MOVING PICTURE** Watch the video. Describe the people. What are they doing?

SPEAK

7 Work in pairs. Ask and answer the questions.

This week's survey:
AGE AND EXPERIENCE

1 In your country, when can you …

start and finish school? ______
get a driver's license? ______
vote? ______

2 When do people in your country usually …

go on a first date? ______
leave home? ______
get married? ______
have children? ______

Workbook, page 80

PHRASE BYTES

You can … at … / when you're …
You can't … until …
People usually … in their twenties / thirties / forties.

MOVE BEYOND

Do the Words & Beyond exercise on page 69.

READING Coming of age

»» Find specific information

SPEAK AND READ

1 Work in pairs. Answer the questions about *coming of age* – the age when a person becomes an adult.

1. At what age do people come of age in your country? Is it the same for boys and girls?
2. What do people do to celebrate their coming of age where you live?
3. What other coming-of-age traditions do you know about? Where are they celebrated?

2 (▶05) Read the texts and answer the questions.

1. Who wrote the texts?
2. Do they mention your country, or a country you talked about in Exercise 1?

3 a Read the tips in the HOW TO box.

HOW TO
find specific information

- ☐ Don't read all of the text.
- ☐ Are there headings? Use them to find the information you need.
- ☐ Read the beginning of each paragraph. Does it have the information you need? If not, read the next paragraph.
- ☐ Look for words connected to the information you need.

b Complete the table with information about all three texts. If a text doesn't include the information, write *doesn't say*.

COMING-OF-AGE TRADITIONS AROUND THE WORLD

We did some research about traditional coming-of-age celebrations and rituals around the world. This is what we discovered. We hope you enjoy reading about them. **Class 3B**

Seijin no Hi
In Japan, the second Monday in January is Seijin no Hi – "Coming-of-Age Day." It's a celebration for girls and boys who have turned 20 in the last year. A 20-year-old is considered an adult and can therefore vote. First there's a ceremony at the local city offices called Seijin-Shiki, and then a party with friends and family. Girls wear a special kimono and boys often wear suits. In the photo above, the girls are wearing traditional kimonos.

Satere-Mawé
The Satere-Mawé tribe in Brazil uses the bullet ant in their coming-of-age ritual. If this ant bites you, it hurts more than any other insect bite in the world, and it continues to hurt for 24 hours. During the ritual, boys have to wear gloves with hundreds of ants in them for 10 minutes, and they mustn't scream. They have to do this 20 times over the coming months or years. Some boys start the ritual when they're just 12.

Quinceañera
A quinceañera is a coming-of-age party for girls on their 15th birthday in many Latin American countries. The girls usually wear a beautiful dress and a crown. The celebration starts with a church ceremony. Then there's a big party. The birthday girl may get a present called *la última muñeca* (the last doll). She dances with it, then she gives it to a younger girl. She's now an adult and can go on her first date.

COMING-OF-AGE CELEBRATIONS AND RITUALS AROUND THE WORLD

Name	Type Party? Ritual?	Boys/Girls	When	Age	Clothes	Activities
Seijin no Hi	*ceremony*		*Second Monday in January*			

4 Which tips in the HOW TO box did you use for help with Exercise 3b? Check (✓) them.

REACT

5 Work in pairs. Discuss these questions.

1. Are you familiar with any of the traditions above? If so, is the description a true reflection of what happens? If not, what else would you like to know about them?
2. What do you think of each tradition? Why?

MOVE BEYOND

Test your memory. Choose a ritual and write down what you remember about it. Then read the text again to check your notes.

»» Workbook, page 81

GRAMMAR Present tenses review

>>> Talk about present actions

READ AND LISTEN >>> Grammar in context

1 06 **Read and listen to the conversation. Where are the girls? What are they doing?**

Miyu: What are these girls doing?
Tina: They're probably at a Sweet 16. It's a typical coming-of-age party here in the USA.
Miyu: What do people usually do at a Sweet 16?
Tina: They do different things. This girl is celebrating with friends. They aren't wearing special clothes because the party is informal. My sister wants a big formal party. She's preparing for it right now, and she talks about it every day. The problem is, I don't think we can afford a big party.

STUDY

2 a Underline nine examples of the simple present in the conversation in Exercise 1 and circle four examples of the present progressive.

b Complete the examples. Use Exercise 1 to help you.

Simple present

Use the simple present for habits, routines, and things that are generally true. Use time expressions such as *usually, never, from time to time,* and *every day.*
What do people ______ do at a Sweet 16?

Present progressive

Use the present progressive for actions in progress now or around now. Use time expressions such as *now* and *right now.*
She's preparing for the party ______.

Stative verbs
Don't use these verbs in the present progressive:
like, need, want (for preferences)
know, understand (for thoughts and opinions)

See GRAMMAR DATABASE, page 64.

PRACTICE

3 07 **Choose the correct options to complete the conversation. Then listen and check.**

Miyu: Why (1) ***do they paint*** / ***are they painting*** this girl's face?
Tina: I (2) ***don't know*** / ***'m not knowing*** a lot about Native American traditions, but I think she (3) ***'s preparing*** / ***prepares*** for the Sunrise Dance. It's a coming-of-age ceremony for Apache girls.
Miyu: So (4) ***do the girls dance*** / ***are the girls dancing*** when the sun comes up?
Tina: I'm not sure, but I know that the ceremony (5) ***lasts*** / ***'s lasting*** for four days and that the girls (6) ***dance*** / ***are dancing*** for hours each day. So it's a very difficult physical test.

4 Complete the questions with the simple present or present progressive form of the verbs.

1 What *are you studying* (you / study) at school these days?
2 ______ (you / think) that your classes prepare you well for adult life?
3 What clothes ______ (most teenagers / wear) right now?
4 ______ (adults / usually / wear) these kinds of clothes?
5 At what age ______ (a person / really / become) an adult?
6 Think of an adult you know well. What ______ (they / do) right now?

SPEAK

5 Work in pairs. Ask and answer the questions from Exercise 4. Ask each other for examples, details, and reasons.

In math class, we're studying geometry.

>>> Workbook, pages 82–83

Recognize informal speech

SPEAK AND LISTEN

1 Work in pairs. Answer the questions.

1. Describe the things in the photos.
2. Do you own any similar things? Describe them.
3. What do you do with things when you stop using them?

2 ▶08 Aidan is leaving home. Listen to the conversation with his sister, Katie. Put the photos in order.

3 ▶08 Listen to the conversation again and decide if the sentences are correct (*C*) or incorrect (*I*).

1. Aidan's father gave him the phone. ____
2. The soccer jersey is big. ____
3. Uncle Harry gave him the jersey on his eighth birthday. ____
4. Katie thinks the action figure is worth a lot of money. ____
5. Katie wants to keep Aidan's CDs. ____
6. She says she likes Aidan's music. ____

4 a Read the tips in the HOW TO box.

b ▶09 Listen to the excerpts from the conversation and complete them with words from the HOW TO box. Then find five contractions.

HOW TO

recognize informal speech

- Listen for contractions (*don't* = *do not*).
- Listen for informal forms (*dunno* = *don't know*, *kinda* = *kind of*, *stuff* = *things*, *ya* = *you*, *yeah* = *yes*).
- Listen for fillers (*hey*, *so*, *um*, *you know*).

Katie: Look at this. It's enormous.
Aidan: (1) ________ , don't laugh. That was my first cell phone. It's (2) ________ … (3) ________ …
Katie: Colorful?

Katie: So if it's special, why are you throwing it away?
Aidan: I (4) ________ . I have too much (5) ________ . I can't keep everything.
Katie: (6) ________ … see (7) ________ .
Aidan: (8) ________ . See ya.

REACT

5 Work in pairs. Answer the questions.

1. Do you think Katie is going to miss Aidan? Why or why not?
2. Which thing might Aidan decide to keep? Why?

WORK WITH WORDS

6 ▶10 When you use more than one adjective before a noun, the adjectives go in the order listed in the table. Complete the table with the adjectives in the box. Then listen and repeat.

antique colorful cotton enormous old
old-fashioned plastic red round ~~special~~
square tiny unusual useful valuable

Opinion	Size	Age	Shape	Color	Material	
____	____	____	____	____	____	+ noun
____	____	____	____	____	____	
____						
____						
special						

SPEAK

7 a Think of an interesting present you gave and one you received. Write a few sentences describing each present. Use more than one adjective.

For my fourth birthday, my mother made an amazing chocolate cake. It was enormous.

b Work in pairs. Talk about your presents.

MOVE BEYOND

Do the Words & Beyond exercise on page 69.

Workbook, pages 84–85

GRAMMAR Past tenses review

>>> Talk about past actions

READ AND LISTEN >>> Grammar in context

1 (11) **Read and listen to the conversation. What kind of object are they talking about?**

George: Where did you get this?
Megan: My dad bought it for me while we were staying in New York.
George: What were you doing that day?
Megan: We were going to Central Park. We were walking down the street when I saw it in a store window. I didn't know how to play it, but I found some videos on the internet. Mom and Dad weren't very happy.
George: Why not?
Megan: Because I played it all the time, and it sounded terrible.

STUDY

2 Complete the explanations. Use Exercise 1 to help you.

Simple past

Use the simple past for completed actions in the past.
Regular past verbs add *-ed* to the base verb.
I ____________ it all the time, and it ____________ terrible.
Irregular past verbs change in form. See page 74.
My dad ____________ it for me.

Past progressive

Use the past progressive for actions in progress in the past.
We ____________ to Central Park.
Use the simple past for actions that interrupt an action in progress.
We ____________ down the street when I ____________ it in a store window.

See GRAMMAR DATABASE, page 64.

PRACTICE

3 Choose the correct options to complete the description.

Megan (1) ***met*** / ***was meeting*** George while she (2) ***visited*** / ***was visiting*** New York. They soon (3) ***became*** / ***were becoming*** good friends, and George (4) ***occasionally went*** / ***was occasionally going*** to Boston to see Megan. One day George and Megan (5) ***sat*** / ***were sitting*** in her room when he (6) ***saw*** / ***was seeing*** the harmonica.

4 (12) **Complete the conversation with the simple past or past progressive form of the verbs. Then listen and check your answers.**

Megan: Mom, I can't find my harmonica.
Mom: When (1) ____________ you ____________ (see) it last?
Megan: I (2) ____________ (see) it last week while George (3) ____________ (visit). We (4) ____________ (talk) when he (5) ____________ (notice) it on my desk. He tried to play it.
Mom: Maybe George (6) ____________ (put) it in your desk drawer while you (7) ____________ (help) me in the kitchen.
Megan: I don't think so. Wait ... I remember now. I (8) ____________ (see) it later the same day while I (9) ____________ (do) my homework. I (10) ____________ (put) it in my desk drawer so I wouldn't lose it.

5 Write the questions using the simple past, past progressive, or both, if necessary.

1 What / you / lose? *What did you lose?*
2 When and where / you / lose / it?
3 What / you / do / when / you / lose / it?
4 How long / you / look / for it?
5 While / you / look / for it, / other people / help / you?
6 you / ever / find / it?

6 Think of something you lost in the past. Write answers to the questions in Exercise 5.

I lost my ...

SPEAK

7 Work in pairs. Talk about things you've lost. Use your answers in Exercise 6 to help you. Ask questions for more information and make notes.

Can you describe it? What did it look like?

What happened next?
And then what happened?

Do you still have ... ?

>>> Workbook, page 86

LANGUAGE & BEYOND

What do you think about group work? To find out, decide which option you think is better, A or B.

1. A An activity is more fun if everybody helps organize it.
   B It's not important who does the work. The important thing is the result.
2. A Some people have ideas, and other people are workers.
   B It's good to hear other people's ideas and add to them.
3. A It's best if one person makes the decisions for everybody.
   B Voting is the best way to make decisions if people don't agree.
4. A Giving people specific jobs makes it easier to organize an activity.
   B Groups work best if people are free to do what they want.

>>> Collaborate to organize a group activity

SPEAK AND READ

1 Work in pairs. Answer the questions about the last time you worked with others to organize an activity.

1 What did you organize?
2 Who did you work with?
3 Who had the most ideas? Who did the most work?
4 What part of the organizing went well? What was hard?

2 Take the survey above about organizing activities.

3 Compare your answers in groups. Which options did most people choose?

4 Make a list of tips for organizing a group activity. Then compare your list with the tips on page 75. What differences are there?

PHRASE BYTES

When should we have ... ?
Why don't we ask ... ?
We could all bring ...
How about making ... ?
Does everyone agree?
Let's vote on it.

DO

5 Work in groups. You're organizing a sale of secondhand things to make money for a school trip. Work together to do the following things:

- choose a day for the sale
- find a place for the sale
- decide how to collect the things to sell
- think about how to advertise the sale
- calculate how many people need to work at the sale
- decide who is going to do the different jobs

6 Tell the class about your decisions.

REFLECT

7 Discuss the questions with your class. Do you agree with the REFLECTION POINT?

1 Which tips from Exercise 4 did you use when you planned your sale?
2 Which tips were easy to follow? Which were harder?
3 Do you think you worked well as a group? Why or why not?

REFLECTION POINT

Group activities are more successful when everybody contributes ideas, has a specific job to do, and does an equal share of the work.

EXTEND

8 Work in groups. Plan your school trip. Decide where to go and what needs to be done. Then give everybody a job to do.

GET ORGANIZED

Workbook, page 89

SPEAKING Invitations

Make and react to invitations

SPEAK

1 Work in pairs. Answer the questions.

1 When was the last time you received a party invitation?
2 Did you go to the party? If so, was it good?
3 Look at the invitation to the right. Would you like to go to Ethan's party? Why or why not?

LISTEN

2 13 Listen to the conversations. Who can't come to the party? Why not?

Ethan: Hi, Alice. (1) ________ come to my birthday party?
Alice: When is it?
Ethan: It's next Saturday, the 6th. I'm having a barbecue.
Alice: Sure. That sounds great. Thanks for inviting me.
Ethan: Great. See you there!

Ethan: Hey, Leo. I'm having a birthday party next Saturday. (2) ________ free?
Leo: I'd love to come, but I can't. I'm visiting my grandparents that day.
Ethan: That's too bad.
Leo: Yeah, but thanks for the invitation!

Ethan: Max, (3) ________ like to come to my birthday party?
Max: Yes, I'd love to. When is it?
Ethan: It's next Saturday.
Max: I'm sorry, but I can't. I'm going to a barbecue in Wilson Park.
Ethan: A barbecue in Wilson Park?
Max: Yeah. Alice is going, and she invited me.
Ethan: Max, that's my party!
Max: Really? Well, I guess I'll see you there!

3 13 Complete the questions in the conversations. Then listen again and check.

4 14 Listen and repeat the invitations.

5 a Underline the following sentences in the conversations. Write the sentences below.

Two ways to accept an invitation:
1 ________ 2 ________
Two ways to refuse an invitation:
3 ________ 4 ________
Two ways to say "thank you" for an invitation:
5 ________ 6 ________

b 15 Listen and check. Then listen and repeat.

ACT

6 Write an invitation to a party that you're organizing. Use Ethan's invitation to help you.
– Student A: Think of a party and invite Student B.
– Student B: Find out the day of the party. Accept or refuse the invitation.

7 Work in pairs. Write your own conversation. Then present it to another pair.

PHRASEBOOK 16

Make an invitation
Can you come to … ?
Would you like to come to … ?
I'm having a … on …
Are you free?

Accept an invitation
Sure. That sounds great.
Yes, I'd love to.
Thanks for inviting me.

Refuse an invitation
Sorry. I'd love to come, but I can't. I'm visiting / going to …
I'm sorry, but I can't come. I have / need to …

Workbook, page 87

WRITING A special object

Make a writing plan

b

SPEAK AND READ

1 Work in pairs. Describe and compare the elephants in the photos. Which do you like best? Why?

2 Read Jessica's description. Which elephant is she describing? What does Lucy's elephant look like?

a

My special object

I'm looking at my special object now. It's a small, black, wooden elephant. It's standing on a shelf in my room with some books and photos. I got the elephant while I was staying with my friend Lucy in Chicago. We were walking through an antique market one day when she saw two elephants. She said they were best friends like us. They weren't expensive, so we bought both of them. I kept one elephant, and Lucy kept the other. People say that elephants never forget. When I see my elephant, it reminds me of that summer and my friend. It's a nice feeling to know that Lucy has an identical elephant.

@ SEND TO TEACHER

c

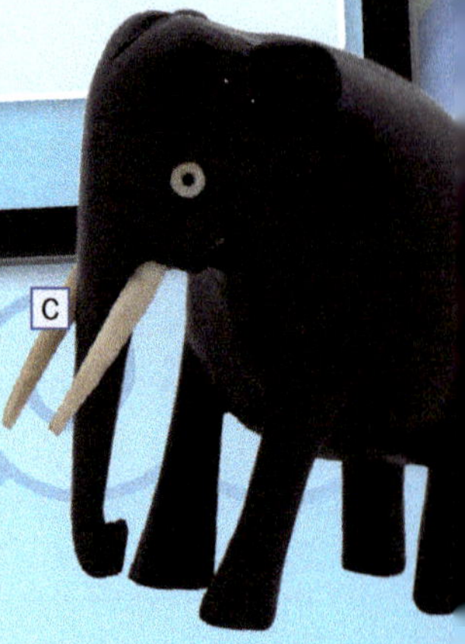

3 a Read the tips in the HOW TO box.

HOW TO

make a writing plan

- Write a heading for each subtopic in your paragraph.
- Write short questions for each subtopic.
- Make notes of the answers to your questions.

b Look at Jessica's writing plan. Did she follow all of the steps and answer all of the questions? Underline the answers to the questions in Jessica's description.

A description of a special object

1 Description – Describe the special object. ☐
What is the object? Is it new or old? What is it made of? Where do you keep it?

2 History – Explain the object's history. ☐
How and when did you get it? Is the object connected to a place or person?

3 Importance – Say why it's special. ☐
What do you think about when you see the object? How does it make you feel?

PRACTICE

4 Correct the order of the steps in this writing plan. Then write a question for each section.

A description of a special photo

☐ Importance: ______

☐ Description: ______

☐ History: ______

DISCUSS

5 Discuss an object that's special to you.

WRITE

6 Write a description of a special object, but don't say what the object is.

1 Answer the questions in the writing plan and write a detailed description of the object. Use complete sentences. Use the tips in the HOW TO box.

2 Use the present tense to describe the object now.

3 Use the past tense as you give the history of the object.

SHARE

7 Read your description to people in your class. Ask your classmates to guess what the object is.

Workbook, pages 88–89

VOCABULARY Special days

1 Tony's 4 years old. Complete his life plan with the words and phrases in the box.

children college driver's license first date high school job married retire school vote

MY LIFE PLAN

- Start (1) ______ next year. Be the best student ever!
- Get my (2) ______ as soon as I'm 16, buy a car, and then go on my (3) ______ .
- Graduate (4) ______ when I'm 18 and go to (5) ______ to get a degree.
- Get a really well-paid (6) ______ when I finish my degree.
- Get (7) ______ on a beach in Hawaii and have five (8) ______ .
- Run for president. Persuade everybody to (9) ______ for me!
- (10) ______ when I'm 50 and spend all day playing golf.

___ /10

Adjectives for describing objects

2 Tony's 16 now. Complete the adjectives in the message to his friends.

Hi, guys!

I need some money to buy a used car, so I'm selling some of my things. Here's a description of what's for sale. Offers welcome!

1 An (1) a______e watch that my great-grandfather gave me. It's broken, so it's not very (2) u______l, and it's too (3) old-f______d to wear, but I think it's made of gold, so it could be (4) v______e.

2 An (5) e______s, brightly (6) c______d (7) c______n carpet. It's (8) s______e in shape, and it was on the floor in my room until recently, but it still looks pretty new.

3 An MP3 player. It's really (9) t______y so you can put it in your pocket. But it has a lot of memory, and it's full of really (10) u______l music – the kinds of songs you never hear on the radio.

___ /10

GRAMMAR Present tenses review

3 Tony's 25. Choose the correct options to complete the conversation.

Stan: Hello? Tony? Is that you?
Tony: Hi, Stan. It's been a long time.
Stan: It has. So what (1) *do you do* / *are you doing* these days?
Tony: Not much. I (2) *don't work* / *'m not working* right now, so I (3) *usually spend* / *'m usually spending* all day at home. I (4) *look* / *'m looking* for a job, but it isn't easy.
Stan: What about Sally? (5) *Do you ever see* / *Are you ever seeing* her?
Tony: No, we're not in touch. I (6) *don't know* / *'m not knowing* where she lives, to be honest.
Stan: That's a shame. She was your first date! But listen, Tony, I (7) *make* / *'m making* dinner right now.
Tony: Oh, OK. I'll call you back later.

___ /14

Past tenses review

4 Tony's 70. Complete his email with the simple past or past progressive form of the verbs.

Hey, Stan!
How are things? I (1) ______ (look) for old friends from high school on the internet, and I (2) ______ (find) your page. The last time we (3) ______ (speak) was over 45 years ago. I (4) ______ (call) you, but you (5) ______ (do) something, and you couldn't talk for long. I remember that you asked me about Sally. Well, I (6) ______ (see) her a few months ago while I (7) ______ (shop) at the mall. She was there with her husband and three adult kids. She (8) ______ (get) married when she was 30. I had no idea! Anyway, get back to me if you have time.
All the best,
Tony

___ /16

Your score: ___ /50

SKILLS CHECK

✓✓✓ Yes, I can. No problem!
✓✓ Yes, I can. But I need a little help.
✓ Yes, I can. But I need a lot of help.

I can find specific information when I read. ______
I can recognize informal speech. ______
I can collaborate to organize a group activity. ______
I can make and react to invitations. ______
I can make a writing plan. ______

Workbook, pages 90–91

UNIT 2

PACK YOUR BAGS

IN THE PICTURE Travel

>>> Talk about travel items

WORK WITH WORDS

1 RECALL **Work in pairs. Do the tasks. You have two minutes.**

a **Make a list of methods of transportation under the headings.**

Air	Rail	Road	Sea
plane	*train*	*bike*	*boat*

b **Complete the sentences with *by* or *to*.**

From Los Angeles .... New York City, it takes five hours .... plane or 42 hours .... car.

c **Match the verbs in the box to the correct methods of transportation.**

drive fly ride sail

You can drive a bus, a …

2 ▶17 **Look at the pictures. Put the items (a–l) in the correct groups. Then listen and check.**

suitcase

luggage/ baggage

personal items

money and documents

3 **a** ▶18 PRONOUNCE **Listen and repeat the words. Pay attention to the /p/ and /b/ sounds.**

backpack brush bag passport shampoo toothpaste

b ▶19 **Listen and circle the word you hear. Then listen and repeat both words.**

1 back / pack 2 beach / peach 3 Ben / pen 4 bear / pear 5 bill / pill

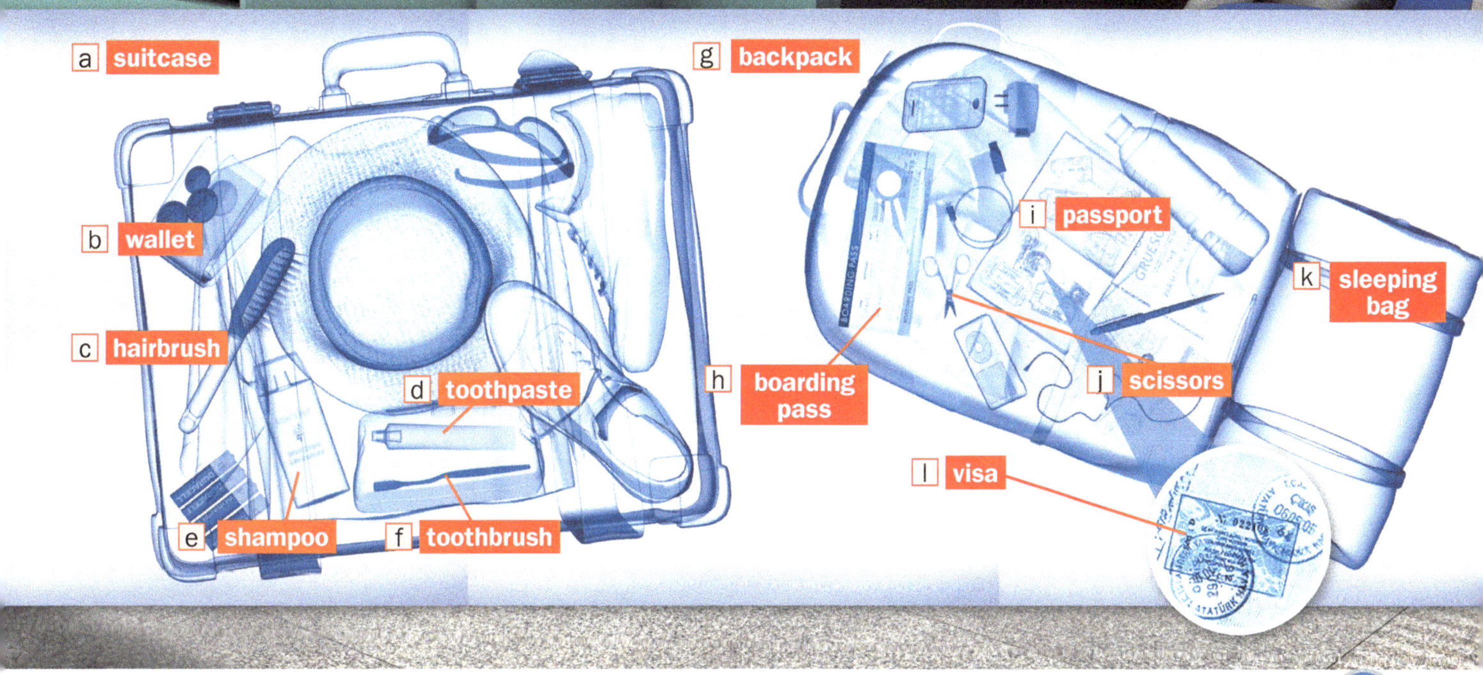

4 **Work in pairs. Describe and guess the objects in Exercise 2.**

You use it to keep your hair neat. *A brush.*

5 **Work in pairs. Look at the pictures again. What other objects are in the backpack and suitcase? Make a list.**

6 **THE MOVING PICTURE** **Watch the video of an airport scanner. Write the names of the items that you see.**

PHRASE BYTES

What about taking / packing … ?

Let's take … / Why don't we take … ?

We definitely need …

I don't think / I'm not sure … is necessary / especially useful.

SPEAK

7 **Work in pairs. You're going on a camping trip in your area.**

- With your partner, decide on the five most important things to pack.
- Look at the pictures for ideas and think of other items.
- Compare your ideas with another pair.

MOVE BEYOND

Do the Words & Beyond exercise on page 70.

Workbook, page 92

READING Be a vacation volunteer

Identify the purpose of a text

SPEAK AND READ

1 Work in pairs. Talk about your best vacation. Answer these questions.

1 Where did you go and who were you with?
2 What kind of vacation was it?
3 Why was it so good?

2 a Read the tips in the HOW TO box.

b 20 Read the first part of the text and identify its purpose.

3 Which tips in the HOW TO box did you use for help with Exercise 2b? Check (✓) them.

HOW TO

identify the purpose of a text

- ☐ Use the headings, layout, pictures, and weblinks to identify the **type of text**.
- ☐ Read the beginning of the text and decide who the readers might be.
- ☐ Identify the **writer** and the **writer's goal** – is it to give information, entertain, or persuade?

VACATION VOLUNTEERS: see the world and change it!

What's a voluntourist?

You know what a tourist is. And you've probably heard of volunteers (people who help others for free). Voluntourists are people who travel to a different place on their vacations to provide aid after a natural disaster or help a local community.

What's Vacation Volunteers?

Since 2001, *Vacation Volunteers* has offered voluntourist programs for 14- to 18-year-old students at home and overseas. For two to four weeks, you can live with a host family and do a program of social or environmental work. All you need is a backpack, your toothbrush, and a positive attitude! We have programs in North and South America, Africa, Asia, Europe, and Australia.

Interested? Click here and read what some of our voluntourists have said.

4 20 Read the voluntourists' stories. Complete the report form for Molly and Alex.

Program report

Area: ____________
Project: ____________
Project length: ____________
How the program has helped you:
____

Molly, 15 (New Zealand)

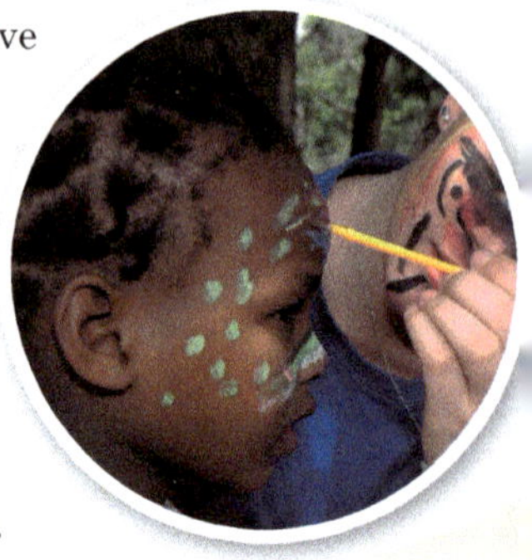

I've just spent four weeks in South Africa. I've been home for a week now, and I haven't gotten used to it yet. I miss everything about South Africa, but especially the people. They were always cheerful and ready to share food or tell stories. I miss the children in the activity center where I worked too. The program gave me the opportunity to experience the world in a new way. I've learned that you don't need a lot of money or material things to enjoy life.

Alex, 16 (USA)

I've never been overseas, and I was a little nervous about traveling outside the USA, so I chose a two-week project in Boston. My team helped elderly people with housework and shopping. It was my first time away from home alone, but I wasn't homesick because I made so many new friends. I can really recommend programs like this. Since the trip, I've felt much more confident. Making a difference as a voluntourist is definitely better than sitting at home!

REACT

5 Work in pairs. Discuss the questions.

1 What helps communities in need more: volunteers or donations of money?
2 As a voluntourist, what kind of program would you choose?
3 Which place, country, or continent would you most like to visit?

MOVE BEYOND

Underline the names of six continents in the text. Which continent is missing?

Workbook, page 93

GRAMMAR Present perfect

»» Talk about how long something has happened

READ »» Grammar in context

1 Read the article. What volunteer activity is the Rawlins family doing and why?

Since 2006, thousands of voluntourists have traveled to New Orleans, USA, to rebuild the city. Hurricane Katrina destroyed 300,000 homes in 2005, and the city hasn't completed rebuilding work yet. The Rawlins family has been in New Orleans for one week.

"We've already finished a playground, and we've just started on a park project," explains Amy Rawlins. "I've never been on a trip like this before," says 16-year-old Elena. "Have you ever worked on vacation? Since we arrived, we've worked for eight hours every day. The weird thing is – I've had a fantastic time!"

STUDY

2 Read the explanations. Then underline examples of the three different uses of the present perfect in Exercise 1.

Present perfect

Use the present perfect for:
1 past actions when the exact time is not mentioned.
2 past actions with *ever/never.*
3 actions in the recent past with *just*, *yet*, and *already.*

Form the present perfect with *have/has* + *(not)* + past participle.

Irregular past participles change in form. See page 74.

3 Underline *for* and *since* in Exercise 1. Then complete the explanations.

Present perfect: with *for* and *since*

Use *for* or *since* to answer the question *How long ...?*
Use .... with specific dates, months, or years.
Use .... with lengths of time.

See GRAMMAR DATABASE, page 65.

»» Workbook, pages 94–95

PRACTICE

4 a Ben wants to be a voluntourist. Complete the interview with the present perfect form of the verbs and the adverbs.

I: (1) .... (you / ever / be) to the USA?
Ben: Yes, I (2) .... (already / visit) Boston on a sight-seeing trip.
I: (3) .... (you / ever / stay) in a tent with 10 people?
Ben: Uh ... no, I (4) .... (never / be) camping. But I (5) .... (sleep) in a sleeping bag at my friend's house.
I: (6) .... (you / ever / work) eight hours in a day?
Ben: No, (7) I .... (not do / that / yet). Um, I think I (8) .... (just / change) my mind ...

b Write your answers to the three questions in Exercise 4a. Use *already*, *not yet*, and *never*.

5 Complete the visitor's form. Write the questions and complete the answers with *for* or *since*.

1 How many years ....?
We've spent our vacations in Orlando *since* I can remember.
2 How many years ....?
We've stayed at the Beach Campsite .... 10 years.
3 How long ....?
We've been here .... Saturday.
4 How many days ....?
We've had good weather .... we came here.
5 How long ....?
I've looked forward to this vacation .... a long time!

WRITE AND SPEAK

6 a Work in pairs. First write five activities you do regularly. Give your list to your partner.

I eat toast for breakfast. I do gymnastics. I go to school with my brother.

b Ask your partner how long he or she has done the activities on the list. Answer your partner's questions.

How long have you eaten toast for breakfast?

For 10 years. / Since I was three.

c Tell the class one interesting thing about your partner.

LISTENING AND VOCABULARY Around the world

Listen for the information you need

SPEAK AND LISTEN

1 Work in pairs. Answer the questions.

1 What are your favorite ways to travel? Why?
2 What are the positive and negative aspects of traveling by boat?

2 Read the beginning of Oscar's blog. Why is he writing a blog?

Hi, I'm Oscar. My family and I are sailing around the world on a two-year voyage in our boat, *Dolphin*. Check me out with the rest of the crew (that's my mom, dad, and my sister, Poppy), and follow our voyage on this blog. I'll probably post some videos too. Enjoy!

3 a Read the tips in the HOW TO box.

b 21 Listen to Oscar's video blog. First listen for the main ideas only and answer the questions. Then listen again and add some details to your answers.

1 What's the family doing now?
2 How does Oscar feel about the trip?
3 At sea, what does he do in the morning?
4 What does he do in the afternoon?
5 Who's Oscar meeting in Brisbane?
6 What are they going to do?

4 Which tips in the HOW TO box did you use for help with Exercise 3b? Check (✓) them.

HOW TO
listen for the information you need

First listen for the main ideas.
- ☐ Don't worry if you can't understand everything.
- ☐ Listen for words you know. They can help you understand important ideas.

Then listen for specific information.
- ☐ Decide what you want to know.
- ☐ Think about the words you might hear.

REACT

5 Work in pairs. What do you think? Tell your partner.

1 What are the good things about living on a boat?
2 What problems are there living in a small space on a boat?
3 Would you like to be homeschooled? Why or why not?
4 Would you like to take a trip around the world? Why or why not?

WORK WITH WORDS

6 22 Complete the map and online ticket with the travel words in the box. Listen and check.

arrival connection delay departure destination fare passenger reservation ~~route~~ seat

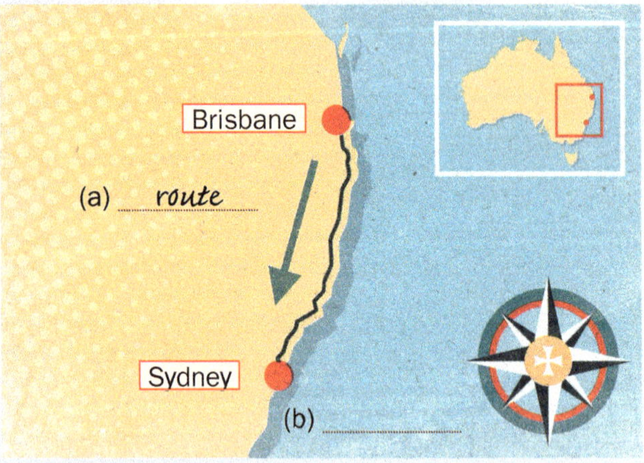

(c) ____________: Brisbane, October 5, 7:30 a.m.
(d) ____________: Sydney, October 5, 9:06 p.m.
(e) ____________s: none (direct train)
Please note that there may be a possible
(f) ____________ because of work at Sydney Central Station.
(g) 4 ____________s (2 adults, 2 children under 16)
(h) 4 ____________s, (i) ____________s: 21, 22, 23, 24 in coach G
Total (j) ____________: $289.52

7 a Make an online ticket like the one in Exercise 6. Change the trip details (destination, arrival and departure times, and the connections). Don't show your ticket to anybody.

b Work in pairs. Ask your partner questions to find out the details of his or her trip and make notes.

MOVE BEYOND
Do the Words & Beyond exercise on page 70.

Workbook, pages 96–97

GRAMMAR The future

»» Talk about events in the future

READ »» Grammar in context

1 Read the chat message. What's an InterRail trip?

DAN: My big sister's starting her InterRail trip on Saturday. Her train to Paris leaves at twelve o'clock, and then she's going to travel around Europe by train for a month.

JUAN: Wow, that'll be amazing. Will she be OK?

DAN: Well, she isn't traveling alone, and my parents will definitely call her every day. So she isn't likely to have any problems.

JUAN: What countries are they going to visit?

DAN: They don't know their final route yet – but it's likely to be a lot! You can travel to 30 countries with an InterRail ticket. They probably won't remember which countries they went to!

STUDY

2 Read the explanations. Then underline an example of each form in Exercise 1.

The future

Form	Use
present progressive	future arrangements
simple present	events on a timetable
be + *going to* + base verb	future plans/intentions
will/won't + base verb + *definitely* = 100% sure + *probably* = 75% sure	predictions
be + *likely to* + base verb	probable events

Place *definitely* and *probably* after *will*, but before *won't*.

My parents will ________ call her every day.

They ________ won't remember which countries they went to!

See GRAMMAR DATABASE, page 65.

PRACTICE

3 23 Felipe and his parents are going on their dream trip on the Ecuador railway from Quito to Guayaquil. Choose the correct options. Then listen and check.

Felipe: We (1) *'ll go* / *'re going* on our trip tomorrow.

Sam: When (2) *does your train leave* / *is your train likely to leave*?

Felipe: In the morning. It (3) *'s arriving* / *arrives* in Cotopaxi National Park for lunch. On the second day, we (4) *'re going to travel* / *'re traveling* through the Avenue of the Volcanoes – the train climbs to over 3,600 meters!

Sam: It sounds exciting. Is it (5) *likely to be* / *being* dangerous?

Felipe: No, it's very safe – well, pretty safe. Only one volcano is active.

Sam: (6) *Are you going to sleep* / *Do you sleep* on the train?

Felipe: No, we aren't. We (7) *'re staying* / *likely to stay* in hotels.

4 Read quotes by students about their plans and dreams. Write the correct future forms.

1 Tomorrow I *'m doing* (do) an audition for a theater school.
2 My judo course ________ (start) next week.
3 Next year I ________ (learn) Japanese.
4 In 10 years I ________ (definitely / be) a pilot.
5 My dream is to be a famous singer, but it ________ (not / likely / come) true.
6 I ________ (probably / get) my driver's license and a car when I'm 17.

WRITE AND SPEAK

5 a Work in pairs. Write three sentences about your plans and dreams using these time phrases. (Don't show your partner.)

1 Next week …
2 In 10 years …
3 Next year …

b Try and predict your partner's future. Write three sentences using your own ideas.

Next week you'll definitely get a good grade on your English test.
In 10 years you'll probably be a musician.
You're not likely to be a teacher.

c Tell your partner your ideas. Then look at your partner's sentences from Exercise 5a. Were any of your predictions correct?

This year you'll make the soccer team.

Yes, I'm definitely going to do that. / Maybe I'll do that. / I'm not sure.

No, I'm not going to do that. / I'm not likely to do that. / No, I probably won't do that.

»» Workbook, page 98

LANGUAGE & BEYOND

Imagine you're in an invisible bubble. This bubble is your personal space – your ideal distance from other people.

The area of the brain that builds this "bubble" is the same area that controls being scared. When you know people well, you allow them to come closer to you. If you don't know people well, you try to leave more space. There are gender differences too. Two girls usually get closer together when they talk than two boys.

Sometimes it's hard to keep a normal distance from people. This often happens when traveling – for example, when you're a passenger on a busy bus or subway, or in line at a ticket office or bus stop. It can also happen at crowded concerts or in an elevator.

Interestingly, personal space is different for different cultures and in different countries. People who live in countries with a large population, like China or India, usually have a smaller personal space. People in North America and northern Europe often need more space than people in South America or Asia.

››› Respect other people's personal space

RESPECT OTHERS

READ

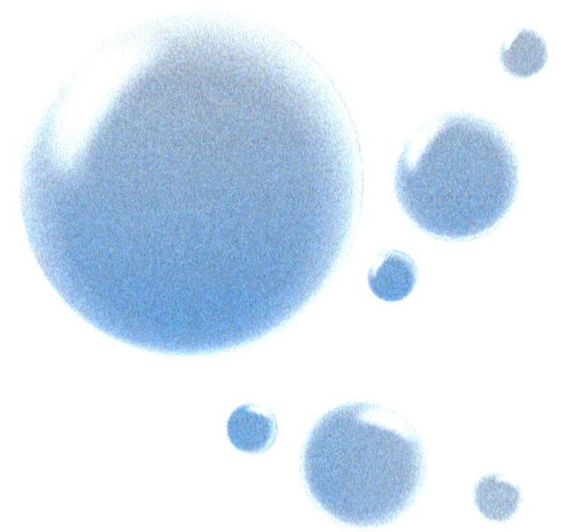

1 Look at the picture to the right. What do you think it shows? Read the article and check.

2 Choose the correct options for you. Compare your answers with your class.

1 I *don't mind* / *like* being in a crowd.
2 I *don't mind* / *like* standing close to somebody in line.
3 I *don't mind* / *like* closed spaces like elevators.

DO

3 Work in groups of three. Do the following task.

1 Two people stand across from each other but pretty far away.
2 Talk about something (free time, your favorite music).
3 Walk slowly toward your partner until you both feel uncomfortable and can't concentrate on your conversation.
4 The third person measures the space between you.
5 Compare your distance with other people in the class.

PHRASE BYTES

I allow my friend / mother / sister to come closer.

I feel annoyed / embarrassed / nervous.

I look at them / move back / say something / shout.

REFLECT

4 Discuss the questions with your class. Do you agree with the REFLECTION POINT?

1 Which people do you allow to come closer to you than other people?
2 How do you feel if somebody comes too close? Think of an example.
3 What do you do if people come too close? Do you say anything?

EXTEND

5 a 24 Listen to the sentences about areas of personal space. Write *agree*, *disagree*, or *not sure* for each sentence.

b Work in pairs. Compare your answers and explain any differences.

REFLECTION POINT

Different people have different ideas about personal space. Protect your own space and respect other people's space.

››› Workbook, page 101

SPEAKING At the airport

Check in at the airport

SPEAK

1 Answer these questions.

1 What's the closest airport to your town or area?
2 What's the best way to get to the airport from your home?
3 How many times have you been to an airport? Did you go there to meet people or fly?

2 Match the airport signs (a–f) to the correct activities (1–6).

1 Planes land at this part of the airport. e
2 Planes take off from this part of the airport. ......
3 You board the plane here. ......
4 You get your boarding pass here and/or check your bags. ......
5 Somebody checks your passport before you enter a country here. ......
6 Somebody sometimes checks your bags after your flight here. ......

LISTEN

3 25 Listen to the conversation. Where's Bella? What other airport places are mentioned?

Bella: Hello, I'd like to check in for the flight to Rome.
Agent: Can I have your passport, please?
Bella: Yes. Here you go.
Agent: How many bags are you checking?
Bella: One suitcase.
Agent: Do you have any carry-on bags?
Bella: I have a backpack.
Agent: OK, that's fine. Do you have any sharp objects in there?
Bella: Sorry, I don't understand. Could you repeat that, please?
Agent: Do you have any sharp objects in your carry-on bag? Scissors, knives, anything like that?
Bella: Uh, yes, I have some scissors.
Agent: I'm sorry, you'll have to put those in your suitcase. Here's your boarding pass. Departures are upstairs.
Bella: Which gate number is it?
Agent: You board at Gate 30.
Bella: Sorry, I didn't hear that. Can you say that again, please?
Agent: Gate 30. Have a good flight.

4 26 Underline sentences in the conversation for 1–4 below. Listen and check. Then listen and repeat.

1 you want to check in
2 you give something to somebody
3 you talk about carry-on bags
4 you ask about the gate

5 a Read the tips in the HOW TO box.

b 27 Complete the phrases from the conversation. Listen and check. Then listen and repeat.

1 Sorry, I don't ...
2 Sorry, I didn't ...
3 Could you ... ?
4 Can you say ... ?

ACT

6 Work in pairs. One student is at the check-in desk, and the other student wants to check in. Decide where you're flying to, how much luggage you have, and if you have sharp objects. Prepare and act out a scene.

HOW TO

check that you understand

- Say you didn't hear or don't understand.
- Ask the other person to repeat the information.
- Be polite: use *sorry* and *please*.

PHRASEBOOK 28

Check in at the airport

I'd like to check in (for) ...
Here you go.
I have a backpack / suitcase.
Where are Departures?
Which gate number is it?

Check that you understand

Sorry, I didn't hear that. Can you say that again, please?
Sorry, I don't understand. Could you repeat that, please?

Workbook, page 99

WRITING Wish you were here

Use correct verb tenses

SPEAK AND READ

1 Work in groups. Answer the questions.

1 Why do people usually write postcards?
2 Who do you receive postcards from?
3 Who do you send postcards to?

2 Read Vicky's postcard. Check (✓) the correct pictures on the front.

Dear Marco,

We've been in Spain for three days now, and I'm having a fantastic time! The trip was terrible – our flight had a three-hour delay. I was getting really tired of waiting in the airport. Then we missed our connection, of course, because of the late departure.

But our campsite is fantastic! There's a huge swimming pool, a game room, and a lot of sports like mini golf and table tennis. The weather isn't bad, but it's a little cloudy. Yesterday we rented bikes and rode along the coast. Then we went to an excellent restaurant. The food here is so delicious! Tomorrow we're taking the train into Barcelona, and we're going to do some sightseeing. I think it'll be exciting.

Wish you were here!

Vicky

3 a Read the tips in the HOW TO box.

HOW TO
use correct verb tenses

- Decide if the action is past, present, or future.
- Look at the rules for past, present, and future tenses in Units 1 and 2.
- Use the correct tense with the correct time words (*yesterday*, *tomorrow*, *right now*, *for two years*, *always*).

b Underline examples of seven different tenses in the postcard.

PRACTICE

4 Write the sentences in another postcard in the correct tense. Use the HOW TO box to help you.

1 We .... (get) here five days ago.
2 I .... (play) tennis here every day.
3 I .... (not play) computer games since we got here.
4 We .... (watch) a show later tonight.
5 It .... (rain) today.
6 I hope it .... (stop) later.

DISCUSS

5 Imagine you're on vacation now. Talk about the fun activities you've done already and the activities you plan to do.

WRITE

6 Write a postcard to a friend while you're on your imaginary vacation.

1 Describe where you're staying and what you're doing. Use the simple present or present progressive to describe your actions.
2 Use the simple past or past progressive to describe what you did previously on vacation. Use the future with *will* or *be going to* to say what you're planning for the next day.
3 Use the present perfect to describe how long you've been doing an action or an action you've already done. Use the tips in the HOW TO box.

SHARE

7 Take turns reading your postcards to the class. Whose trip sounds the most interesting? Why?

Workbook, pages 100–101

VOCABULARY Travel items

1 Complete the conversation with the correct words.

Teacher: How many bags do you have, Luke?
Luke: Uh, just two big (1) s________ with my clothes and shoes.
Teacher: That's a lot for five days in Lima! Your (2) b________ looks heavy too.
Luke: I have my (3) s________ b________ so I can sleep on the plane. And my (4) t________ and (5) t________ so I can brush my teeth after lunch, my (6) h________, of course, for my hair. Oh, and (7) s________, to wash my hair later. I like to be prepared!
Teacher: OK, everybody, did you all check in online? Good, get your (8) b________ p________ ready. Ping, do you have your (9) v________ for Peru? All right, let's take our baggage to the desk. Remember, no sharp items like (10) s________ in your carry-on bags. Yes, Luke?
Luke: Um, I think I've forgotten my (11) p________ and my (12) w________ with all my money in it.

___ /12

Travel

2 Choose the correct options to complete the travel plan.

Tuesday

Our flight is at 2:25 p.m. Hopefully there will be no (1) delays / fares. Please check in online with your (2) connection / reservation number and choose a (3) seat / destination. We'll meet at the airport an hour before (4) arrival / departure. Please remember not to disturb other (5) seats / passengers during the flight. After our (6) arrival / departure in Lima, we'll get our (7) passenger / connection to our hotel, which is our final (8) delay / destination. We'll take a private bus, which is the quickest and cheapest (9) passenger / route. The (10) reservation / fare for the bus is included in the price of the trip.

Wednesday

Visit to the famous Archeological Museum.

___ /10

GRAMMAR

Present perfect

3 Write the verbs in the present perfect and choose *for* or *since*.

Guide: This vase is the museum's most expensive item. It (1) ________ (be) in the museum (2) for / since I started working here. I (3) ________ (work) here (4) for / since 30 years. (5) For / Since the last two years a rich collector (6) ________ (want) to buy the vase. We (7) ________ (just / decide) to sell it, but the collector (8) ________ (not take) it away yet. Don't touch it, young man!
Luke: Oh, uh … sorry.

___ /16

The future

4 Choose the teacher's next sentence (A or B).

1 It's our last day today.
  A We're flying back home.
  B We're likely to fly back home.
2 We need to be at the airport at 5:00 p.m.
  A The plane leaves at 6:00 p.m.
  B The plane is leaving at 6:00 p.m.
3 You have a free afternoon.
  A You're enjoying it.
  B I hope you'll enjoy it.
4 I've checked the weather for later today.
  A It doesn't rain.
  B It isn't likely to rain.
5 Let's meet at the hotel at 4:00 p.m.
  A We're going to travel to the airport by bus.
  B We travel to the airport by bus.
6 Luke, please make sure you're on time.
  A We aren't waiting for you.
  B We won't wait for you.

___ /12

Your score: ___ /50

SKILLS CHECK

✓✓✓ Yes, I can. No problem!
✓✓ Yes, I can. But I need a little help.
✓ Yes, I can. But I need a lot of help.

I can identify the purpose of a text. ____
I can listen for the information I need. ____
I can respect other people's personal space. ____
I can check in at the airport. ____
I can use correct verb tenses. ____

Workbook, pages 102–103

READ

1 Read the article and decide if the sentences are correct (*C*) or incorrect (*I*).

1 Woolton was part of Liverpool in 1957. ......
2 Paul McCartney met John Lennon after a concert. ......
3 The Beatles were more popular in the past. ......
4 Lennon lived in Mendips when he was an art student. ......
5 Lennon lived in Mendips for a short time with his first wife. ......
6 People have had the opportunity to visit Mendips since 2003. ......
7 McCartney met Lennon before he moved to Forthlin Road. ......
8 Lennon and McCartney met at Paul's house to practice their first songs. ......
9 The tour guides for the two houses live in the houses. ......
10 You can only go into the houses if you're on a National Trust tour. ......

TEST-TAKING TIPS

do a true/false activity

- Read the sentences carefully before you read.
- Look at any pictures that can help you understand the text.
- Read the text carefully and choose the correct answers.
- Check details: if any part of the sentence is false, then it's incorrect.

LIVERPOOL HIGHLIGHTS:

The Beatles' childhood homes

On a summer afternoon in 1957, a group called The Quarrymen gave a concert in a field behind a church in Woolton. Now a suburb of Liverpool, Woolton was a separate village at that time. The same evening, The Quarrymen played again, this time in the church hall. A boy named Paul was in the audience for both performances. While they were setting up for the evening concert, a friend of his introduced him to John, the group's singer. It was the moment when John Lennon and Paul McCartney met for the first time.

Over half a century has passed since that first meeting, but interest in the Beatles, the group they formed together, has not decreased. People from all over the world still come to Liverpool to see where the Beatles lived and played. Two of the most popular destinations are the houses where Lennon and McCartney grew up.

Mendips is the house on Menlove Avenue where Lennon lived from the age of five until he left home to study at Liverpool Art College in the late 1950s. He briefly moved back into the house in the early 1960s with his first wife. Lennon's second wife, Yoko Ono, bought the house in 2003. It was restored and opened to the public the same year. The highlight for Beatles fans is a trip upstairs to the tiny bedroom in the front where Lennon slept.

Paul McCartney's childhood home on Forthlin Road is smaller and simpler. The McCartney family moved into the house in 1955 when Paul was in middle school. It's often referred to as "the birthplace of the Beatles" because this is where Lennon and McCartney practiced their earliest songs. Like Mendips, the house has been restored. Visitors can stand in the McCartney sitting room, with its colorful curtains, antique television, and old-fashioned wallpaper, and imagine how the teenage McCartney lived.

Today custodians live in both houses. Their job is to care for the houses and to show groups of visitors around when they arrive four times a day, five days a week.

If you want to see inside the houses, you have to go on a minibus tour organized by the National Trust. It's important to reserve a place online in advance, because visits are limited to 15 people at a time. It's also important to be punctual. Passengers need to arrive 15 minutes before the minibus departs, and the tour doesn't wait for people who arrive late.

Reading: ______ /10

LISTEN

2 29 **You'll hear an adventure camp organizer talking to a group of teenagers. Listen and write the missing information in the blanks.**

"Goodbye talk" to group

About Adventure Weeks:
- The first Adventure Week was (1) ________ ago.
- Two main objectives for campers:
  Personal: to keep in touch with new friends
  Skills: to learn about (2) ________

Practical things:
- Bus leaves for the airport at 10 a.m.
- We can't wait if you're late.
- Alternative transportation: taxi fare is (3) ________ .
- Print your (4) ________ before you leave.
- Bus to (5) ________ leaves at 11 a.m.

Listening: ______ /10

TEST-TAKING TIPS

listen and complete notes

- Read the information carefully before you listen.
- Decide what kind of information is missing.
- Listen for the words before the missing information.
- Write the exact words that you hear.

WRITE

3 For each question, complete the second sentence so that it means the same as the first. Use no more than three words.

1 We met when we were in math class in college.
  We met while we ________ math in college.
2 Can you come to our housewarming party?
  Would ________ to come to our housewarming party?
3 We moved into our new house two weeks ago.
  We've lived in our new house ________ .
4 We're still waiting for John to answer our email.
  John ________ our email yet.

______ /4

4 You decide to send a short message to an Australian friend named Neil. Write your message (35–45 words).

- Say if you are having a good week and say why or why not.
- Say what you have done.
- Tell him what you plan to do on the weekend or next week.

______ /6

Writing: ______ /10

TEST-TAKING TIPS

do sentence transformations

- Read the instructions. How many words can you use?
- Read both sentences carefully.
- Decide if the missing words are nouns, verbs, or other parts of speech.
- Check that the meaning is the same and your spelling is correct.

TEST-TAKING TIPS

write a short message or blog post

- Read the task carefully.
- Answer all the questions in the task.
- Use the correct tense(s): past, present, or future.
- Use the correct number of words – count them.

Progress check score ______ /30

UNIT 3

MY MUSIC

IN THE PICTURE Live music

>>> Talk about music and music events

b

c

d

e

f

WORK WITH WORDS

1 RECALL **Work in pairs. Do the tasks. You have three minutes.**

a **Make lists of words. Use the pictures to help you.**

Kinds of music	Instruments	People	Kinds of groups	Places & events
rock	*guitar*	*singer*	*band*	*concert*

b **Match the verbs *listen* and *play* to the correct categories.**

You can listen to rock music/a guitar ...

2 **Match two words to each photo. Add them to the table above.**

audience ~~band~~ brass band conductor flute folk
jazz opera orchestra performance trumpet ~~venue~~

a – band, venue

3 30 **Listen and match the speakers (1–6) to the photos (a–f).**

4 **a** 31 **Use the words in Exercise 2 to complete the sentences. Then listen and check.**

1 The .... is amazing. I've never been to a concert in a place like this with all these hills and rocks. And the .... is performing really well.

2 Thank you for coming to the Newton .... Festival. Now please welcome one of the greatest .... players of all time.

3 I usually perform .... songs ... a mix of old traditional songs and more modern stuff. If I give a good .... , then people give money.

4 I've played the .... since I was 12. I also play the trumpet in the school ....

5 I don't like .... very much, but a friend gave me tickets, and I'm really enjoying it. I think the rest of the .... is having a good time too.

6 The sound of the .... in the concert hall is fantastic. I've seen the .... before, but I've never seen him conduct Beethoven.

b 32 **Listen and repeat the words in Exercise 2.**

5 **a** 33 PRONOUNCE **Listen and repeat the words. Pay attention to the /ɔ/ and /ɑ/ sounds.**

/ɔ/ hall /ɑ/ opera

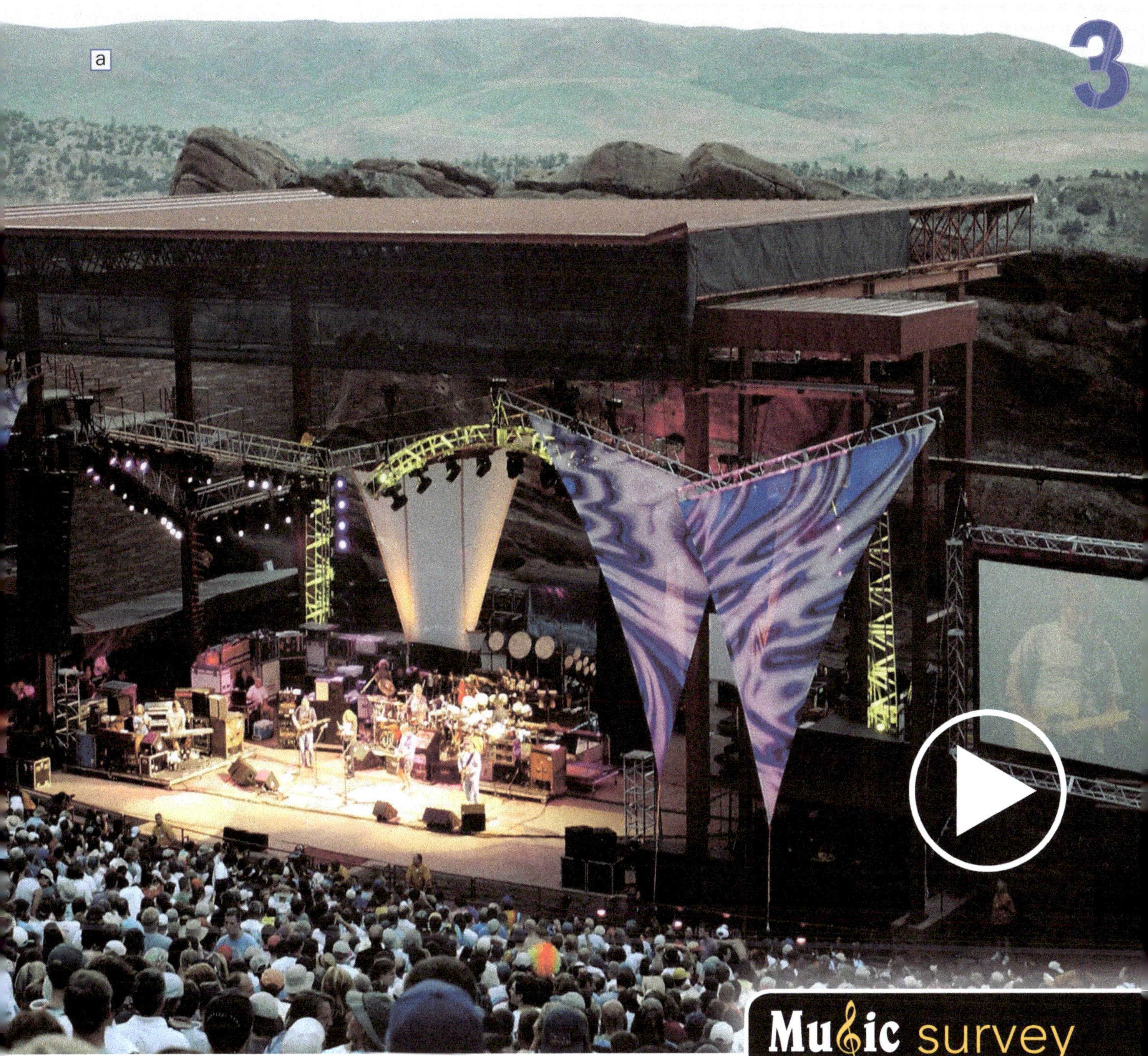

b 34 **Listen and circle the words with the /ɔ/ sound. Underline the words with the /ɑ/ sound. Then listen and repeat.**

stop audience concert song modern lost

6 **THE MOVING PICTURE** **Watch the video. Work in pairs. Describe what you see. What kind of performance is it?**

7 **Complete a music survey. Student A looks at the music survey on page 75. Student B looks at the music survey to the right. Answer the questions in your music survey.**

Music survey

1. Which music genres do you like/dislike?
2. When and where do you sing?
3. Have you ever been to a rock concert or music festival?
4. What music venues are there where you live?
5. In your opinion, which is better, going to a live concert or listening to recorded music?

SPEAK

8 **Work in pairs. Ask your partner the questions in your music survey and compare your answers. Make notes of your partner's answers and tell the class one interesting thing about your partner.**

MOVE BEYOND

Do the Words & Beyond exercise on page 71.

Workbook, page 104

READING A dream concert

>>> Understand new words

SPEAK AND READ

1 What kind of concert is in the picture?

2 35 Read the concert program and answer the questions.

1. Why did José Ángel Salazar become famous?
2. Who is the most important person in an orchestra?
3. What does José Ángel want to do in the future?

3 a Read the tips in the HOW TO box.

b Read the text again and try to understand the underlined words.

4 Match the dictionary definitions to the underlined words in the text.

1. *(adj)* knowing about a situation or a fact
2. *(v)* communicate ideas or feelings
3. *(v)* criticize someone for doing something wrong
4. *(n)* the ability to understand something
5. *(v)* performed a short song, dance, or act, hoping to be selected for a play or concert
6. *(n)* movements that communicate a feeling or instruction

5 Which tips in the HOW TO box did you use for help with Exercises 3b and 4? Check (✓) them.

REACT

6 Work in pairs. What do you think? Tell your partner.

1. Why is José Ángel Salazar's story unusual?
2. What characteristics does a conductor need?
3. Would you be a good conductor? Why or why not?

HOW TO
understand new words

- ☐ Identify the part of speech (verb, noun, adjective, adverb).
- ☐ Is there a similar word in your language? Does its meaning help you?
- ☐ Look at the words and sentences before and after the new word.
- ☐ Guess what the new word might mean and check your idea in the sentence.

When José Ángel Salazar was 14 years old, he became the youngest conductor in the world. Born in Nueva Esparta, Venezuela, José Ángel didn't listen to much classical music during his childhood. When he was eight years old, his father and grandfather took him to a brass band concert, and his life changed forever. He stopped going to karate lessons and learned to play the flute. Soon afterward, he decided to learn the violin.

In 2011 José Ángel auditioned to join the Symphony Orchestra of Nueva Esparta, where he continued studying violin and music theory. The following year, he was asked to become the orchestra's conductor. Although conductors usually have their backs to the audience, they are the most important person in an orchestra. Apart from indicating the beat of the music, the conductor interprets how the music is played. He uses different movements, gestures, and expressions to communicate with every individual musician.

There are between 70 and 80 musicians in the Youth Orchestra of Nueva Esparta, and more than half of them are older than José Ángel. "It's hard because I have to find the way to communicate, or sometimes tell off kids who are much older than me," he said in an interview with the *Guardian* newspaper. "Conducting is a wordless language. I have to convey confidence to the musicians in order to get a confident performance back from them … I have to coordinate my body's movements with the music." José Ángel is also aware of the importance of words for a conductor. "I'd like to study languages. I don't want to go on tour and have to use a translator. Or if I'm interpreting Mahler, there are certain criteria, or feelings, that I'd have a better grasp of if I spoke German."

PHRASE BYTES

I think his story is unusual because …

A conductor needs to be / have / be able to …

I would be a … conductor because …

MOVE BEYOND

Read about José Ángel Salazar again and write different questions about the text. Then ask a partner.

>>> Workbook, page 105

GRAMMAR Verbs followed by gerunds or infinitives

>>> Talk about things you enjoy doing

READ >>> Grammar in context

1 Read the advertisement. Would you like to go to The Rock School? Why or why not?

Do you enjoy singing? Are you learning to play the guitar, drums, keyboard, or bass? Do you want to become a rock star? If your answer is "yes" and you'd like to turn your dream into reality, come to The Rock School. At The Rock School you can practice playing music with other young people like you. We love helping talented young people achieve their ambitions. The official school motto is "To inspire kids to rock on stage and in life." If you live in the USA or Mexico, are between eight and 18, and hope to be a rock star, call us now!

STUDY

2 Complete the examples with verbs from Exercise 1.

Verbs followed by gerunds or infinitives

Use a gerund after the verbs *enjoy, practice, don't mind,* and *imagine.*

Do you enjoy ________ ?

Use an infinitive after the verbs *learn, want, would like, hope, plan,* and *decide.*

Do you want ________ a rock star?

Some verbs can be followed by a gerund or an infinitive with little or no difference in meaning. Examples of these verbs are *like, hate, love,* and *prefer.*

See GRAMMAR DATABASE, page 66.

PRACTICE

3 Read Marta's interview. For each sentence, choose the correct option or both options.

Jeff: Why would you like (1) *coming* / *to come* to The Rock School?
Marta: I've always imagined (2) *being* / *to be* famous.
Jeff: Are you learning (3) *playing* / *to play* any instruments or do you want (4) *being* / *to be* a singer?
Marta: I don't mind (5) *singing* / *to sing*, but I prefer (6) *playing* / *to play* the guitar and piano.
Jeff: So what else do you enjoy (7) *doing* / *to do* in your free time?
Marta: I love (8) *swimming* / *to swim*.

4 Complete the text with the correct form of the verbs in the box.

become	give	~~go~~	learn	make	perform

When he was a teenager, Paul Green planned (1) *to go* to college, but he didn't have enough money. A lot of young people in his neighborhood wanted (2) ________ the guitar, so he decided (3) ________ guitar lessons at his home. His classes were popular, and two years later he opened the Paul Green School of Rock Music. It was a place where teenagers could enjoy (4) ________ music and learn (5) ________ in front of an audience. Today there are more than 90 schools in the United States and Mexico. Paul Green hopes he can inspire more young people (6) ________ better musicians.

5 Write the questions. Use the infinitive or the gerund form of the words in blue.

1 Which instruments / you / learn / **play** / right now?
2 Which other instruments / you / would like / **learn** ?
3 you / enjoy / **sing** ?
4 you / like / **perform** / in front of people ?
5 What / you / hope / **do** / in the future ?
6 What other things / like / **do** / in your free time ?

SPEAK

6 Work in pairs. Take turns asking and answering the questions in Exercise 5.

>>> Workbook, pages 106–107

LISTENING AND VOCABULARY Talking music

>>> Transfer spoken information to a table

SPEAK AND LISTEN

1 Work in pairs. Answer the questions.

1 What kind of music do you listen to while you're relaxing?
2 Which music, if any, do you listen to while you're doing these other activities?

doing homework   running (or other exercise)   studying for a test

HOW TO
transfer spoken information to a table

- ☐ Read all the information in the table.
- ☐ Decide what information you need.
- ☐ Listen for the information you need and write notes in the table.

2 a Read the tips in the HOW TO box.

b 36 You'll hear different people talking about the music they listen to. For each person, complete the missing information in the table.

Name	*Marty*	*Jeannine*	*Sergio*	*Sheila*
Activity	(1)	(2)	*studying for test*	(5) ....
Kind of music	*rock music*	*heavy metal*	(4)	*pop songs*
How music helps	*helps him think creatively*	(3)	*helps him get focused*	(6) ....

3 Which tips in the HOW TO box did you use for help with Exercise 2b? Check (✓) them.

REACT

4 Work in pairs. Answer the questions.

1 Which person in the interviews in Exercise 2b is most similar to you? Why?
2 Do you think listening to music could help you study? If so, what would be the best kind of music?

WORK WITH WORDS

5 37 Write the adverbs of degree in the correct column. Listen and check. Then listen and repeat.

a little   a lot   extremely   fairly   incredibly   pretty   really   terribly   totally   very

1 ▪	2 ▪▪	3 ▪▪▪
a little	*a lot*	*extremely*

6 38 Listen to excerpts from the interviews and complete the sentences (1–10) with the adverbs from Exercise 5.

1 It's .... good for your brain.
2 It has a .... steady rhythm of 60 beats a minute.
3 That sounds .... boring.
4 It's .... extreme.
5 It helps me get into the rhythm .... quickly.
6 They're .... good to listen to before a test.
7 They help me get .... focused.
8 He's .... powerful.
9 It doesn't help me work .... better.
10 I find it .... distracting.

WRITE AND SPEAK

7 Work in pairs. Write an answer to the question below. Include at least three adverbs of degree. Then discuss with a partner.

Does music help you do things better?

MOVE BEYOND
Do the Words & Beyond exercise on page 71.

>>> Workbook, pages 108–109

GRAMMAR Comparison of adverbs

››› Compare how people do things

READ AND LISTEN ››› Grammar in context

1 ▶39 **Read and listen to the music teacher. Does he believe that practice is positive?**

"It takes a lot of time and practice to play a musical instrument well. At first, beginners play more slowly than the usual tempo. They try to play as accurately as possible. Later, when they are familiar with the notes, they can play faster and more confidently. Music students sometimes use a metronome to help them keep the tempo. They have to play as quickly as the metronome beat. If they practice longer, they'll improve more quickly. The students who practice the hardest are usually the students who play the most successfully. Students who practice the least often play the worst."

STUDY

2 Complete the examples. Use Exercise 1 to help you.

Comparative and superlative adverbs

Use comparative adverbs to compare how people or things do something.
For one-syllable adverbs, add *-er* to the adverb.
For two or more syllables, use *more* + adverb.
If they practice ______ *, they'll improve* ______ .

Use superlative adverbs to compare actions by more than two people or things.
For one-syllable adverbs, add *-est* to the adverb.
For two or more syllables, use *the most* + adverb.
The students who practice ______ *are usually the students who play* ______ .

Some adverbs have irregular forms:
______ *, best, the best / badly, worse,* ______

3 Complete the examples. Use Exercise 1 to help you.

Comparative adverbs with *as … as*

Use *(not) as* + adverb + *as* to say two people or things do or don't do something the same.
They try to play as ______ *as possible.*
They have to play as ______ *as the metronome beat.*

See GRAMMAR DATABASE, page 66.

PRACTICE

4 Choose the correct options.

1 There were eight top runners in the semi-final, but the American ran *the fastest* / *the most fast*.
2 The Chinese team is performing *well* / *better* than last year.
3 The German isn't swimming *as fast as* / *faster* the Australian.
4 The British team is playing *more carefully* / *most carefully* than the French team.
5 The Mexican has jumped *higher* / *the highest* of all the competitors.
6 He's running *the best* / *as well as* the US champion.

5 ▶40 **Complete the talent show conversation using comparative and superlative adverbs or adverbs that show equality or inequality. Then listen and check.**

Simon: Which of the three singers do you think has performed (1) *the best* (well)?
Millie: Amanda can sing (2) ______ (loudly) than anyone I know.
Simon: That's true. But she doesn't sing (3) ______ (well) as Katy.
Millie: I think Amy sings (4) ______ (beautifully) than the others.
Simon: I disagree. Amy can't sing (5) ______ (high) as Amanda or Katy.
Millie: But she's a star. She's worked (6) ______ (hard) of the three.
Simon: She practices (7) ______ (long) than the others because she needs to.
Millie: But which of them is going to become famous (8) ______ (fast)?

6 Complete the sentences with names to give your opinion.

IN MY OPINION …

1 ______ sings better than ______ .
2 ______ doesn't play ______ (the guitar, soccer) as well as ______ .
3 ______ acts as well as ______ .
4 ______ is the most hard-working student in the class.
5 ______

DO YOU AGREE?

SPEAK

7 Work in pairs. Complete the tasks.

1 Read one of your opinions from Exercise 6.
2 Your partner gives his or her opinion and explains why.

In my opinion, X sings better than Y.

I don't agree. Y sings better than X. X's last album was terrible.

LANGUAGE & BEYOND

Stay on task and avoid distractions

SPEAK AND READ

1 Work in pairs. Read the comic strip. What reasons does Dom give for not finishing his homework?

2 Work in pairs. Think of more possible reasons for Dom not finishing his homework.

PHRASE BYTES

I think he couldn't finish because ...

He was distracted by ...

He was feeling ...

DO

3 Work in groups. Look at the tips for staying on task. Which of the tips should Dom follow?

1 If you don't understand the task – ask.
2 Find a quiet place to work.
3 Work with another person.
4 Make sure you have everything you need to complete the task.
5 Set a time limit for the task.
6 If it's a long task, plan a break after completing part of it.
7 Get some exercise if you're sitting for a long time or feeling bored.
8 Have a snack if you feel hungry.

4 What other things should Dom do to stay on task?

REFLECT

5 Discuss the questions with your class. Do you agree with the REFLECTION POINT?

1 How often do you find it difficult to stay on task? Which tasks are the most difficult?
2 What's similar or different about Dom's homework situation compared to yours?
3 Which of the tips in Exercise 3 do you regularly follow? Which other tips do you think you should follow?

REFLECTION POINT

Learning to stay on task helps you work better at school, at home, and in other areas of life.

EXTEND

6 Work in groups. Look at the jobs below. When is it important for these people to stay on task? Add other jobs to the list.

pilot teacher surgeon electrician

GET ORGANIZED

Workbook, page 113

SPEAKING My sister thinks …

››› Present other people's opinions

SPEAK

1 Work in pairs. Complete the tasks.

1 Individually, write down the names of your top five favorite singers or groups.
2 Compare each other's lists. How many names appear on both lists?
3 What do you think of the other singers or groups on your partner's list?

LISTEN

2 ▶41 Listen to the conversation. What does Veena want to ask Finn's sister?

Veena: What do you think?
Finn: My sister thinks they're great. She has all their (1) ____________ .
Veena: You're lucky. My sister really hates them.
Finn: Why?
Veena: She says they can't sing. She says they're terrible.
Finn: Oh, yeah. A lot of people didn't like their last (2) ____________ .
Veena: People are always saying bad things about them.
Finn: Maybe they're right. My brother says they don't play their (3) ____________ .
Veena: I don't care what other people think. I think they're totally amazing.
Finn: Good.
Veena: So what's your opinion?
Finn: What?
Veena: You've told me what everyone else thinks. What about you? What do you think?
Finn: Honestly? I don't have an opinion.
Veena: Liar. I'll have to ask your (4) ____________ .

3 ▶41 Can you remember the missing words? Listen again to check or complete your answers.

4 ▶42 Listen and repeat. Pay attention to which words are stressed.

1 My sister thinks they're great.
2 My sister really hates them.
3 She says they can't sing.
4 She says they're terrible.
5 People are always saying …
6 My brother says …

5 Work in pairs. Answer the questions.

1 What do you think Finn really thinks of the music?
2 Why doesn't he tell Veena?
3 What do you think Finn's sister will say?

ACT

6 Work in groups of three or four. Complete the tasks.

1 Talk about things you like (music, movies, sports). Find something you have different opinions about.
2 Prepare a scene similar to the one in Exercise 2. Talk about your different opinions and include the opinions of your classmates, friends, or family.
3 Present your scene to another group.

PHRASEBOOK ▶43

Asking for and giving opinions

What do you think (of …)?
What's your opinion?
I think they're great / amazing.
I don't care what other people think.
I don't have an opinion.

Presenting other people's opinions

My sister / brother thinks / says …
My sister really likes / hates …
She says they …
A lot of people …
People are always saying …

››› Workbook, page 111

WRITING My music profile

>>> Link contrasting ideas

SPEAK AND READ

1 **Work in pairs. Look at the man in the photo. What kind of music do you think he plays?**

PHRASE BYTES

He looks like a ...

I think he plays pop / jazz.

2 **Read the music profile to check your answer to Exercise 1.**

I LOVE ROCK MUSIC. However, my music hero is Lang Lang, the Chinese pianist. He grew up in a poor area of Beijing and started playing when he was three years old. His parents thought he would become a famous pianist, but his piano teacher told him he had no talent and should stop playing.

Although his family didn't have much money, they continued to support Lang Lang. He practiced night and day, and by the age of 17, he was a star. Since then he has performed at concerts around the world.

Even though he's a successful classical pianist, some people don't like his playing. Everyone has different ideas about music, of course. In my opinion, however, he's a great player. He also encourages young people to make music.

3 **a** **Read the tips in the HOW TO box.**

HOW TO

link contrasting ideas

- Use *but* to join two parts of a sentence.
- Use *although* and *even though* at the beginning of a two-part sentence.
- Use *however* at the beginning, the middle, or the end of a contrasting sentence.

b **Underline five examples of contrasting ideas in the profile. Which linking word appears twice?**

PRACTICE

4 **Link the sentences using the words in parentheses.**

1. Lang Lang's teacher said he had no talent. He managed to become successful. (although)
2. He grew up in China. When he was 15, he moved to the United States. (however)
3. He normally records classical music. He has also recorded music for video games. (but)
4. He lives a rock star's life. He finds time to help young people play music. (even though)

DISCUSS

5 **Talk about your favorite musicians or bands and why you like them.**

WRITE

6 **Write a profile about a musician or a member of a band you like.**

1. Begin with where and when the person was born. Add interesting facts about how the person became interested in music or when the person became famous.
2. Give your opinion. Include where you first heard this musician and why you like the music. Compare this musician with others that you like. Use comparatives.
3. Contrast your opinion with the opinions of other people. Use *but*, *although*, *even though*, and *however*. What do other people think of your taste in music? Use the tips in the HOW TO box.

SHARE

7 **Read your profile to people in your class. What kind of music and which musicians are the class favorites?**

Workbook, pages 112–113

VOCABULARY Music words

1 Complete the poster with the words in the box.

audience bands brass band conductor flute folk jazz opera orchestra performance trumpet venue

TONIGHT! *Be part of the (1) ________ at the world's most exciting music (2) ________ and enjoy tonight's concert by international superstar Justin!*

January 9

For one night only! A (3) ________ of *Cosi Fan Tutte*, possibly Wolfgang Amadeus Mozart's most famous (4) ________ . With the Chicago Symphony (5) ________ and guest (6) ________ , José Ángel Salazar.

March 5

A night of (7) ________ music, celebrating the music of one of the world's greatest (8) ________ players, Miles Davis.

May 8

Traditional (9) ________ music from England, Scotland, and Wales. Sing along to the old songs and listen to Mary Martyn play the (10) ________ .

June 23 & 24

The annual International (11) ________ competition is back! Come and listen to (12) ________ from 12 different countries compete to win this year's prize.

___ /12

Adverbs of degree

2 Complete the quotes by members of the audience after Justin's concert.

"It was a (1) r________ great concert."
"It was (2) f________ boring at the beginning, but it got a (3) l________ better."
"His band was (4) t________ amazing! And they all look (5) p________ cool."
"I'm (6) e________ happy that I came."
"It wasn't (7) v________ good. I thought Justin gave a (8) t________ bad performance."
"I was (9) i________ lucky to get a ticket. I'm still (10) a l________ surprised.

___ /10

GRAMMAR Verbs followed by gerunds or infinitives.

3 Complete the interview with the gerund (*-ing*) or the infinitive (*to* + verb) form of the verbs.

Interviewer: Are you feeling nervous about the concert?
Justin: No. I love (1) ________ (**come**) to your country. I always enjoy (2) ________ (**play**) here.
Interviewer: Can you tell us about your new album? Is it finished?
Justin: Not yet. We hope (3) ________ (**finish**) the album this summer.
Interviewer: Do you prefer (4) ________ (**work**) in the studio or (5) ________ (**play**) live?
Justin: I really love (6) ________ (**perform**). I like (7) ________ (**be**) with the fans. I'd like (8) ________ (**spend**) my whole life on stage.

___ /16

Comparison of adverbs

4 Complete the news story about Justin's concert with the correct form of the adverbs. Add *as* where necessary.

What has happened to superstar Justin? Two years ago his albums sold (1) ________ (**fast**) than any other pop star. He was the star who worked (2) ________ (**hard**). But at last night's concert he didn't play (3) ________ (**well**) as he did in the past. In fact, he wanted to get off stage (4) ________ (**quickly**) as possible. His fans have waited (5) ________ (**long**) than two years for a new album. If you can hear me, Justin – try (6) ________ (**hard**) next time!

___ /12

Your score: ___ /50

SKILLS CHECK

✓✓✓ Yes, I can. No problem!
✓✓ Yes, I can. But I need a little help.
✓ Yes, I can. But I need a lot of help.

I can understand new words when I read. ________
I can transfer spoken information to a table. ________
I can stay on task and avoid distractions. ________
I can present other people's opinions. ________
I can link contrasting ideas when I write. ________

Workbook, pages 114–115

UNIT 4 VERY IMPORTANT PEOPLE

IN THE PICTURE Relationships

>>> Talk about people you know

WORK WITH WORDS

1 RECALL **Work in pairs. Do the tasks. You have three minutes.**

a Complete the answers with the words in the box.

a small nose | bad-tempered | patient | shy | tall | wavy hair

What's she like?

She's ________ / ________ / ________ .

What does she look like?

She's ________ . *And she has* ________ / ________ .

b Make a list of four other ways to complete each answer.

2 Work in pairs. Take turns describing a person in the photos. Can your partner identify the person?

3 (44) **Listen and match the relationship words to the twelve definitions that you hear.**

___ acquaintance	___ boyfriend/girlfriend	___ classmate
1 close friend	___ enemy	___ friend of a friend
___ guest	___ neighbor	___ old friend
___ online friend	___ relative	___ teammate

4 (45) **Listen and check. Then listen again and repeat the words.**

5 (46) **Louise is talking about people on her relationship tree. Listen and write a relationship from Exercise 3 next to the names. Note their personality too if you hear it.**

Name	Relationship	Personality	Photo
Mel	________	________	________
Nicola	________	________	________
Jack	________	________	________
Matt	________	________	________
Donna	________	________	________

6 (46) **Listen again and match the people to some of the photos.**

7 THE MOVING PICTURE **Watch the video of Alexa making a relationship tree. Make a note of the names of the people and their relationship to her.**

2

7

SPEAK

8 a **Draw your own relationship tree and write the names of at least six people on the leaves. Include people you know very well but also acquaintances or relatives you don't know well.**

b **Work in pairs. Ask and answer questions about the people on your relationship tree.**

MOVE BEYOND

Do the Words & Beyond exercise on page 72.

PHRASE BYTES

Who's this boy / girl with the green eyes / in the blue T-shirt?

His / Her name's … He's / She's a classmate / an online friend.

We met … years ago in / at …

We've known each other since / for …

We keep in touch online / by email.

READING Close friends

Recognize examples

SPEAK AND READ

1 Work in pairs. Answer the questions.

1 What's your definition of a close friend?
2 How many close friends do you think people generally have?

2 47 **Read the article. Match the qualities of a close friendship in the box to the headings (1–5). Also find out how many close friends we have.**

Good company Honesty Respect Support Trust

Best of friends?

How many friends do you have?

The answer, of course, depends on how you define "friend." For instance, if you count everybody you know – relatives, classmates, neighbors, and other acquaintances – the answer could easily be 20, 30, 40, or more. And if you include people you don't usually meet, like online friends, you might have hundreds or even thousands of friends.

What about *close* friends? According to a recent survey, we have fewer close friends than you might think. (Read to the end to find out how many.)

So how can you know who your close friends are? As a general rule, a close friendship should have all of these qualities.

1 ________ A close friendship won't survive unless this quality is present. It means that you accept your close friends the way they are and don't want them to change.

2 ________ We all want to hear nice things about ourselves, but if it's necessary, a really good friend will also tell you things you *don't* want to hear, such as pointing out your mistakes.

3 ________ Close friends are generous with their time. They'll listen patiently if you need to talk and will help if you have a problem. They'll also defend you if other people are giving you a hard time.

4 ________ A close friend is somebody you can share your ideas with. You may not have things like hobbies and interests in common, but your friend will always take an interest in what you do.

5 ________ This could be the most important quality of all. If you tell your friend private information, he or she won't tell anybody else about it. And your friend won't talk about you behind your back.

(The survey says we generally have just two close friends.)

3 a Read the tips in the HOW TO box.

b Underline four words or phrases in the article that come before examples.

c Under two of the headings, the first sentence is an example. Which sections?

4 Which tips in the HOW TO box did you use for help with Exercises 3b and 3c? Check (✓) them.

HOW TO

recognize examples

- ☐ Look at the words after *like* and *such as* in the middle of sentences.
- ☐ Look at the words after *For example* and *For instance* at the beginning of sentences.
- ☐ Look under headings. The first sentence is sometimes an example.

REACT

5 Work in pairs. What do you think? Tell your partner.

1 Are you surprised that we generally have only two close friends? Why or why not?
2 Which two qualities in the article are the most important in a close friendship? Why?

MOVE BEYOND

Think of one more quality of a close friendship. Then write two sentences to explain what the quality is and why it's important.

Workbook, page 117

GRAMMAR First conditional with *if/unless*

>>> Talk about possible situations in the future

READ AND LISTEN >>> Grammar in context

1 (48) **Read and listen to the conversation. Who does Olga want at her birthday barbecue?**

Jay: Are you going to invite Tim to your birthday barbecue?
Olga: I don't know. If I invite Tim, he'll probably argue with Dan. But Bea won't come unless I invite Tim. And what will Tim say if I don't invite him? He's one of my oldest friends.
Jay: If you talk to Tim and Dan, they might stop arguing for one day.
Olga: You're right. I'd really like all three to be there.

STUDY

2 Choose the correct option. Use Exercise 1 to help you.

First conditional with *if/unless*

Use the first conditional to talk about possible situations and their future results.

Use the present tense after *if* and *unless* to indicate the possible situation.
Use *will*, *may*, or *might* to indicate the result.
If you ***talk*** */* ***will talk*** *to Tim and Dan, they might stop arguing for one day.*
Bea won't come unless I ***invite*** */* ***will invite*** *Tim.*
Use *unless* + an affirmative verb to mean the same as *if ... not*.
These sentences have the same meaning:
Dan will come unless Olga invites Tim.
If Olga invites Tim, Dan won't come.

See GRAMMAR DATABASE, page 67.

PRACTICE

3 Complete the second sentence so that it means the same as the first. Use no more than three words. (Contractions count as one word.)

1 I won't enjoy the barbecue if Sabrina doesn't come.
Unless Sabrina comes, I won't enjoy the barbecue.
2 Unless you send invitations, people won't remember when it is.
If ________ invitations, people won't remember when it is.
3 Vincent won't come unless he can bring his girlfriend.
Vincent won't come ________ bring his girlfriend.
4 If you don't invite the neighbors, they may complain about the noise.
________ the neighbors, they may complain about the noise.
5 My parents won't let me have another barbecue if we don't clean up afterward.
My parents won't let me have another barbecue ________ up afterward.
6 I might not have time to clean up unless people help me.
I might not have time to clean up ________ help me.

4 (49) **Choose the correct options to complete the conversation. Then listen and check.**

Olga: I'm going to invite Dan to my barbecue.
Tim: I (1) *don't* / *won't* come if he (2) *'s* / *'ll be* there. He told lies about me.
Olga: If he (3) *says* / *'ll say* he's sorry, (4) *do* / *will* you change your mind?
Tim: But he won't.
Olga: He (5) *says* / *might say* he's sorry if he thinks you (6) *stop* / *'ll stop* being so angry.
Tim: I have a good reason to be angry.
Olga: Yes, but unless you (7) *'re* / *'ll be* more friendly, people (8) *stop* / *will stop* talking to you. And not just Dan.
Tim: OK, you're right. I'll talk to him.

WRITE AND SPEAK

5 Complete the sentences about friends and other relationships with your ideas.

1 If you forget a good friend's birthday ...
2 You won't have many good friends unless ...
3 Unless you make mistakes ...
4 If you're always honest ...
5 People will respect you if ...

6 Work in pairs. Compare your sentences in Exercise 5. Do you agree with your partner's sentences? If not, explain why.

>>> Workbook, pages 118–119.

Use stress and intonation to help you understand

SPEAK AND LISTEN

1 Work in pairs. Look at the picture and answer the questions.

1 Describe the situation. What do you notice about the face in the mirror?
2 The picture represents a story. What do you think happened?

2 a Read the tips in the HOW TO box.

b 50 Listen to a podcast. Were your predictions in Exercise 1 correct?

3 Which tips in the HOW TO box did you use for help with Exercise 2b? Check (✓) them.

HOW TO

use stress and intonation to help you understand

☐ People stress the most important words when they speak. Listen for stressed words.

☐ When people express strong feelings, their voices go up and down more. Listen for these changes.

4 50 Listen again and choose the correct options.

1 The story *is* / *isn't* true.
2 Naomi *heard* / *didn't hear* another person's voice.
3 She *recognized* / *didn't recognize* the face in the mirror.
4 She was suffering from *a common* / *an unusual* condition.
5 She *still remembered* / *didn't remember* that she had a child.
6 Her memory came back *slowly* / *quickly*.

WORK WITH WORDS

5 Match the underlined extreme adjectives in the podcast excerpts (1–10) to the definitions.

1 … amazing real stories.
2 I'd be furious!
3 … she was shocked …
4 … she looked ancient …
5 She looked exhausted …
6 … with huge black bags under her eyes.
7 That's awful.
8 I'd be terrified.
9 That's unbelievable!
10 That really is a fascinating story.

…… very good or surprising
…… very interesting
…… very surprised (in a negative way)
…… very angry
…… very old
…… very bad
…… very scared
…… very tired
…… very big
…… very hard to believe

6 51 Listen and repeat the adjectives from Exercise 5.

7 a Choose three adjectives from Exercise 5 and write a true sentence for each one.

b Work in pairs. Take turns reading your sentences to each other. Ask your partner at least one question about each sentence.

I was furious with my little sister on Thursday.

Why? What did she do?

She broke my game console.

REACT

8 Imagine that you wake up in the morning and you're 34 years old. Work in pairs. Answer the questions.

1 Where are you? Describe the room and the house.
2 How do you feel?
3 You look in the mirror. What do you look like? How do you feel now?

MOVE BEYOND

Do the Words & Beyond exercise on page 72.

Workbook, pages 120–121

GRAMMAR Second conditional

Talk about imaginary situations in the present and future

READ AND LISTEN Grammar in context

1 52 **Read and listen to the conversation. What kinds of parents do Raj and Kim think they might be?**

Raj: It's a shame you couldn't come to the movie. It was terrifying!
Kim: You know my parents. If I had kids, I wouldn't be so strict. I'd be much more easygoing.
Raj: I'm not so sure.
Kim: So what about you? What would you be like if you were a parent?
Raj: If I were a dad, I'd be pretty strict, I think. It's a big responsibility!

STUDY

2 Complete the examples. Use the words in orange in Exercise 1 to help you.

Second conditional

Use the second conditional to talk about unlikely or imaginary situations in the present or future and their results.

Use the past tense after *if* to indicate the imaginary situation. Use *would* or *wouldn't* to indicate the result.

If I ________ kids, I ________ be so strict.

Questions and short answers
Use *would* or *wouldn't* and the past tense in questions. Use *would* in short answers.

________ you be strict if you were a parent?
Yes, I ________ . / No, I ________ .

See GRAMMAR DATABASE, page 67.

PRACTICE

3 Match the two parts of the sentences.

1 If I were a parent, *d*
2 My kids would have to do housework ____
3 I wouldn't let my kids have a house party ____
4 If their friends invited them to go on vacation, ____
5 They couldn't go out at night ____
6 If we went shopping, ____

a I wouldn't let them choose their clothes.
b if they wanted an allowance.
c unless they came home before 10 p.m.
d I'd be very strict.
e unless I were there.
f I'd tell them they couldn't go.

4 Are the sentences in Exercise 3 true for you? If not, change them to make them true.

5 Complete the sentences with the correct form of the verbs.

1 If I ________ (wake) up with superpowers, I'd fly around the world.
2 I ________ (live) in Japan if I could study in another country.
3 If I ________ (have) a special talent, I'd want to be an amazing singer.
4 I ________ (spend) the extra day relaxing if there ________ (be) eight days in a week.
5 If I ________ (can) travel back in time for a day, I ________ (go) back to the time of the dinosaurs.
6 My family ________ (give) the money to charity if we ________ (win) the lottery.

6 Write questions for the sentences in Exercise 5.

1 If you … , what / do? *If you woke up with superpowers, what would you do?*
2 Where / live if … ?
3 If you … , what / want to be?
4 What / do on the extra day if … ?
5 If you … , where / go?
6 What / your family / do if … ?

7 a 53 PRONOUNCE **Second conditional sentences often have two stressed words or phrases in each part. Listen and underline the stressed words or phrases.**

A: If you woke up with superpowers, what would you do?
B: I'd fly around the world.
C: I wouldn't do anything. I'd go back to sleep.

b 54 **Listen and repeat the sentences. Pay attention to their rhythm.**

SPEAK

8 Work in pairs. Ask and answer the questions in Exercise 6. Give reasons for your answers.

Workbook, page 122

LANGUAGE & BEYOND

What's really important?

Do the activities to find out what's really important to you.
Name and age: *Claire Tate, age 15*

Activity 1

Write two options for each question and a short explanation of your choices.

1 If you won a six-day Caribbean cruise for two, who would you take with you?
A: *I'd take my best friend, Lola. We never stop talking when we're together!*
B: *I'd take my sister, because she'd be unhappy if I didn't.*

2 If your house were on fire and you could only take one thing, what would you take?
A: *I'd take my violin, because it's really old and valuable.*
B: *I'd take my tablet, because it has all my photos and music on it.*

3 If you could do whatever you wanted with your time tomorrow, what would you do?
A: *I'd clean up my room. It's a real mess, and I can never find anything.*
B: *I'd do nothing at all, just sit and read. I love reading!*

Activity 2

Quickly choose one of your options. Don't think too much – choose the option that feels better to you.

»» Decide what's important to you

KNOW YOURSELF

SPEAK AND READ

1 **Read Claire's answers on the activity sheet. What do you think she's like? Choose two adjectives and then compare with a partner.**

bad-tempered creative friendly kind patient serious shy smart

2 **Work in pairs. Talk about Claire's answers. Which options do you think she'll choose in Activity 2? Explain why.**

PHRASE BYTES

I think she'll take … with her because …

I (don't) agree. I think she'll take … in the end because …

I think she'll try to save her … from the fire because …

But if she saved her … she'd / she wouldn't …

If she had the choice, I think she'd prefer to …

DO

3 **Do Activity 1 on the activity sheet.**

4 **Do Activity 2. Don't take longer than 30 seconds.**

5 **Work in pairs. Explain your choices to your partner. After speaking, are there any choices you'd like to change?**

REFLECT

6 **Discuss the questions with your class. Do you agree with the REFLECTION POINT?**

1 What area of life is each question in Activity 1 about?
2 Did you find it hard to choose just one alternative in Activity 2? Why or why not?
3 Why is it sometimes hard to make the choices we want?

REFLECTION POINT

It's good to know what's important to you in different areas of your life. It can help you decide what you really want to do and not what you think you should do.

EXTEND

7 **Repeat Exercises 3, 4, and 5 for these questions. What do your answers tell you about you and your plans for the future?**

1 If you had to choose just three school subjects to continue studying, which ones would you choose?
2 If you could decide now what job you'll do in the future, what job would it be?

»» Workbook, page 125

SPEAKING Do you mind?

»» Make and react to requests

SPEAK

1 Work in pairs. Look at the situations. Who would you talk to? What would they say?

1 You need somebody to drive you somewhere.
2 You need to borrow some money.
3 You need to call somebody but don't have your cell phone.

LISTEN

2 ▶55 Listen to the conversations. Who does Leo talk to in each situation? Who says "no" to his requests?

Leo: Dad, can you drive me to the festival?
Dad: All right. But you'll have to wait 20 minutes.
Leo: No problem. Can we (1) ______ Jack too?
Dad: OK.
Leo: Thanks. And can you come and get me later?
Dad: Sorry, I can't. Mom needs the car tonight.

Leo: Jack, could you (2) ______ me some money for a drink?
Jack: Sure.
Leo: And do you mind if I (3) ______ your phone to call Kate?
Jack: No, go ahead.
Leo: Thanks.

Leo: Mr. Gibb, could I (4) ______ you a favor?
Mr. Gibb: Of course.
Leo: Would you (5) ______ me home, please? My dad can't come and get me, and I think I missed the last bus.
Mr. Gibb: I'm sorry, but there's no space in the car.
Leo: OK. Would you mind if I (6) ______ your phone to call my mother?
Mr. Gibb: No, of course not. Here you go.
Leo: Thank you.

3 ▶55 Complete the conversations with the verbs in the box. Then listen again to check.

ask drive lend take use used

4 Choose the best option or options for formal situations (with people you don't know very well). Use the conversations to help you.

1 Use *Could* / *Can* / *Would you …* ?
2 *Say* / *Don't say* "please" and "thank you."
3 Use *Do* / *Would you mind if …* ?
4 Accept a request with *Of course* / *Sure*.
5 Refuse a request with *Sorry, I can't.* / *I'm afraid …*

5 ▶56 Listen again and repeat the requests and the reactions.

PHRASEBOOK ▶57

Make and react to requests

Can / Could I borrow / use … , please?
Can / Could you lend me / take … , please?
Would you drive / call … , please?
✓ OK. / All right.
Sure.
Of course.
✗ Sorry, I can't.
I'm afraid …
Do you mind if I use / borrow … ?
Would you mind if I used / borrowed … ?
✓ No, go ahead.
Not at all.
✗ I'm afraid …

ACT

6 Work in pairs. Prepare a conversation for each situation below. Make one formal and the other informal. Then present your conversations to another pair. Can they guess who's talking?

1 You want to change channels and watch a different TV show.
2 You want someone to check your English homework.

»» Workbook, page 123

WRITING A poem about true friends

Use a dictionary

SPEAK AND READ

1 Work in pairs. Answer the questions.

1 Do you ever read poems? If so, what kinds of poems do you like? If not, why not?
2 Have you ever written a poem? If so, what was it about?

2 Read the poem about friends and answer the questions.

1 Which lines do you agree with? Check (✓) them.
2 Do you like the poem? Why or why not?

Best Friends

True friends accept you how you are
And don't try to change you
They'll help you dry a tear
And they'll share the good times with you
If you want to talk, they'll be there
But if you need some space, they'll understand
And even if you had a fight
And said "I never want to see you again!"
You know you'd miss them if they left
They're like your sister or your brother
You'd do anything for each other
And that's because you're best friends

3 a Read the tips in the HOW TO box.

HOW TO
use a dictionary

- Use a bilingual dictionary to translate words. Use a monolingual dictionary to see definitions in English.
- Look for the correct part of speech: noun, verb, adjective, or adverb.
- Make sure you choose the correct translation or definition if there's more than one. Look at the examples.
- Read the phonetic transcription to see how you pronounce the word.

b Read the poem again and answer the questions.

1 Circle words in the poem that are new for you. Are they nouns, verbs, adjectives, or another part of speech?
2 Two of the lines rhyme. Which ones?

PRACTICE

4 Use the dictionary entry and the tips in the HOW TO box to help you answer the questions about the word *tear* in the poem.

1 What part of speech is *tear*?
2 Which definition of *tear* in the dictionary is the correct one? Check (✓) it.
3 Does this meaning of *tear* rhyme with *there* or with *here*?

☐ **tear** /ter/ verb
to pull something so that it separates into pieces: *How did you tear your jeans?*

☐ **tear** /ter/ noun
a hole in a piece of paper or cloth where it has been torn: *There was a tear in her coat.*

☐ **tear** /tɪr/ noun
a drop of liquid that comes from your eye when you cry: *Her eyes filled with tears.*

DISCUSS

5 Think of your best friend. Discuss what he or she does for you as a true friend.

WRITE

6 Write a poem about your friend. Start each line of your poem with a green phrase from Exercise 2.

1 Complete the lines in the poem with your own ideas or ideas from your discussion.
2 Use a bilingual dictionary to translate words you want to use. Check the meaning with a monolingual dictionary. Use the tips in the HOW TO box.
3 Make at least one rhyme. Use a dictionary to check the pronunciation.

SHARE

7 Read your poem to a partner or display it in the classroom. Which lines in the poems do you especially like?

Workbook, pages 124–125

VOCABULARY People and relationships

1 Match the people and relationships in the box to the definitions.

MyFriends.com
close friends, girlfriends/boyfriends, old friends, online friends, classmates, teammates, guests, friends of friends, parents, relatives, neighbors, acquaintances, enemies

1 You've known them for a long time: ....
2 You're having a romantic relationship: ....
3 They're members of your family who don't usually live with you: ....
4 You met on the internet: ....
5 You dislike each other: ....
6 You're really good friends: ....
7 They play for your team: ....
8 They live near you: ....
9 They're in your class at school: ....
10 You know them a little: ....
11 They're invited to your party: ....
12 They're friends' friends: ....

___ /12

Extreme adjectives

2 Complete the adjectives in the description of the picture.

Harry's (1) h__________e and although he's only 16, he looks (2) a__________t. He's (3) t__________d of Farah. She gets (4) f__________s, and her face turns bright red when he doesn't show enough interest in her (5) f__________g stories. Eric's always (6) e__________d from laughing so much at his own jokes and is (7) s__________d when we tell him how (8) a__________l they are. (They really are terrible!) And Amy has (9) a__________g white teeth and she always has the most (10) u__________e hairstyles. They're my best friends, and I love them!

___ /10

GRAMMAR First conditional with *if/unless*

3 Complete the messages with the first conditional form of the verbs.

Nina, we (1) __________ (miss) you if you (2) __________ (go) to live in another city!
Your best friends — Like

Kevin, unless you (3) __________ (respect) people more, you (4) __________ (not have) any friends, just enemies!
A close friend — Like

Mark, if you (5) __________ (not send) Lucy a card, she (6) __________ (be) really unhappy. She always remembers your birthday!
An old friend — Like

___ /12

Second conditional

4 Choose the correct options to complete the messages.

What (1) *did* / *would* you do if your best friend (2) *left* / *would leave* her bag at your house with her diary in it? (3) *Did* / *Would* you read it? — **Elena**

If I (4) *found* / *'d find* a friend's diary, I (5) *took* / *'d take* a look at it. Why not? Your friend (6) *never knew* / *would never know*! — **Aiden**

Aiden, that's terrible! I'm sure you (7) *didn't* / *wouldn't* say the same if it (8) *were* / *would be* your diary! You can't have friendship without trust. — **Trish**

___ /16

Your score: ___ /50

SKILLS CHECK

✓✓✓ Yes, I can. No problem!
✓✓ Yes, I can. But I need a little help.
✓ Yes, I can. But I need a lot of help.

I can recognize examples. ....
I can use stress and intonation to help me understand. ....
I can decide what's important to me. ....
I can make and react to requests. ....
I can use a dictionary. ....

Workbook, pages 126–127

READ

1 You want to buy a music album as a present for the following people. Read the album reviews and decide which album would be the best choice for each person.

1 Kylie downloads a lot of songs to listen to on the move. She's a big fan of pop music, especially songs and artists currently in the music charts.

2 Danny is Kylie's boyfriend, but they have very different tastes in music. Although he likes some pop music, Danny prefers American rock or folk music.

3 Holly doesn't buy much music. She prefers going to The Basement, a local venue for new bands. She enjoys discovering new music, but it has to be rock.

4 Jorge wants to be a conductor. He loves listening to classical music at home. He often plays music loudly and pretends to conduct an orchestra.

5 Max really likes traditional jazz. He mostly listens to jazz music from the 1940s and 50s. He likes jazz singers, but he doesn't like contemporary jazz music.

TEST-TAKING TIPS

do a matching exercise (people and texts)

- Read all the texts carefully.
- In the people profiles, underline important words or phrases.
- In the reviews, look for ideas that match the important words.
- Make sure <u>all</u> the information about the people matches the review.

This week's album reviews

A Room for More

If you enjoy listening to traditional jazz music, such as Louis Armstrong, then this isn't the album for you. If, however, you like extremely loud and incredibly fast modern jazz music, then you'll love this new CD from trumpeter Lilo Watts. It's not easy to listen to, but it's fascinating.

B Ancient Monsters

If I had to pick the best pop album of the year, this would be my last choice. These pop superstars may have been the greatest thing on the planet in prehistoric times but not anymore. The album title says it all. It's awful!

C The Brass Ring

Although I like classical music, I'm not a huge fan of opera or brass bands. I didn't expect to enjoy this album, but the brass band's performance of excerpts from Wagner's *Ring* is surprisingly good, and I didn't miss the orchestra or the singers.

D Step Back

Surprisingly, the new album from boy band OneStep is even better than last year's debut album. It includes this week's number one hit "New Acquaintance." The members of this New Orleans band are performing more confidently all the time. It looks as if they're here to stay.

E Undercover

This week's top choice is a live recording by the new rock band Classmates. Listen to the audience reaction to the performance! If the band continues producing amazing rock music like this, Classmates will be together for a long, long time.

F Moonrise

I don't normally enjoy classic songs from the Big Band era like "What a Wonderful World," but this collection of rare performances by well-known jazz vocalists is unbelievably good. You'll love it – unless your heart is made of stone (or rock!).

G Double H

If you decide to buy just one album this year, make it this one. In the past I've been pretty critical of traditional American folk music such as last year's *Arthur*. However, Beth Hands has transformed the genre and sings beautifully on this album.

H The Essential Collection V

Even though the composer of the music on this album was born almost 250 years ago, his compositions still sound totally fresh and exciting today. I was exhausted after listening to this collection of greatest hits from his symphonies. Inspiring.

Reading: ______ /10

LISTEN

2 58 **You'll hear a guest on a radio show talking about her work on a magazine. Check (✓) the correct box for each question.**

1 Belinda Vine …
- **A** helps people with their problems. ☐
- **B** writes letters for an advice column. ☐
- **C** tells people how to be happy. ☐

2 Belinda thinks we can see problems more clearly …
- **A** in a magazine. ☐
- **B** if we write them down. ☐
- **C** when we talk to our friends. ☐

3 Kate has a problem with her …
- **A** classmates. ☐
- **B** parents. ☐
- **C** best friend. ☐

4 If Belinda answered Kate's message, first she'd …
- **A** suggest giving her friend space. ☐
- **B** ask some questions. ☐
- **C** tell her to do something else. ☐

5 Belinda has given advice to teens …
- **A** since the magazine first appeared. ☐
- **B** for more than 10 years. ☐
- **C** all around the world. ☐

Listening: _______ /10

TEST-TAKING TIPS

answer multiple-choice questions

- Read the instructions. What are you going to hear?
- Read the questions and choices. Underline important words.
- Listen. Decide which choices are not possible.
- Listen again. Choose the best possible option.

WRITE

3 Read part of a letter from your aunt who lives on the other side of the world. Then write a letter answering your aunt's questions. Write 90–100 words.

> It's been so long since I saw you. Write and tell me about yourself. What do you like doing? Who are your friends? Are you studying hard?

Writing: _______ /10

Progress check score _______ /30

TEST-TAKING TIPS

reply to a letter

- Read the task. Who are you writing to?
- Read the letter and underline the points to include.
- Plan your letter before you write.
- Include phrases to start and end your letter.

UNIT 5

FIVE SENSES

IN THE PICTURE Can you feel it?

Talk about how we use our senses

WORK WITH WORDS

1 RECALL **Work in pairs. Do the tasks. You have three minutes.**

a **Write down the letters of the alphabet. Write the names of parts of the body for as many letters as you can. Use the photos to help you.**

b **Which of the words can you match to the five icons in Exercise 2a?**

2 **a** **Write the names of the five senses below the correct icons.**

hearing sight smell taste touch

1 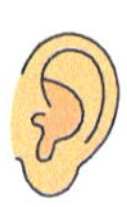	2 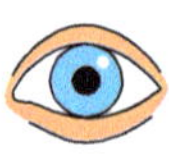	3 	4 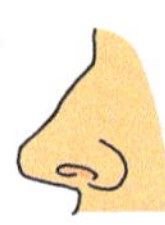	5 

b 59 **Listen and check. Then listen and repeat.**

3 **a** **Match the verbs to the five senses. Write them in the table in Exercise 2a.**

feel hear listen look see smell sound taste touch watch

b 60 **Listen and check. Then listen and repeat the verbs.**

4 61 **Listen and match the sentences (1–10) to the photos (a–e).**

5 62 **Complete the sentences with the correct form of the verbs in Exercise 3. Listen and check.**

1 It's so good not wearing shoes. The grass .... so soft under my feet.
2 There's so much traffic. Everything .... so noisy here.
3 "What do you think of this one?" "Wow! That .... fantastic."
4 There's so much to .... in the city. It's huge.
5 It's so hot here, and that water .... so cool.
6 I like Mexican food. This .... really good.
7 I can't .... anything apart from amazing music.
8 Sometimes I lie on the grass and imagine I can .... the clouds in the sky.
9 I love .... the ocean. It's so blue under the sky.
10 I like .... to music while I walk. It's relaxing.

a

5

6 a ▶63 **PRONOUNCE** **Listen to the consonant combinations in the words. Underline the consonant combinations.**

smell taste sound strong grass text message sky hand soft

b **Listen and repeat the words. Pay attention to the consonant combinations.**

7 **THE MOVING PICTURE** ▶ **Watch the video and imagine you're in each scene. Say something using the sense verbs.**

8 **Some sense verbs can also be nouns. Choose the correct nouns for these sentences.**

1 I like the *smell* / *sound* of fresh bread. It reminds me of home.
2 I hate the *taste* / *sound* of motorcycles. They're so noisy.
3 I really like the *look* / *taste* of honey. It's sweet.
4 I don't like the *sight* / *smell* of graffiti on buildings. It's ugly.

SPEAK

9 **Work in pairs. Write the names of things you love or hate. Tell your partner.**

1 I *love* / *hate* the smell of ....
2 I *love* / *hate* the taste of ....
3 I *love* / *hate* the sound of ....
4 I *love* / *hate* the sight of ....

MOVE BEYOND

Do the Words & Beyond exercise on page 73.

Workbook, page 128

READING Fragrance fact file

››› Use pictures to help you understand

SPEAK AND READ

1 Work in pairs. Answer the questions.

1 Which perfumes and fragrances can you name?
2 What different kinds of products use fragrances?

2 a Read the tips in the HOW TO box.

b Before you read, look at the text and pictures and answer the questions.

1 Where do you think the text comes from – an encyclopedia, a magazine, or a history book?
2 What is it about?
3 What information do you think it includes?

HOW TO

use pictures to help you understand

- ☐ Before you read, look at any pictures or other visuals.
- ☐ Think about the connection between the pictures, the title, the topic, and the style of text (news story, manual).
- ☐ Look at the visuals when you read. They can help you understand new words.

9 things you should know about FRAGRANCES

1 The world's first chemist was a woman named Tapputi, who made perfumes in Mesopotamia in the 2nd millennium BC.

2 The word "perfume" comes from the Latin *per fumom* which means "through smoke." The first form of perfume was incense. It was produced from burning wood or plants and was used in religious ceremonies.

3 Ancient Egyptians and Romans created the first liquid perfumes using water and oils. In Rome, perfume was used by both women and men on their bodies and in their houses.

4 Today, perfumes are often called fragrances. A new fragrance appears almost every day, and many of them are promoted by celebrities.

5 When you buy a fragrance, the cheapest thing you are buying is the actual fragrance. The bottle and the box cost more to produce.

6 It's almost impossible to tell the difference between fragrances that have been created for women and for men. The first popular unisex fragrance for both women and men was first sold in 1994.

7 Companies that create perfume for fragrances also make the fragrances that are used for cleaning products, air fresheners, and potato chips.

8 More than 4,000 ingredients are used in the fragrance industry. The formula of each perfume is kept secret, and the ingredients aren't listed on the bottle.

9 Some fragrances can cause headaches or allergic skin reactions in some people. Many people don't like the smell of fragrances and hope they will be banned in public places.

3 ▶64 Read the text and decide if the sentences are correct (*C*) or incorrect (*I*).

1 The very first perfumes were oils and water. ____
2 New fragrances appear every day. ____
3 The world's first perfume maker was named Mesopotamia. ____
4 The first fragrance for men appeared in 1994. ____
5 Each fragrance has more than 5,000 ingredients. ____
6 The fragrance bottle is often more expensive to produce than the fragrance. ____

4 Which tips in the HOW TO box did you use for help with Exercises 2b and 3? Check (✓) them.

REACT

5 Work in pairs. What do you think? Tell your partner.

1 Which facts in the article surprised you? Why?
2 Should fragrances be banned in some public places? If so, which?

MOVE BEYOND

A picture caption is a short text that usually appears under a picture. Write captions for the pictures in the text. Use information from the text.

››› Workbook, page 129

GRAMMAR Passives (past, present, and future)

5

>>> Use the past, present, and future passives to talk about senses

READ >>> Grammar in context

1 Read about Molly's breakfast. Answer the question at the end of the text.

When Molly had breakfast yesterday, her senses were working hard. First, visual messages were sent to her brain. (*Eggs on toast! They look good, but maybe they're bad.*) Then some cells that are found in the nose sent another message. (*They smell OK up here!*) Finally, the thousands of taste buds that are located on the tongue sent a final message. (*They taste really good!*) When all the messages were received by her brain, she was given the OK to eat them. Unfortunately, today Molly has a cold. Tomorrow she'll be given eggs again, but she won't be given the OK by her brain. Why not?

STUDY

2 Complete the examples. Use Exercise 1 to help you.

Passives (past, present, and future)

Use passives when the action is more important than the person or thing that does the action.

Form the passive with the verb *to be* + past participle.

Some cells that ________ *found in the nose sent another message.*

Visual messages ________ *sent to her brain.*

Tomorrow she ________ *given eggs again, but she* ________ *given the OK by her brain.*

Form questions with the verb *to be* + subject + past participle.

________ *taste buds located on the tongue?*

When ________ *she given the OK to eat?*

Use *by* + subject to explain who or what did the action.

Molly was sent many messages by her senses.

See GRAMMAR DATABASE, page 68.

PRACTICE

3 Complete the news story with the future passive form of the verbs.

A new fast-food restaurant, *Sixth Sense*, (1) *will be opened* (open) by superstar singer Justin next Tuesday. At the new restaurant, customers (2) ________ (not allow) to see the food they eat. All the food (3) ________ (serve) in the dark. *Sixth Sense* chef, Gerard LePong, says people (4) ________ (give) the chance to experience fast food in a new way. I asked Gerard: "(5) ________ (people / tell) what they're eating?" His answer was "No. If you eat at *Sixth Sense*, you (6) ________ (not show) the menu until after you've eaten. Enjoy!"

4 Complete the sentences with the correct passive form of the verbs.

1 In the past, most fruits and vegetables *were sold* (sell) in markets.
2 They ________ (choose) for their taste and not for the way they looked.
3 In the USA, these days most fruits and vegetables ________ (sell) in supermarkets.
4 They ________ (often / reject) by supermarkets because they don't look good.
5 The supermarkets say that if they start putting ugly fruit on their shelves, it ________ (leave) on the shelves by customers.
6 But if tomorrow's fresh food ________ (grow) only to look good, its taste ________ (lose) forever.

5 Rewrite the sentences using the passive form of the verbs in blue.

1 In the USA, people spend more than $100 billion on processed foods each year.
In the USA, more than $100 billion is spent on processed foods each year.
2 People often choose a product because of the photo on the packaging.
3 However, when they prepare the food, it can look very different.
4 Companies receive a lot of complaints each year.

SPEAK

6 Work in pairs. Compare the information in Exercises 4 and 5, talking about your country. How will people eat food in the future?

LISTENING AND VOCABULARY The power of color

Follow a conversation

SPEAK AND LISTEN

1 a What do you associate each color in the box with? Write the first word you think of. Then compare your words with your partner.

black blue brown gold green gray
orange pink purple red silver yellow

black – night

b Find as many of the colors as you can on the color wheel.

2 a Read the tips in the HOW TO box.

b 65 Listen to the interview with Amy Shore about the National Color Wheel and order the topics.

a The ways in which different cultures interpret colors. ......
b A survey carried out in Manchester. ......
c The reasons for doing the new survey. ......
d How people can take part in the survey. ......

3 65 Listen again and choose the correct answers.

1 Amy Shore basically wants people to …
A visit a website. **B** take a street survey. **C** visit Manchester.
2 The main purpose of the survey is to …
A know what colors mean. **B** make people more aware of color. **C** create an international database.
3 She gives an example of how white is associated with death in …
A China. **B** countries with jungles. **C** the West.
4 The show's host associates the color green with …
A grass. **B** the environment. **C** Ireland.

4 Which tips in the HOW TO box did you use for help with Exercises 2b and 3? Check (✓) them.

HOW TO
follow a conversation

☐ *Basically* and *The thing is* introduce an important point.
☐ *For example* and *For instance* introduce examples.
☐ *Although*, *Even though*, and *However* add contrasting information.

REACT

5 Work in pairs. Look at the color wheel and answer the questions.

1 Which of the colors reflects the way you feel now?
2 What's your favorite color? Why do you like it?
3 Work in pairs. Complete the colors task. Student A looks at page 75. Student B looks at page 76.

WORK WITH WORDS

6 Match the color idioms and phrases (1–10) to the definitions (a–j).

1	as black as night	**a**	suddenly feel angry
2	black and white	**b**	tell a small lie to make someone feel better
3	as white as a sheet	**c**	clear and simple
4	get the green light	**d**	very dark
5	be in the red	**e**	be sad or depressed
6	once in a blue moon	**f**	very pale, especially when scared or sick
7	out of the blue	**g**	get permission to do something
8	tell a white lie	**h**	spend more money than you have
9	feel blue	**i**	very rarely
10	see red	**j**	suddenly and unexpectedly

7 Work in pairs. Make a list of things that …

… make you see red.
… make you feel blue.
… are black and white.
… only happen once in a blue moon.

MOVE BEYOND
Do the Words & Beyond exercise on page 73.

Workbook, pages 132–133

GRAMMAR (*In order*) *to* … , *so* (*that*) …

Talk about the purpose of doing things

READ >>> Grammar in context

1 Read the story of Braille. Do young people today still use it?

Blind people

have restricted or no sight. They depend on their other senses in order to live independently. They use their sense of touch to read Braille. A form of Braille was used by Napoleon's soldiers so that they could communicate silently at night. However, it was a French teenager named Louis Braille who developed the idea so blind people could use it. These days, young people prefer using electronic screen readers so that they don't have to use Braille.

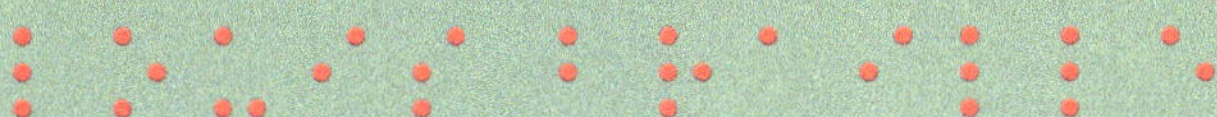

STUDY

2 Complete the explanations. Use Exercise 1 to help you.

***(In order) to* … , *so (that)* …**

Use *to, in order to, so,* and *so that* to explain why someone does, did, or will do something.

Use the base verb after *to* and *in order to.*
They use their sense of touch to ________ Braille.
In order to is more formal than *to.*

Use a subject after *so* and *so that.*
Young people prefer using screen readers so that ________ don't have to read Braille.

Use *could* or *would* + verb after *so* and *so that* to indicate the past.
Louis Braille developed the idea so blind people ________ use it.

See GRAMMAR DATABASE, page 68.

PRACTICE

3 Choose the correct option to complete the sentences.

1. When he was 10, Louis Braille went to one of the first schools for the blind *in order* / *so that* he could study with other blind boys.
2. At that time, blind people used their fingers *to* / *so* feel the shape of normal letters.
3. A soldier named Charles Barbier visited the school *in order* / *so that* to demonstrate a system he'd created for soldiers.
4. He created his system *in order* / *so that* soldiers could pass messages at night.
5. Louis adapted Barbier's system *to* / *so* make it possible for blind people to read and write.

4 (66) Complete the conversation with *to* or *so*. Then listen and check your answers.

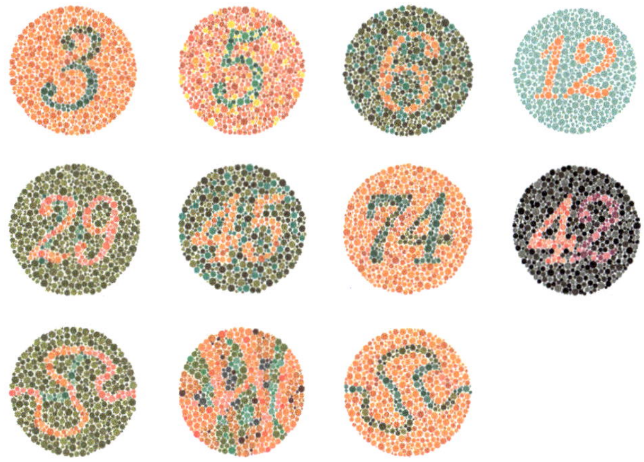

Mike: We're talking to Jackie today (1) ________ we can learn something about being color-blind. How did you find out you were color-blind, Jackie?

Jackie: My art teacher asked me to stay after class one day (2) ________ talk to me. She thought it was strange that I had painted the sky purple. I took a test (3) ________ find out if I was color-blind.

Mike: What's the test like?

Jackie: They show you a circle with a lot of colored dots (4) ________ find out if you can see a number in the dots. They also do the test (5) ________ they can discover which type of color-blindness you have.

Mike: Is it a problem being color-blind?

Jackie: Not really. But I usually buy clothes with a friend (6) ________ I don't choose colors that look bad together.

5 Complete the sentences in your own words using *in order to* / *to* or *so that* / *so*.

1. I use my phone's touchscreen …
2. Elevators have Braille on the buttons …
3. You try clothes on before you buy them …
4. We often use our sense of touch …
5. Signs often use the color red …
6. You enter your PIN at an ATM …

SPEAK

6 Work in pairs. Answer the questions.

1. Why do we need each of the five senses?
2. Which sense is the most important to you? Why?

We need our sense of smell in order to sense dangers, such as fire.

Hearing is the most important sense to me because I love music.

Workbook, page 134

LANGUAGE & BEYOND

»» Recognize nonverbal communication

COMMUNICATE & COOPERATE

SPEAK AND READ

1 **Work in pairs. Choose one of the phrases in the box. Communicate the phrase to your partner without speaking. Can your partner understand you?**

Be quiet. I can't hear you. I'm hungry. I'm tired.
It tastes disgusting. OK. What's that smell? What time is it?

2 **Read about body language. Based on your experience, check (✓) the points (1–6) you think are true. Then compare your answers with your partner.**

DO

3 **Work in groups. Take turns demonstrating the examples of body language in Exercise 2. Think of other examples.**

REFLECT

4 **Discuss the questions with your class. Do you agree with the REFLECTION POINT?**

1 How accurate do you think the article is?
2 Is it possible to misunderstand someone's body language? In what situations?
3 How aware are you of your own body language? Do you ever try to control or change it? If so, in what situations?

EXTEND

5 **Work in groups. Create a scene from a silent movie.**

1 Think of a situation for the scene and who the characters are.
2 Decide what happens in the scene. Think about how the characters feel and how they can express this with body language.
3 Rehearse your scene and then perform it for the rest of the class. Can the other students describe what happens?

We often use gestures, facial expressions, and eye movements to communicate with each other. Although we often do this deliberately in order to say something specific, our expressions and body movements also communicate things we don't mean to say. Look at these examples.

1 To find out if people are telling the truth, look at their movements. If they touch things a lot while they are talking, then they might be lying. ☐

2 How much do people like you? The closer they stand to you, the more they possibly like you. ☐

3 The way people stand can say a lot about their character. If they stand with their arms folded, they might be trying to build a wall between you and them. ☐

4 We communicate best when we look each other in the eye. If people look down while they are talking, they might be hiding something. ☐

5 If people move their heads to one side while you're talking to them, it can mean that they're interested. ☐

6 When people "mirror" your body language and make the same movements as you do, this means they might like you or they want you to like them. ☐

REFLECTION POINT

Sometimes our body language can reveal a lot about the way we think and feel. However, there might be other reasons for our expressions and body movements, so it isn't always accurate.

Workbook, page 137

SPEAKING At the pharmacy

»» Ask for help with words at the pharmacy

SPEAK

1 Work in pairs. Look at the photos and answer the questions.

1 What's wrong with the people in the photos?
2 What should they do?
3 Which of the situations have you been in?

a
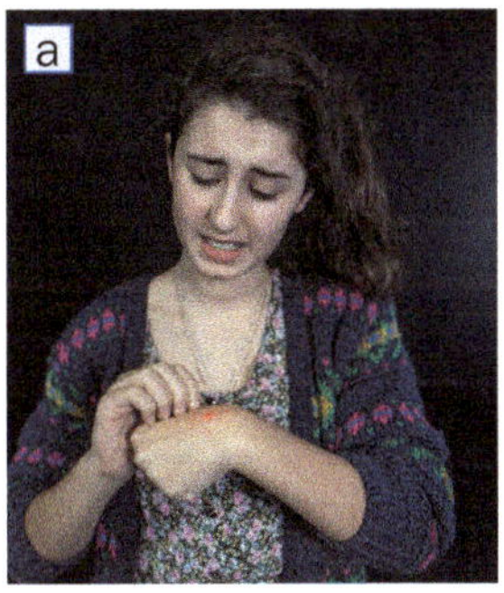
b
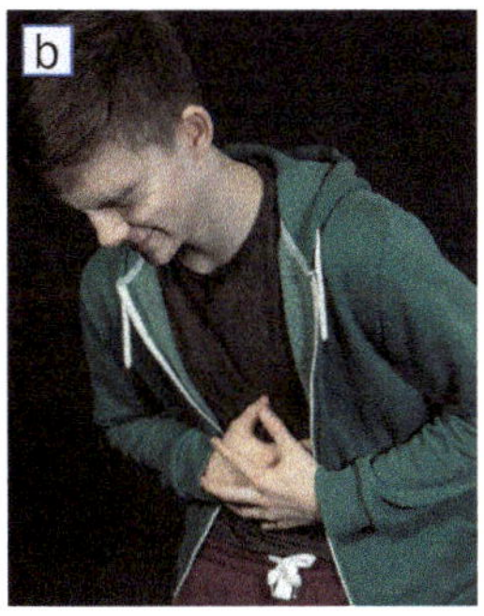
c

LISTEN

2 67 Listen to the conversations. Which problem in Exercise 1 isn't talked about in the conversations?

1

Pharmacist: Are you all right?
Adele: I need something for my (1) ____________ . I have … I'm not sure how to say it in English. It's a pain.
Pharmacist: You mean a (2) ____________ ?
Adele: Yes. Is this the right thing for a (3) ____________ ?
Pharmacist: Yes, it is.
Adele: And I don't understand what this means. Can you help me?
Pharmacist: Let me see. Oh … FD&C 6. It's a color they use in the medicine.
Adele: I see. Does this sign mean that it's bad for you?
Pharmacist: It can be bad for some people. Are you allergic to anything?
Adele: No, I don't think so.
Pharmacist: Then you're probably OK.

2

Pharmacist: Can I help you?
Takeshi: Yes. I need some of that spray you put on your (4) ____________ . I don't know what it's called. It's a special spray for keeping (5) ____________ away.
Pharmacist: Do you mean (6) ____________ repellent?
Takeshi: I think so.
Pharmacist: This one is very good.
Takeshi: What does "light fragrance" mean?
Pharmacist: It means the spray has a fragrance, but it's not very strong. Here. Smell it.
Takeshi: Hm. That's not too bad.
Pharmacist: We also have this in a lotion.
Takeshi: What's the difference between the spray and the lotion?
Pharmacist: Just the price. The spray is cheaper.
Takeshi: OK. I'll take the spray.

3 67 Listen again and write the missing words.

4 a Read the tips in the HOW TO box.

b 68 Complete the phrases from the conversations. Then listen and repeat. Pay attention to which words are stressed.

1 I'm not ____________ how to say it in English.
2 I don't understand what this ____________ .
3 I don't know what it's ____________ .
4 It's a special spray ____________ keeping insects away.
5 What's the ____________ between the spray and the lotion?

5 Match the phrases in Exercise 4b to the tips in Exercise 4a.

ACT

6 Work in pairs. Complete the tasks.

1 Think of another product you buy at the pharmacy.
2 Role-play a conversation between a pharmacist and a customer at the pharmacy. The customer doesn't know the name of the object and needs help with words.
3 Change roles and repeat steps 1 and 2.

»» Workbook, page 135

HOW TO

ask for help with words

When you don't know the name of something:

- Say that you don't know the word.
- Explain what it's for (*it's for* + verb + *-ing*).

When you don't understand a word:

- Say that you don't understand.
- Ask the other person for more information.

PHRASEBOOK 69

Explaining what you need

I need something for … / It's for …
I need some of that spray / stuff.
I'm not sure how to say it in English.
I don't know what it's called.

Asking for help

I don't understand what this means.
Does that mean … ?
Is this the right thing for … ?
What's the difference between … and … ?

WRITING A place I really like

Link similar ideas

SPEAK AND READ

1 **Work in pairs. Look at the photo and describe it. What similar places do you know?**

2 **Read the description. Which part of the description doesn't fit the photo?**

PHRASE BYTES

It's a photo of ...

It reminds me of ...

I've never seen any place like this.

My grandma lives in a big, old house in Maine. We go to stay there three or four times a year. Other relatives often come too, so the house is always full of people.

The house is in the middle of nowhere, and there aren't any stores or movie theaters nearby, but we never get bored. There are hills to climb and a forest to explore. There's the ocean as well. We spend hours on the beach. I love the feeling of the wind on my face and the sand under my feet. I also love swimming, although the water is freezing!

My grandma is not only one of the coolest people on the planet, but she's also an amazing cook. There's always the smell of cooking and baking in the house. At night it sometimes feels a little scary because it's so dark and quiet, but I love my grandma's house.

3 **a** **Read the tips in the HOW TO box.**

HOW TO

link similar ideas

- Use *and* to join two parts of a sentence.
- Use *also*, *too*, and *as well* to add another fact.
- Use *also* after *be*, but before other main verbs.
- Use *too* and *as well* at the end of a sentence.
- Use *not only* + *but also* to say that two things are true.

b **Underline examples of all the linking words in Exercise 2.**

PRACTICE

4 **Rewrite the sentences using the words in parentheses.**

1 There's a park near my house. I go there once or twice a week. (and)
2 It's a good place to meet friends. It's a good place to play sports. (not only + but also)
3 There are some basketball courts. There's an area for skateboarding. (also)
4 Once a month there's a market. They have concerts in the summer. (too)
5 I go there to have fun. I sometimes go there to read. (as well)
6 You see a lot of different people there. People take their pets there. (too)

DISCUSS

5 **Talk about the home of a relative or family friend. Describe what you do when you're there.**

WRITE

6 **Write a description of the home you discussed.**

1 Give basic information about the place. Tell who lives there and where it is.
2 Describe the place in more detail. Mention several activities you can do there. Use linking words to connect similar ideas: *and*, *also*, *too*, *not only ... but also*. Use the tips in the HOW TO box.
3 Use your senses. Describe how the place makes you feel. What can you see, hear, taste, smell, and touch?

SHARE

7 **Read your description to a partner. As you read, your partner will draw the place. Compare your story and the picture to see if your partner understood the details.**

Workbook, pages 136–137

VOCABULARY The senses and sense verbs

1 Complete Casper Wright's introduction to his video game with the words in the box.

feel hear hearing listening look see sight smell sounds taste touch watch

Don't just sit and (1) ________ boring TV. With SensaWorld, you can use your sense of (2) ________ to (3) ________ our amazing 3D visuals. Stop (4) ________ to boring music and really use your sense of (5) ________. You'll be amazed when you (6) ________ the sound effects in the game. It (7) ________ incredible! And that's not all. (8) ________ at these other great features! With SensaWorld, you can use your fingers to (9) ________ and (10) ________ the objects around you. And with our special five senses system you can (11) ________ fragrances and (12) ________ food. With SensaWorld you really are part of the action.

___ /12

Color idioms

2 Complete the conversation from the game with colors.

Sally: Hello? I can't see anything, it's as (1) ________ as night here.
Avatar: Why are you here? People only come here once in a (2) ________ moon. You look as (3) ________ as a sheet.
Sally: Are you … a ghost?
Avatar: Maybe. Nothing's ever (4) ________ and white in SensaWorld. Do I look like a ghost?
Sally: No … no. You look fine.
Avatar: Are you telling (5) ________ lies? Don't make me angry. I see (6) ________ very easily.
Sally: I'm sorry.
Avatar: I'm the creator of SensaWorld. Life was good when I got the (7) ________ light to make SensaWorld. But then I had money problems, and soon I was in the (8) ________. Then out of the (9) ________ I had an idea. I could escape the real world and live inside SensaWorld. But I feel sad and (10) ________ being alone in a virtual world.

___ /10

GRAMMAR Passives (past, present, and future)

3 Complete the encyclopedia entry with the passive forms of the verbs.

SensaWorld (1) ________ (create) by the inventor Casper Wright in 2011. He (2) ________ (inspire) by science fiction movies. In 2012 he (3) ________ (interview) by a newspaper and said: "I want to create a video game that (4) ________ (use) by young people for the next 100 years. I think in the future, players (5) ________ (connect) to other players on other planets." Soon after giving the interview, Casper Wright (6) ________ (report) missing by his family. Today the game (7) ________ (play) by millions of people around the world. Casper Wright (8) ________ (remember) for a very long time.

___ /16

(In order) to … , so (that) …

4 Write the SensaWorld rules using *in order to/to* or *so that/so*.

HOW TO PLAY SENSAWORLD

1. In SensaWorld, you use your senses ________ complete tasks.
2. You complete the tasks ________ you can collect points.
3. You collect points ________ exchange them for tickets.
4. You need the tickets ________ travel to the next world.
5. You are given a wallet ________ you won't lose your tickets.
6. You need your tickets ________ you'll be able to get home.

___ /12

Your score: ___ /50

SKILLS CHECK

✓✓✓ Yes, I can. No problem!
✓✓ Yes, I can. But I need a little help.
✓ Yes, I can. But I need a lot of help.

I can use pictures to help me understand. ________
I can follow a conversation. ________
I can recognize nonverbal communication. ________
I can ask for help with words at the pharmacy. ________
I can link similar ideas when I write. ________

Workbook, pages 138–139

READ

1 Look at each sign and text. What does it say? Choose the correct summary (A, B, or C).

NO ENTRANCE
WITH DOGS OR OTHER ANIMALS.
Guide dogs for the blind are permitted to enter with their owners.

1 What animals can come into this place of business?
- A All animals with their owners.
- B Dogs with their owners.
- C Dogs with blind people.

New mail | Reply | Forward

Hi Kelly,
I'm visiting my grandparents out in the country. I love listening to my grandfather's stories and eating the delicious foods my grandma makes. You would love it out here. It's so beautiful.
Cheri

2 Which senses is Kelly writing about?
- A hearing, smell, touch.
- B hearing, taste, sight.
- C sight, smell, touch.

Chocolate bars won't be sold in schools starting next year.

3 Will chocolate bars be available in the future?
- A Not this year.
- B Not next year.
- C Not ever.

TEST-TAKING TIPS

match short texts to summaries

- Look at each text. What type of text is it?
- Read the text. What's its general meaning?
- Read the three summaries carefully.
- Look for specific information in the text to help choose your answer.

12:30

Where are you???? I've been here for half an hour!! Suri

4 How is Suri feeling?
- A She's angry.
- B She's embarrassed.
- C She's excited.

PHARMACIST AVAILABLE
Monday through Saturday, 9 am to 6 pm, except during lunch hour from 12 pm to 1 pm.

5 When can customers talk to the pharmacist?
- A Any day of the week, any time.
- B Monday through Saturday, from 6 to 9.
- C Monday through Saturday, except during lunch.

Reading: _______ /10

LISTEN

2 70 **You will hear a conversation between Ellen and Ken about sense of smell. Check (✓) T if each sentence is true or F if it's false.**

		T	F
1	Ellen says she likes the smell of strong fragrances.	☐	☐
2	Ken wants to get something at the pharmacy so that Ellen feels better.	☐	☐
3	Ken has a strong sense of smell.	☐	☐
4	There's a strong smell of cheese.	☐	☐
5	Ken says that the shopping center smells bad.	☐	☐

Listening: ______ /10

WRITE

3 For each question, complete the second sentence so that it means something similar to the first. Use no more than three words.

1 I like the smell of fresh bread.
Fresh bread ______ so good.
2 The cafeteria has received complaints about their food.
Complaints ______ about the cafeteria food.
3 Blind people use Braille so that they can read.
Blind people use Braille ______ to read.
4 She is feeling sad.
She ______ sad.

______ /4

4 You want to share a description about summer camp with a friend. Write a short informal email to Josh (35–45 words).

- Tell Josh some basic information about the camp.
- Describe some of the activities you are doing.
- End with a friendly close and state when you expect to see him again.

______ /6

Writing: ______ /10

Progress check score ______ /30

TEST-TAKING TIPS

answer true/false questions

- Read the sentences carefully before you listen.
- Every part of the sentence must be true: listen carefully for the details.
- When you listen again, check your answers.
- If you don't know, guess – you have a 50 percent chance!

TEST-TAKING TIPS

write a message

- Read the task carefully. Who are you writing to?
- Plan your message before you write.
- Include phrases to start and end your message.
- Remember the difference between formal and informal language.
- Use *because* before a reason and *so* before a result.
- Link your ideas with *and*, *also*, *too*, *as well*, and *not only … but also*.

EXTRA READING The Wizard of Oz

BEFORE YOU READ

1 Look at the cover of the book. What kind of story is *The Wizard of Oz*?

a love story b mystery c fantasy d science fiction

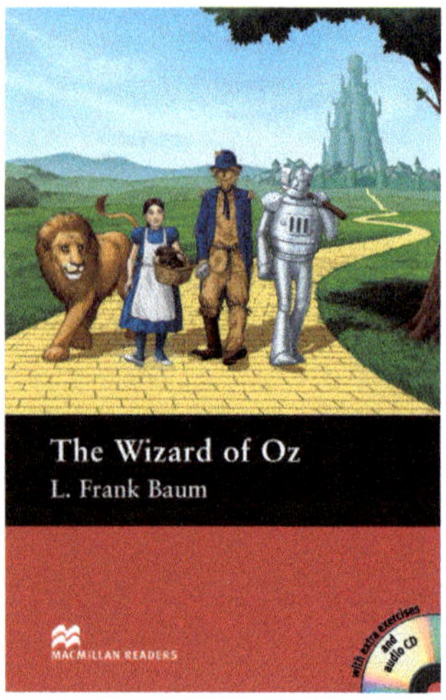

2 Describe the characters in the pictures. What qualities do you think they have?

WHILE YOU READ

3 (71) Read the excerpt from *The Wizard of Oz* and check your answers to Exercises 1 and 2. Is the excerpt from the beginning, the middle, or the end of the story?

The Wicked Witch of the West had only one eye, but she could see everything. She saw Dorothy first. The girl was fast asleep with her friends all around her.

The Wicked Witch was very angry, and she blew on her silver whistle. Almost at once, a pack of wolves ran toward her. The animals had long legs, red eyes, and sharp teeth.

"Go and tear those strangers to pieces!" the Wicked Witch told the Leader of the wolves.

"Don't you want to use them for slaves?" the Leader of the wolves asked.

"No, they are no use to me," the Wicked Witch replied. "One is made of tin and one of straw. The girl and the lion won't be able to work for me. Tear them to pieces."

"We will!" the Leader said and the wolves all ran toward the strangers.

The Scarecrow and the Tin Man saw the wolves coming.

"Leave this to me," the Tin Man said, and he raised his axe. As the Leader ran up, the Tin Man swung his axe. The wolf's head was cut from its body.

There were forty wolves. The Tin Man raised his axe forty times. Forty heads were cut off, and all the wolves were dead. Then the Tin Man sat down and smiled.

"That was a good fight," he said to the Scarecrow.

When Dorothy woke up in the morning, she saw the wolves' heads and bodies all around her. At first she was afraid, but then the Tin Man told the girl everything.

"Thank you for saving my life," she replied. Then she hugged him.

After a good breakfast, the friends started on their way.

The Wicked Witch looked out of the door of the castle. First she saw all the dead wolves. Then she saw the strangers walking through her country, and she was very, very angry. The Witch blew her silver whistle and a flock of black crows flew toward her.

"Peck out the strangers' eyes! Tear them to pieces!" the Wicked Witch said to the King Crow.

"Right away!" the King Crow replied.

When Dorothy saw the black crows coming she was very afraid.

"Don't worry," the Scarecrow said. "Leave this to me."

When the crows saw the Scarecrow at first they were afraid of him. But then the King Crow said, "He's only stuffed with straw. I'll peck his eyes out."

The King Crow flew down, but the Scarecrow caught him. He twisted the bird's neck until it was dead.

One by one, the crows flew at the Scarecrow. He caught each one and twisted its neck. Soon the forty black crows were dead.

"You're safe now," the Scarecrow said to his friends. They started on their way again.

When the Wicked Witch saw the dead crows, she was angrier than before. She blew three times on her silver whistle and a swarm of black bees came flying toward her.

"Sting those strangers to death!" she cried. "Be quick!"

But the Scarecrow saw the bees coming, and he knew what to do.

"Take out my straw and cover the girl, the dog, and the Lion with it," the Scarecrow said to the Tin Man. "Then the bees can't sting them."

So when the bees came, there was only the Tin Man to sting. But when they flew at him, the bees broke their stingers, and they all died.

Then Dorothy and the Lion got up. They helped the Tin Man put the straw back into the Scarecrow, and they all started on their way again.

The Wicked Witch was so angry that she jumped up and down. Then she called the Winkies, who were her slaves. She gave them sharp spears to fight with.

"Go and kill those strangers," she said. "Don't come back until they are dead – or I'll kill you!"

The Winkies didn't like fighting, but they were afraid of the Wicked Witch. They soon found Dorothy and her friends. But when the Cowardly Lion roared, the Winkies were very afraid, and they ran back to the Witch's castle.

The Wicked Witch was very angry because all her plans were going wrong. She beat the Winkies and gave them a lot of hard work to do in her castle. Then she sat down and thought hard.

Soon she had an idea. The Wicked Witch had a magic Golden Cap. The owner of the Golden Cap could ask for the help of the Winged Monkeys. The Winged Monkeys would help three times and three times only. Then the magic would stop working. The Wicked Witch had already used the Golden Cap twice.

"I'll use the Golden Cap for the third time," the Wicked Witch said to herself. "The Winged Monkeys will kill these strangers for me, I'm sure of that."

AFTER YOU READ

4 Copy the organizer. Then complete the information for the excerpt.

Title: ______________________
Main character: ______________________
Other characters: ______________________
Setting (place, time): ______________________
Story (most important events)
Event 1: ______________________
Event 2: ______________________
Event 3: ______________________
Event 4: ______________________

5 a What do you think the Winged Monkeys look like?

b 72 Listen to the audio to check your answers. What lesson do you learn in this part of the story?

6 Write the answers to the questions in your own words.

1 Which attack scared you the most – the wolves, the crows, or the bees? Why?
2 In what way does the Scarecrow show intelligence, the Tin Man show feeling, and the Lion show courage?
3 Why did the Wicked Witch decide to use her Golden Cap for the third time?

7 Answer the questions.

1 What's the climax in *The Wizard of Oz* excerpt?
2 What "fantasy story" ingredients does the author include in the climax?
3 What do you think happens next? Make a note of your ideas.

climax
Noun
The most exciting or important moment in a story, event, or situation, usually near the end.

Workbook, pages 140-141

EXTRA READING *The Call of the Wild*

BEFORE YOU READ

1 Look at the cover of the book and read the plot summaries. Which is a summary of *The Call of the Wild*?

a An old yellow dog is a companion to a boy on a Texas farm. The dog becomes a protector and saves the family from wolves.

b A big, strong dog is taken to Canada and sold as a sled dog. He has many masters, good and bad, and finally learns to live free in the far North.

c A dog tells the story of her life with a family. She describes the joys and problems of being a dog, and how she risks her life to save the new baby from a fire.

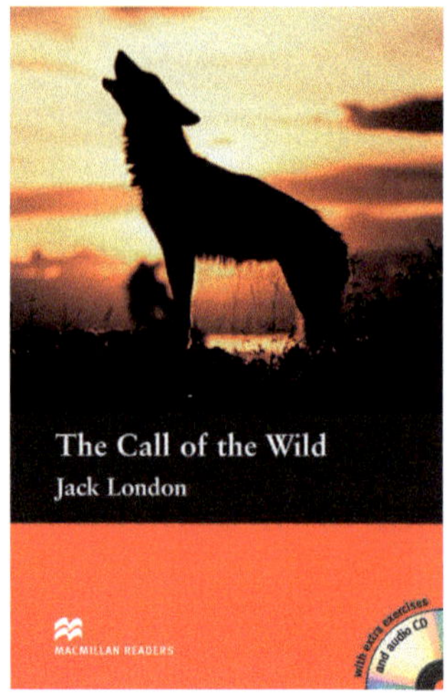

WHILE YOU READ

2 73 Read the excerpt from *The Call of the Wild* and check your answer to Exercise 1. Do you know the titles of the other two books?

When Buck arrived with the other dogs at the Americans' camp, he could see at once that these people were not well organized. The tent was badly put up, the plates were unwashed, and there were things lying everywhere. As well as Charles and Hal, there was also a young woman. Her name was Mercedes and she was Charles's wife and Hal's sister.

Buck watched these people, feeling worried, as they took down the tent and put their things on the sled. They worked slowly, but not sensibly or carefully. When the men put a big bag at the front of the sled, Mercedes told them to put it at the back. Then, after they had moved it and put other things on top, she said that she needed it again.

Three men from another tent came out to watch, smiling at each other and laughing.

"Do you think it will move?" one of the men asked.

"Why wouldn't it?" said Charles, annoyed.

"I was just asking," the man said quickly. "You have a big load there. It looks very heavy."

Charles turned his back and got the sled ready, then Hal took out his whip. "Mush!" he called to the dogs. "Let's go!"

The dogs pushed against the harness for a few moments, then stopped. They couldn't move the sled.

"Lazy animals! I'll teach them," shouted Hal, getting ready to hit them with his whip.

"No, Hal, don't!" cried Mercedes, pulling the whip from him. "Poor darlings! You must promise you'll be good to them, or I won't come."

"You know nothing about dogs," said her brother. "You have to whip them to make them work. You ask anyone. Ask one of those men."

Mercedes looked up at the men, who were still watching.

"They're weak as water, if you want to know," said one of the men. "They need a rest."

"Rest! Huh!" said Hal, and his whip fell on the dogs. They pushed against the harness with all their strength, but they couldn't move the sled.

"I don't care what happens to you," said the man. "But to help those poor dogs, I'll tell you that you should break out that sled. It's frozen in the snow, and you need to push it out."

Hal did what the man said, and this time Buck and his team were able to pull the sled forward. They moved ahead, trying as hard as they could with the whip coming down on them. But they hadn't gone far when the road turned and went around a bend into Skagway's main street. With such a heavy load, it would be difficult even for an experienced driver, but Hal was new to driving dogs. The sled fell over, and half the things came off it. The dogs didn't stop. Buck was angry because of the heavy load and the whipping, and he started to run, with the rest of the team following.

"Stop! Stop!" cried Hal, but he fell over and the half-empty sled went over him. People stopped to watch and laugh as the dogs ran on through the town. Things went flying from the sled and lay all over Skagway's main street.

Some kind people caught the dogs, picked everything up, and explained a few things to the Americans. They needed a small load and more dogs, they were told. Charles and Hal listened unhappily, and then began to take things off of the sled.

Buck

Hal

Charles Mercedes

Mercedes cried when things were taken out of her clothes bags and thrown away. She cried about everything and said she wouldn't go with them. Then, at last, she stopped crying and began to throw away all their things, even those things that they really needed.

That evening, Charles and Hal went out and bought six new Outside dogs – dogs that were not from the Northland. Together with Buck and his old team, and Teek and Koona, the two huskies that had been bought on a previous trip, Charles and Hal now had fourteen dogs. But the Outside dogs knew nothing, and they didn't like the harness or the trail, and the old dogs were exhausted. Only the two men were happy – and proud too – because they had never seen another sled with fourteen dogs. They didn't know that this was because in the Northland, one sled could never carry enough food for fourteen dogs.

Late the next morning, Buck led the long team slowly up the street. He had traveled between Salt Water and Dawson four times now, and his heart wasn't in the work. This woman and these two men didn't know anything. They loaded the sled so badly that every day they had to stop more than once to reload it. And it took them so long to put up and take down camp that some days they traveled fewer than twenty kilometers.

AFTER YOU READ

3 Copy the organizer. Then make notes about the different characters in the excerpt. Think about their relationships, goals, feelings, and experiences. What do they do in the excerpt?

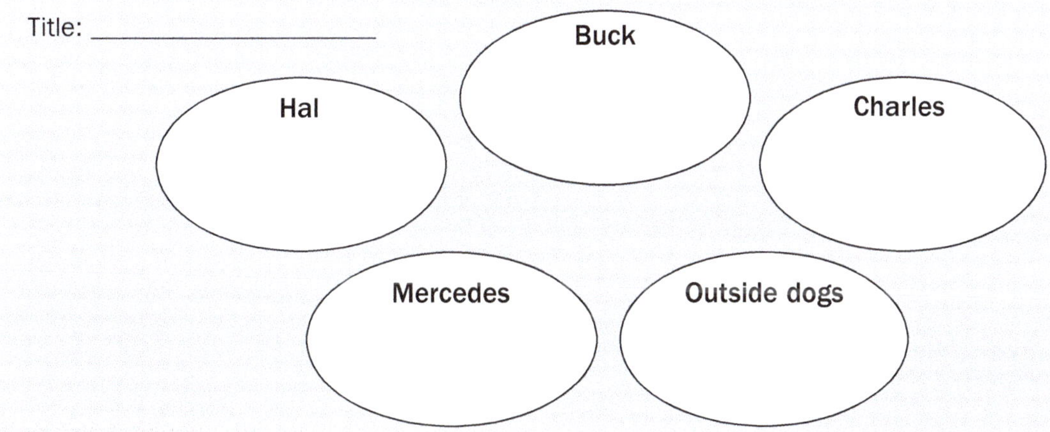

4 Write the answers to the questions in your own words.

1 Why was Buck worried about Charles, Hal, and Mercedes when he first saw them at camp?
2 What happened when the dogs pulled the sled around the bend?
3 Why were the Americans wrong to take 14 dogs with them?

5 74 Listen to an audio excerpt from the next part. How has life in the Northland changed or not changed Mercedes?

6 Read about *The Call of the Wild* and answer the questions.

1 The main character of a novel is usually a human. What are the advantages or disadvantages of telling a story through the eyes of an animal?
2 What does the author mean when he says, "They didn't know how to work the dogs, and they didn't know how to work themselves either."
3 What do you think happens in the story? Does this group of Americans survive and find gold?

The Call of the Wild was written in 1903, around the time of the "gold rush," when people came by ship in search of gold in the Yukon in northwestern Canada. In the winter, the Yukon River was frozen and people carried their things on sleds pulled by dogs. Because of this, they needed strong dogs with warm coats to pull their sleds. Some people found gold and became very rich, but most people found nothing at all.

Workbook, pages 142-143

Present progressive and simple present

USE

Present progressive

- Use the present progressive to talk about things happening now or around now:
  *She **is preparing** for the Sunrise dance.*
  *In this photo the girl **isn't wearing** special clothes.*
  *What **are** these girls **doing**?*
- Use time expressions such as *now, right now, at the moment,* and *these days* with the present progressive:
  *My sister's **preparing** the food for her party **at the moment**.*
- You can also use the present progressive to talk about temporary situations:
  *My brother has gotten a summer job. He's **working** in a café.*

Simple present

- Use the simple present to talk about habits, routines, and things that are generally true:
  *The celebration **starts** with a ceremony.*
- Use adverbs and expressions of frequency such as *usually, sometimes, every day* with the simple present:
  *The girls **usually wear** special clothes for their parties.*

Stative verbs

Don't use the present progressive with **stative verbs**. Use the simple present. Stative verbs often express mental states and opinions (e.g., *believe, know, remember, think, understand*) and preferences (e.g., *hate, like, love, need, want*):

*She **wants** a big party.* (not ~~*She is wanting*~~ …)

*I **don't understand** what he's saying.*

FORM

	Simple present	Present progressive
Affirmative	I usually **wear** jeans to school.	I'**m wearing** jeans today.
	You/We/They usually **wear** jeans to school.	You'**re**/We'**re**/They'**re wearing** jeans today.
	He/She usually **wears** jeans to school.	He'**s**/She'**s wearing** jeans today.
Negative	I **don't** usually **wear** jeans to school.	I'**m not** wearing **jeans** today.
	You/We/They **don't** usually **wear** jeans to school.	You/We/They **aren't wearing** jeans today.
	He/She **doesn't** usually **wear** jeans to school.	He/She **isn't wearing** jeans today.
Questions and short answers	**Do** I/you/we/they usually **wear** jeans to school? Yes, I/you/we/they **do**. No, I/you/we/they **don't**.	**Am** I **wearing** jeans today? Yes, I **am**. No, I'm not. **Are** you/we/they **wearing** jeans today? Yes, you/we/they are. No, you/we/they **aren't**.
	Does he/she usually **wear** jeans to school? Yes, he/she **does**. No, he/she **doesn't**.	**Is** he/she **wearing** jeans today? Yes, he/she **is**. No, he/she **isn't**.

Spelling of *-ing* forms

- If a verb ends in *-e*, remove the final *-e* before adding *-ing*: *tak~~e~~ – taking*   *us~~e~~ – using*
- If a verb ends in a vowel (e.g., *a, i, o*) and a consonant (e.g., *m, p, t*), double the consonant before adding *-ing*: *swim – swimming*   *hit – hitting*
- If a verb ends in *-ie*, change the *-ie* to *-ying*: ~~*lie*~~ *– **lying***

Simple past and past progressive

USE

- Use the simple past for completed actions in the past:
  *My mom and dad **bought** me a new cell phone.*
- Use the past progressive for actions in progress at a particular time in the past:
  *We **were walking** down the street one day.*
- Use the simple past and past progressive together to say something happened while another action was in progress. You usually use *while* before the progressive:
  *My dad bought it for me **while** we were staying in Rome.*
  You usually use *when* before the simple past:
  *We were walking down the street one day **when** I saw it in a store window.*
- You can also use the past progressive to describe background events, often to set the scene in a story:
  *It **was raining**. I **was reading** a book in my bedroom when I suddenly heard a loud bang.*

Stative verbs

Don't use the past progressive with stative verbs such as *know*, *like*, *need*, *understand*, and *want*:

*I **didn't know** how to use it.* (not ~~*I wasn't knowing*~~ …)

FORM

	Simple past	Past progressive
Affirmative	I **walked** to work.	I **was walking** down the street.
	You/We/They **walked** to work.	You/We/They **were walking** down the street.
	He/She **walked** to work.	He/She **was walking** down the street.
Negative	I **didn't walk** to work.	I **wasn't walking** down the street.
	You/We/They **didn't walk** to work.	You/We/They **weren't walking** down the street.
	He/She **didn't walk** to work.	He/She **wasn't walking** down the street.
Questions and short answers	**Did** I **walk** to work? Yes, I **did**. No, I **didn't**.	**Was** I **walking** down the street? Yes, I **was**. / No, I **wasn't**.
	Did you/we/they **walk** to work? Yes, you/we/they **did**. No, you/we/they **didn't**.	**Were** you/we/they **walking** down the street? Yes, you/we/they **were**. No, you/we/they **weren't**.
	Did he/she **walk** to work? Yes, he/she **did**. No, he/she **didn't**.	**Was** he/she walking down the street? Yes, he/she **was**. No, he/she **wasn't**.

Present perfect

USE

- Use the present perfect to talk about past actions when you don't know the exact time:
  *They've **visited** a lot of countries.*

ever

- Use the present perfect with *ever* to ask about an experience that occurred at some time in the past:
  ***Have** you **ever worked** as a volunteer?*

never

- Use the present perfect with *never* to say something has not occurred at any time in the past:
  *I've **never been** to Egypt.*

just

- Use the present perfect with *just* to talk about very recent events:
  *She's **just spent** four weeks traveling around America.*

already

- Use the present perfect with *already* to talk about actions completed before now:
  *They've **already finished** building the new school.*

yet

- Use the present perfect with *yet* in questions to ask if an action is completed or not:
  ***Have** you **finished** your homework **yet**?*
- Use the present perfect with *yet* in negative sentences to talk about an action that isn't completed:
  *I **haven't written** my essay **yet**.*

for

- Use the present perfect with *for* to answer the question *How long ...?*, and answer with periods of time:
  *My brother **has played** in a band **for** three years.*

since

- Use the present perfect with *since* to answer the question *How long ...?*, and answer with dates or points in time:
  *We've **lived** in this house **since** I was two.*

FORM

Affirmative

- Form the present perfect with *have/has* + past participle of the verb:

I/You/We/They	**have**	never	**been**	to the USA.
He/She	**has**			

Contractions

I've/You've/We've/They've	never	**slept** in a tent.
He's/She's		

Past participles

- Many verbs have irregular past participles. You have to learn these:
  make – ***made*** *write* – ***written*** *see* – ***seen***

See page 140 for a list of irregular past participles.

Negative

- Form the present perfect negative with *have/has* + *not* + past participle of the verb:

I/You/We/They	**haven't (have not)**	**flown** on an airplane.
He/She	**hasn't (has not)**	

Questions and short answers

- Form questions in the present perfect with *have* + subject + past participle of the verb:

Questions			Short answers
Have	you/we/they	ever **eaten** Chinese food?	**Yes**, I/we/they **have**. **No**, I/we/they **haven't**.
Has	he/she		**Yes**, he/she **has**. **No**, he/she **hasn't**.

WATCH OUT! Don't use contractions in affirmative short answers:
Yes, I have. (not ~~*Yes, I've*~~.)

The future

USE

- Use different future forms to express different types of activities.

Present progressive

- Use the present progressive for future arrangements:
  *We're **going** on vacation tomorrow.*

Simple present

- Use the simple present for events on a timetable:
  *Our flight **leaves** at 12.*

be going to

- Use *be going to* + base verb for future plans and intentions:
  *I'**m going to spend** a lot of time in the hotel pool.*

will/won't

- Use *will/won't* for predictions about the future:
  *We'**ll have** a fantastic time!*
  *We **won't want** to come home.*
- Use *will definitely* when you're 100 percent sure:
  *We'**ll definitely try** the local food.*
- Use *will probably* when you're 75 percent sure:
  *We'**ll probably go** on a boat trip.*
- In affirmative sentences with *will*, the adverb (*probably, definitely*) comes AFTER *will*. In a negative sentence, the adverb comes BEFORE *won't*:
  will + *probably, definitely* + base verb
  probably, definitely + *won't* + base verb

be likely to

- Use *be likely to* to talk about probable events in the future:
  *It's **likely to be** very hot!*

Verbs followed by gerunds or infinitives

USE

- When a verb comes after another verb, its form depends on the first verb.

FORM

- You can use the gerund (e.g., *doing*) after these verbs: *don't mind, enjoy, imagine, practice*
  *I **enjoy listening** to music.*
  *I **practice playing** the piano every day.*
- You use *to* + base verb (e.g., *to do*) after these verbs: *decide, hope, learn, plan, want, inspire, would like*
  *My sister's **learning to play** the guitar.*
  *She'd also **like to sing** in a band one day.*
- Some verbs can be followed by *-ing* or *to* with little or no difference in meaning, such as: *hate, like, love, prefer*
  *I prefer **dancing** to salsa music.*
  *I prefer **to dance** to salsa music.*

WATCH OUT! Some verbs can be followed by *-ing* or *to* but the meaning changes: *forget* and *remember*.
*I forgot **to shut** the door. (I didn't do it.)*
*I forget **shutting** the door. (I may have done it, but I don't remember.)*
*He doesn't remember **doing** his homework. (He did his homework, but now he's forgotten he did it.)*
*He didn't remember **to do** his homework. (He forgot to do his homework.)*

Remember! Some verbs change their spelling in the *-ing* form:
*shop – **shopping*** *use – **using***

Comparative and superlative adverbs

USE

- To compare how people or things do something, use comparatives and superlatives:
  *She sings **better** than me.*
  *The Australian swimmer swam **the fastest**.*
  *Tom runs **as fast as** his brother.*
  *He **doesn't** practice **as hard as** his brother.*
- To compare how two or more people or things do something, use comparatives.
- To compare one thing with all the others in a group, use superlatives.

FORM

Comparative adverbs

- Add *-er* at the end of one-syllable adverbs followed by *than*:
  *He practices **harder than** the others.*
- Use *more* with adverbs that end in *-ly* followed by *than*:
  *She swims **more quickly than** I do.*

Superlative adverbs

- Use *the* + *-est* with one-syllable adverbs:
  *She jumped **the highest** at the high jump competition.*
- Use *the most* with adverbs longer than one syllable:
  *The Russian gymnasts performed **the most confidently**.*

Irregular adverbs

- Some adverbs have irregular comparative and superlative forms:

Adverb	Comparative	Superlative
well	better	the best
badly	worse	the worst
far	farther further	the farthest the furthest

(not) as … as …

- Use *as* + adverb + *as* to say two people or things do something the same:
  *My sister can run **as fast as** me.*
- Use *not as* + adverb + *as* to say two people or things don't do something the same:
  *She can't jump **as high as** me.*
  *She doesn't sing **as loudly as** me.*

First conditional with *if/unless*

USE

- Use the first conditional to talk about the future. The *if* clause describes a possible action in the future. The other clause describes its result:
  ***If** I **don't finish** my homework, my parents **won't let** me go to the party.*
  ***If** you **don't go** to the party, I **won't go** either.*

FORM

- Use the simple present in the *if* clause and *will (not)* + base verb in the result clause:
  if clause (action) result clause
  If + simple present + (subject) + *will (not)* + base verb
  ***If** he **asks** me, I'**ll say** yes.*
- Use the simple present in the *if* clause and *may or might* (*not*) + base verb in the result clause if you aren't sure about the result:
  ***If** Tom **goes** to the party, I **might not go**.*
- You can start the sentence with either clause:
  ***If** you talk to them, they might let you go.*
  *They might let you go **if** you talk to them.*

WATCH OUT! If the *if* clause comes second, don't use a comma:
I won't come to the party if you invite Tom.

- Use *unless* with an affirmative verb in the *if* clause to mean "*if ... not*":
  ***Unless** I **finish** my homework, my parents **won't let** me go to the party.*
  (= If I don't finish my homework, my parents won't let me go to the party.)

Second conditional

USE

- Use the second conditional to talk about an unlikely or imaginary situation in the present or future and its result:
  ***If** I **were** a parent, I'**d be** pretty strict.*
  ***If** I **had** kids, I **wouldn't let** them stay up late during the week.*

FORM

- Use the simple past after *if* or *unless* in the *if* clause. Use *would (not)* + base verb without *to* in the result clause. The contracted form of *would* is *'d*:
  if clause result clause
  If/unless + simple past + subject + *would (not)* + base verb
  ***If** I **won** the lottery, I'**d buy** a house with a swimming pool.*
  ***Unless** my kids **helped** with the housework, I **wouldn't give** them an allowance.*
- To form questions, use *would* + subject + base verb:
  ***Would** you **be** strict **if** you **were** a parent?*
  *Yes, I **would**. / No, I **wouldn't**.*
  *What **would** you **do if** you **won** the lottery?*
- You can start the sentence with either clause:
  ***If** I were president of our country, I'd ban all cars.*
  *I'd ban all cars **if** I were president of our country.*
- Remember: if the *if* clause comes second, don't use a comma.

Passives (past, present, and future)

USE

- Use the passive when the person or thing that did the action is unknown, obvious, or less important than the subject of the sentence. Compare the two sentences:
  Active: *They make chocolate out of cocoa beans, milk, and sugar.*
  Passive: *Chocolate is made out of cocoa beans, milk, and sugar.*

FORM

Simple present passive

- Form the simple present passive with *am/are/is (not)* + past participle:
  Chocolate ***is enjoyed*** *by people all over the world.*
  Cocoa beans ***are grown*** *in hot places such as Africa and Central and South America.*
- To form questions in the simple present passive, put *am/is/are* before the subject:
  Are *chocolate bars* ***sold*** *in schools in your country?*
  Yes, they ***are****. / No, they* ***aren't****.*

Simple past passive

- Form the simple past passive with *was/were (not)* + past participle:
  Chocolate ***was brought*** *to Europe in the 16th century by Hernán Cortés.*
- To form questions in the simple past passive, put *was/were* before the subject:
  Was *sugar* ***added*** *to chocolate by the Europeans?*
  Yes, it ***was****. / No, it* ***wasn't****.*

Future passive

- Form the future passive with *will/won't be* + past participle:
  Chocolate ***won't be sold*** *in schools starting next year.*
- To form questions in the future passive, put *will* before the subject:
  Will *chocolate* ***be produced*** *in this factory in the future?*
  Yes, it ***will****. / No, it* ***won't****.*
- To say who or what does the action, use *by*:
  Many different kinds of chocolate bars are produced ***by*** *thousands of chocolate companies.*

(In order) to … , so (that) …

USE

- Use *in order to …* or *so that …* to explain the reason why someone does, did, or will do something:
  I turned up the TV ***in order to*** *hear it better.*
  I turned up the TV ***so that*** *I could hear it better.*

FORM

- Use *in order to …* with the base form of the verb:
  Lisa watches movies without subtitles ***in order to practice*** *her English.*
- You can also use the shorter form *to* + base verb (without *in order*). It's more informal than *in order to*:
  Lisa watches movies without subtitles ***to practice*** *her English.*
- Use *so that* + subject + verb when the reason is negative:
  I always check my spelling ***so that*** *I* ***don't*** *make any mistakes.*
- Use *so that* with *can*/simple present to talk about now or in general:
  We learn foreign languages ***so that*** *we* ***can*** *communicate with people from other countries.*
- Use *so that* with *can/will*/simple present to talk about the future:
  Jared is studying hard ***so that*** *he'****ll*** *get a good job when he's older.*
- Use *so that* with *could/would*/simple past to talk about the past:
  I turned on the light ***so that*** *I* ***could*** *see.*
- You can use the shorter form of *so* without *that*:
  I turned on the light ***so*** *I could see.*

WATCH OUT! **If the subject of the sentence changes, use *so (that)*, not *(in order) to*:**
Braille developed the idea ***so (that)*** *blind people could use it.* (not ~~*Braille developed the idea (in order) to blind people could use it*~~.)

WORDS & BEYOND

UNIT 1

Page 4

RECALL

STAGES OF LIFE

baby
child
college student
middle-aged person
parent
senior
teenager
(young) adult

WORK WITH WORDS

TIP: To remember words, try to associate them with people or things you know well.

TASK: Make a list of people you know who are at each of the stages of life.

Pages 4 and 5

SPECIAL DAYS

get a driver's license
get a job
get married
go on a first date
go to college
graduate from high school
have children
leave home
retire
start school
vote

MOVE BEYOND

1. **Which things on the list have you already done? Write them down.**
2. **Which things would you like to do in the next five years?**

Page 8

ADJECTIVES FOR DESCRIBING OBJECTS

antique
colorful
cotton
enormous
old-fashioned
square
tiny
unusual
useful
valuable

MOVE BEYOND

Think of five objects you have. Write a sentence describing each one. Use as many adjectives from the list as you can.

OTHER IMPORTANT WORDS

celebrate
celebration
ceremony
coming of age
crown (n)
diving
doll
election
identical
miss (someone)
packaging
remind
ritual
secondhand
stuff
throw out
traditional
turn + age
wooden
work together

Page 14

RECALL

METHODS OF TRANSPORTATION

AIR	RAIL	ROAD	SEA
helicopter	subway	bike	boat
plane	train	bus	ferry
		car	ship
		horse	
		motorcycle	
		scooter	
		taxi	

WORK WITH WORDS

TIP: When you learn a word, learn it with verbs and prepositions as phrases.

TASK: Can you use *in*, *on* (or both) with each method of transportation? Use a dictionary or search online to check.

Pages 14 and 15

TRAVEL ITEMS

backpack
boarding pass
hairbrush
passport
scissors
shampoo
sleeping bag
suitcase
toothbrush
toothpaste
visa
wallet

MOVE BEYOND

1. **Which word on the list has a silent letter? Circle it.**
2. **Which word exists in its plural form only? How would you describe "one" of this thing? Use a dictionary to check.**

Page 18

TRAVEL

arrival
connection
delay
departure
destination
fare
passenger
reservation
route
seat

MOVE BEYOND

Write the verbs for the following nouns.

1. connection ....
2. delay ....
3. departure ....
4. reservation ....

OTHER IMPORTANT WORDS

abroad
aid (n)
attitude
baggage
bubble
check in (v)
community
compartment
crew
customs
distance
flight
gate
homeschooling
homesick
host family
invisible
journey
land (v)
line (n)
luggage
material goods
natural disaster
passport control
sharp object
take off
trip (n)
voyage

WORDS & BEYOND

Page 26

RECALL

KINDS OF MUSIC	INSTRUMENTS	PEOPLE	KINDS OF GROUPS	PLACES & EVENTS
classical	drum	conductor	band	concert
heavy metal	guitar	musician	orchestra	concert hall
hip hop	keyboard	singer		festival
pop	piano			
R&B	violin			
reggae				
rock				

WORK WITH WORDS

TIP: Listening to songs in English is a great way to improve your vocabulary.

TASK: Make a list of English song titles you know. Then write the name of the person or group who performs the song and the style of music.

Pages 26 and 27

MUSIC WORDS

audience
band
brass band
flute
folk
jazz
opera
performance
trumpet
venue

MOVE BEYOND

Add at least five more music words to the list.

1
2
3
4
5

Page 30

ADVERBS OF DEGREE

a little
a lot
extremely
fairly
incredibly
pretty
really
terribly
totally
very

MOVE BEYOND

Write the title of a movie, a book, and a TV show you've watched recently. Give your opinion of each one using an adverb of degree.

1
2
3

OTHER IMPORTANT WORDS

audition (n & v)	confidence	extreme	music theory	steady
aware	convey	focused	perform	talent
beat (n)	creatively	gesture (n)	powerful	tell off
childhood	criteria	grasp (n)	rhythm	terrible (adj)
conductor	distracting	inspire	stage (n)	wordless

Page 36

RECALL

APPEARANCE

GENERAL	HAIR	EYES	MOUTH/NOSE
good-looking	dark	big	big
old	light	small	small
short	straight		
tall	wavy		
young			

PERSONALITY

ambitious
brave
cheerful
competitive
confident
creative
sensitive
generous
patient
polite
rude
serious
shy

WORK WITH WORDS

TIP: To help you remember new words, write definitions in English.

TASK: Choose three of the personality words from the list and write a definition in English.

Pages 36 and 37

PEOPLE AND RELATIONSHIPS

acquaintance
boyfriend/girlfriend
classmate
close friend
enemy
friend of a friend
guest
neighbor
old friend
online friend
relative
teammate

MOVE BEYOND

Think of someone you know for each of the people and relationships, and write the name of the person, e.g., *Denis is a close friend*.

Page 40

EXTREME ADJECTIVES

amazing
ancient
awful
exhausted
fascinating
furious
huge
shocked
terrified
unbelievable

MOVE BEYOND

Divide the words into syllables, and then underline the stressed syllable, e.g., a-<u>maz</u>-ing. Practice saying the words.

OTHER IMPORTANT WORDS AND PHRASES

accept
argue
condition
cruise (n)
friendship
give somebody a hard time
good company
have something in common
honesty
point out
quality
recognize
respect (n & v)
row (n & v)
shame (n)
strict
suffer (from something)
support (n & v)
survey (n)
take an interest in someone/something
talk behind somebody's back
trust (n)

WORDS & BEYOND

UNIT 5

Page 48

RECALL

PARTS OF THE BODY

ankle
arm
back
chest
ear
eye
face
finger
foot
hand
head
knee
leg
mouth
neck
nose
shoulder
teeth
throat
thumb
toe

WORK WITH WORDS

TIP: Make drawings and label the parts to help you remember vocabulary.

TASK: Draw a human body and label the different parts without looking at the word list. How many words did you remember?

Pages 48 and 49

THE SENSES

hearing
sight
smell
taste
touch

SENSE VERBS

feel
hear
listen
look
see
smell
taste
touch
watch

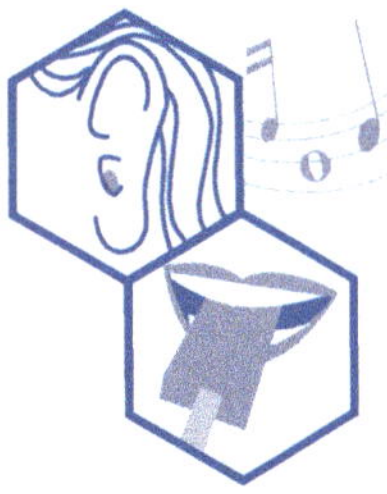

MOVE BEYOND

Match 10 of the body parts above to the five senses. Then write sentences with the sense verbs, for example, *We use our eyes to see.*

Page 52

COLOR IDIOMS

as black as night
as white as a sheet
be in the red
black and white
feel blue
get the green light
once in a blue moon
out of the blue
see red
tell a white lie

MOVE BEYOND

Choose three idioms from the list. Write three sentences about you or the world today using the idioms.

OTHER IMPORTANT WORDS AND PHRASES

air freshener
allergic
ban (v)
blind (adj)
cell
cloud
complaint
formula
fragrance
incense (n)
independently
insect repellent
liquid
lotion
noisy
pale
perfume
pharmacist
potato chips
processed foods
promote
restricted
taste buds
tongue
unisex

IRREGULAR VERBS

base verb	simple past	past participle
agree	agreed	agreed
be	was/were	been
become	became	become
break	broke	broken
bring	brought	brought
built	built	built
buy	bought	bought
can	could	been able to
catch	caught	caught
choose	chose	chosen
come	came	come
cost	cost	cost
do	did	done
drive	drove	driven
eat	ate	eaten
fall	fell	fallen
feel	felt	felt
find	found	found
fly	flew	flown
get	got	gotten
give	gave	given
go	went	gone
grow	grew	grown
have	had	had
hurt	hurt	hurt
keep	kept	kept
knit	knit/knitted	knit/knitted
know	knew	known
leave	left	left
make	made	made
meet	met	met
must	had to	had to
pay	paid	paid
put	put	put
ride	rode	ridden
run	ran	run
say	said	said
see	saw	seen
sit	sat	sat
sleep	slept	slept
speak	spoke	spoken
spend	spent	spent
take	took	taken
teach	taught	taught
tell	told	told
think	thought	thought
understand	understood	understood
wake	woke	woken
wear	wore	worn
write	wrote	written

STUDENT A

UNIT 3 IN THE PICTURE

Page 29, Exercise 7

Music survey

1. Who is your favorite musical artist or group?
2. Can you play any musical instruments? If so, which ones? If not, which ones would you like to learn?
3. Have you ever been to an opera or a classical concert?
4. How do you usually listen to music – a) on the radio, b) online, c) on a CD, or d) on a cell phone?
5. In your opinion, which is more important in a song – a) the words or b) the music?

UNIT 5 LISTENING AND VOCABULARY

Page 54, Exercise 5

Read each word out loud to your partner. Your partner says the color that he or she associates with the word.

tomato ocean planet car fire sky ice cream grass love happiness

TIPS

UNIT 1 LANGUAGE & BEYOND

Page 12, Exercise 4

TIPS FOR ORGANIZING AN EVENT

- Make sure all the people in the group give their ideas.
- Make decisions as a group. You can vote on things if people disagree.
- When planning and preparing the activity, give everyone a specific job to do.
- Make sure that everyone does his or her equal share of the work.

UNIT 5 LISTENING AND VOCABULARY

Page 54, Exercise 5

Read each word out loud to your partner. Your partner says the color that he or she associates with the word.

jeans

soccer

home

chocolate

sun

space

bus

apple

coffee

anger

Move Beyond 5

WORKBOOK

macmillan education

Lynda Edwards
Ingrid Wisniewska

Macmillan Education
4 Crinan Street
London N1 9XW
A division of Springer Nature Limited

Companies and representatives throughout the world

ISBN 978-1-380-00772-8

Written by Lynda Edwards and Ingrid Wisniewska

Go Beyond First published 2015
First edition entitled *Beyond* published 2014

Designed by EMC Design Ltd.

Illustrated by John Batten (Beehive Illustration) p. 133; Zara Picken p. 99.

Cover design by EMC Design Ltd.
Cover photograph by Getty Images/Lonely Planet Images/Ariadne Van Zandbergen
Picture research by Lorraine Beck and Tessa Hammond

The authors and publishers would like to thank the following for permission to reproduce their images:

Alamy/bobo p. 92(5), Alamy/Danita Delimont/Adam Jones p. 94, Alamy/dpa picture alliance p. 105, Alamy/Findlay p. 104(tr), Alamy/Alamy/David Gowans p. 81(t), Alamy/imagebroker p. 120, Alamy/Imagedoc p. 92(4), Alamy/JLImages p. 87(A), Alamy/Petr Malyshev p. 92(1), Alamy/Melba Photo Agency p. 129(cheese), Alamy/Jeff Morgan 02 p. 104(tm), Alamy/Christine Osborne Pictures p. 111(b), Alamy/Radius Images p. 105(br), Alamy/Realimage p. 96(c), Alamy/Dmitry Rukhlenko p. 93(t), Alamy/Aleksandr Ugorenkov p. 84(tr);
BananaStock p. 80(tl, tc, tml, tr);
Brand X Pictures pp. 85(bl), 87(c);
Comstock Images pp. 85(cl), 92(2);
Corbis pp. 85(tr), 101(r), 108, 122(br), Corbis/Gareth Brown p. 113, Corbis/Julian Calder p. 104(tl), Corbis/Envision p. 92(6), Corbis/Ocean/2/Jacqueline Veissid p. 117, Corbis/Reuters/Neil Hall p. 131, Corbis/Tetra Images/Tom Grill p. 122(tr);
Getty Images pp. 87(b), 92(8), Getty Images/AFP p. 104(bl),Getty Images/John W Banagan p. 111(a), Getty Images/Blend Images/Ariel Skelleyp. 80(b), Getty Images/E+/kevinjeon00 p. 128(C), Getty Images/Pawel Gaul p. 122(bl), Getty Images/The Image Bank/Tim Kitchen p. 88(t), Getty Images/jonya p. 116(e), Getty Images/Jupiterimages p. 128(t), Getty Images/Jason Lugo p. 116(b), Getty Images/Moment Open/grasslifeisgood p. 93(cr), Getty Images/OJO Images Ltd/Floresco Productions p. 123, Getty Images/PhotoDisc pp. 80(tmr), 85(cr), 92(3), 96(a), 128(A), 129(cup), Getty Images/PhotoDisc/Buena Vista Images p. 96(B), Getty Images/PNC p. 81(b), Getty Images/RooM/JamieB p. 92(11), Getty Images/Vstock LLC p. 84(br), Getty Images/Rachel Watson p. 109(l, m, r);
Goodshoot p. 118;
Image Source pp. 98, 112, 116(c, d), 122(tl), 129(cake);
Macmillan Publishers Ltd p. 93(bl), Macmillan Publishers Ltd/Macmillan Education/Stuart Cox p. 129(lemons), Macmillan Publishers Ltd/David Tolley/Dean Ryan p. 92(7), Macmillan Publishers Ltd/Raymond Turvey (Turvey Books Ltd) p. 129(tongues);
PhotoAlto p. 85(tl);
PhotoDisc pp. 84(bl), 85(br), 101(l);
Stockbyte/PunchStock p. 129(woman);
Thinkstock pp. 84(c), 94(10), 128(B, D), Thinkstock/Julie Birch p. 88(br), Thinkstock/Fuse p. 106, Thinkstock/iStock pp. 88(bl), 92(9), 100, Thinkstock/johavel p. 84(d), Thinkstock/Joshua Rainey Photography p. 88(background), Thinkstock/omgimages p. 87(D), Thinkstock/Ron Sumners p. 84(tl), Thinkstock/Lisa F Young p. 116(a).

The authors and publishers are grateful for permission to reprint the following copyright material:
Extract and illustration from "Macmillan Readers Call of the Wild Pre-Intermediate no CD Reader" ©Macmillan Publishers Limited, originally written by J. London; retold by R. Bladon 2011, Published by Macmillan Publishers Limited. Used by Permission. All rights reserved. p. 142;
Extract and illustrations from "Macmillan Readers Wizard of Oz Pre-Intermediate Reader Without CD" ©Macmillan Publishers Limited, originally written by F.L Baum; retold by E. Walker 2007, Published by Macmillan Publishers Limited. Used by Permission. All rights reserved. p. 140.

Printed and bound by CPI Group (UK) Ltd, Croydon CR0 4YY

2021 2020 2019
10 9 8 7 6

CONTENTS

LIFE STAGES

VOCABULARY 1 >>> Special days

1 Rearrange the letters to make words for people of different ages.

1 trapne ___*parent*___
2 gouny tudla ______
3 agretene ______
4 irones ______
5 leeclog tunsted ______
6 ledimd-dega sopren ______
7 dilhc ______
8 yabb ______

2 Label the pictures with the words from Exercise 1.

1 ______
2 ______
3 ______

4 ______

5 ______

6 ______

7 ______ and
8 ______

3 Look at the picture below. Write sentences about the people in Emily's family using the words from Exercise 1.

Emily is a child.
______
______
______
______
______

4 Complete the phrases with the words in the box.

get (x3)   go (x2)   have   graduate   leave   retire   vote

1 ___*get*___ a job
2 ______ married
3 ______ in an election
4 ______ from your job
5 ______ from high school
6 ______ home
7 ______ to college
8 ______ children
9 ______ on a first date
10 ______ a driver's license

5 Complete the messages with words and phrases from Exercise 4.

Hey, Jin! It's my 16th birthday tomorrow, and I can't wait – I can get my (1) ______!

Hi, Franca! Awesome! In my country we can't drive until we're 18 ☹.

That's the same age as when we (2) ______ from high school and go to (3) ______. I can't wait to go – it'll be so cool to be independent.

Yes, and when I finish, I can (4) ______ and finally earn some money!

Yeah! Do you want to (5) ______, though? I want three or maybe four!

You're crazy! I only want one! I just want to work hard so I can (6) ______ early, maybe at 50.

50?! And then what? Maybe I can come visit you ☺.

READING

Find specific information

1 Complete the tips with the words in the box.

REMEMBER HOW TO ...

find specific information

all beginning information words

- Don't read (1) ________ of the text.
- Are there headings? Use them to find the (2) ________ you need.
- Read the (3) ________ of each paragraph. Does it have the information you need? If not, read the next paragraph.
- Look for (4) ________ connected to the information you need.

2 Read the information in the table. Then, read the text and complete the table.

	Gretna Green	Las Vegas
Number of marriages	(1) ________	2,000,000+
Reasons it's popular	geography and a long tradition (2) ________ a lot of (3) ________ where you can get married	cheap can (5) ________ immediately
Unusual things people do	marry in the famous (4) ________	dress up as Elvis or (6) ________ characters

A DAY TO REMEMBER?

Home Memories

A pretty village with a lot of history

Gretna Green in Scotland is a very popular place to get married. Each year there are over 5,000 weddings there. Why do so many people choose to get married in this tiny place?

Well, traditionally it's because of geography. If you travel from England to Scotland, it's the first village across the Scottish border. Differences in marriage rules between England and Scotland were the reason for its popularity in the past, because you could marry at a younger age.

So why is Gretna Green still such a popular place to get married? First, it has a long tradition of weddings, so it's a very romantic place. There are also a lot of places to get married and to celebrate. One famous place to get married is in the historic blacksmith's* shop. Finally, it's also a very beautiful place – as you can see from the picture!

*A blacksmith is a person who makes shoes for horses.

Anything goes in this city

Las Vegas couldn't be more different from Gretna Green, but it's an even more popular place to get married. Each year over 2 million couples choose to get married there!

Las Vegas is in the middle of the desert in Nevada, USA, but people still travel from all over the world to get married in this city. The main reason it's so popular is that it's easy and cheap to get married there. In many places in the USA, couples have to wait to get married, but in Las Vegas, they can get married immediately.

It's also a fun place to get married because many places let you dress up in costumes* for the wedding. Some people choose a Hawaiian style; others dress up as Elvis or as characters from *Star Trek*! In Las Vegas, anything is possible!

*A costume is clothes you wear to look like someone else.

MOVE BEYOND

What's the perfect place to get married in your country? Write information about it. Write some facts, download some pictures, and tell your class.

____

____

GRAMMAR 1 Present tenses review

Talk about present actions

1 Complete the grammar tables.

Simple present

Affirmative			
I/We/You/They	go out every Saturday with friends.		
He/(1) ______	wants a party this year.		
Negative			
I/We/You/They	(2) ______	dress up for special occasions.	
(3) ______ /She	does not/doesn't	want to go to the school dance on Friday.	
Questions and short answers			
(4) ______	I/we/you/they	celebrate coming of age?	(5) ______ , I/you/we/they do. No, I/you/we/they don't.
Does	he/she	like parties?	Yes, he/she (6) ______ . No, he/she doesn't.

Present progressive

Affirmative		
I am (7) (______)	studying.	
He/She is ('s)	preparing for a party now.	
We/You/They are (8) (______)	listening to music.	
Negative		
I am not ('m not)	doing anything special today.	
He/She is not (9) (______)	wearing special clothes right now.	
We/You/They are not (aren't)	doing their homework.	
***Yes/No* questions and short answers**		
Am I	laughing in the picture?	No, I'm not.
Are you/we/they	dancing?	Yes, you/we/they (10) ______ . No, you/we/they aren't.
(11) ______ he/she	cutting the cake?	Yes, he/she is. No, he/she (12) ______ .
***Wh-* questions**		
What (13) ______ you celebrating?	I'm celebrating my birthday.	
(14) ______ is he writing an invitation?	Because he's having a party.	

2 Match the uses of the present tenses (1–6) to the sentences (a–f).

1 to talk about habits and routines ______
2 to talk about things that are happening around now with expressions like *these days* and *nowadays* ______
3 to talk about things that are generally true ______
4 to talk about how often we do things with adverbs and expressions of frequency like *never*, *usually*, and *always*. ______
5 with stative verbs (verbs that express mental states, preferences, and opinions, for example, *think*, *understand*, *like*) ______
6 to talk about things that are happening now with expressions like *right now* ______

a I think that parties are really fun.
b My friend always has a party on her birthday.
c I'm waiting to take my driving test right now, and I'm sweating!
d Weddings are getting more and more expensive these days.
e My sister comes home from college on weekends.
f Smartphones cost a lot of money.

3 › Choose the correct option to complete the sentences.

1 In my country, people usually ***are retiring*** / ***retire*** when they're in their 60s.
2 My sister ***makes*** / ***'s making*** a big cake for my parents' wedding anniversary right now!
3 My parents often ***are organizing*** / ***organize*** a big party for my birthday.
4 The children ***are watching*** / ***watch*** a movie on TV right now.
5 I ***'m never wearing*** / ***never wear*** black clothes because they're boring.
6 When my parents are away, we ***stay*** / ***'re staying*** at our Aunt Betty's house.

4 a › Complete the table with the words in the box.

believe celebrate dance do enjoy know like need paint prepare remember want

Stative verbs	Action verbs

b › Add two more verbs to each column of the table.

5 ›› Find and correct the mistakes.

1 Are you needing some help with that project?
....
2 He doesn't want to study physics next year because he's preferring biology.
....
3 Freddie isn't wanting to go to college when he graduates from high school.
....
4 I save money right now to go on vacation next year.
....
5 Jess gets ready to go out now.
....
6 How often are you visiting your grandparents?
....

6 ›› Complete the sentences with the correct present form of the verb in parentheses.

1 My dad .... (know) a lot about cars.
2 Jane speaks French, but she .... (not speak) Italian.
3 I .... (enjoy) the movie. Thanks for inviting me!
4 I .... (exercise) every day after school.
5 I .... (not study) right now.
6 Billy must work harder. His English .... (not improve)!

7 ››› Complete the conversation with the words in the box. Use the correct present tense.

call drive need pass ride (x2) see talk

Tom: Hi, Mark! Can you (1) .... ?
Mark: Hi, Tom! I (2) .... my bike to school right now.
Tom: Really?
Mark: I (3) .... my bike to school every day.
Tom: Good for you!
Mark: Why (4) .... you .... me?
Tom: My dad (5) .... me to school. We (6) .... your house now, but I don't think you (7) .... a ride.
Mark: No, not today.
Tom: (8) .... you at school!

8 ››› Use the prompts to make questions for the answers.

1 **A:** *Do you like Indian food*?
(like / Indian food)
B: Yes, I love Indian food!
2 **A:** ....?
(what / do)
B: Nothing right now, why?
3 **A:** ....?
(brother / play / soccer)
B: Yes, every Saturday.
4 **A:** ....?
(your teacher / usually / give a lot of homework)
B: Yes, we get a lot these days.
5 **A:** ....?
(where / Amy and Sue / go / now)
B: I don't know. Maybe to the cafeteria?
6 **A:** ....?
(what time / history class / start)
B: At 1:30 p.m., I think.

LISTENING

Recognize informal speech

1 Complete the tips with the words in the box.

REMEMBER HOW TO …

recognize informal speech

can't d'ya stuff um yeah

- Listen for informal pronunciation: *dunno*, *kinda*, and (1) ________ .
- Listen for informal word choices: (2) ________ and (3) ________ .
- Listen for contractions: *don't* and (4) ________ .
- Listen for fillers: *you know*, *hey*, and (5) ________ .

2 ▶75 Look at the pictures and listen to the conversation. Check (✓) the things Mark plans to take with him.

A ☐

B ☐

C ☐

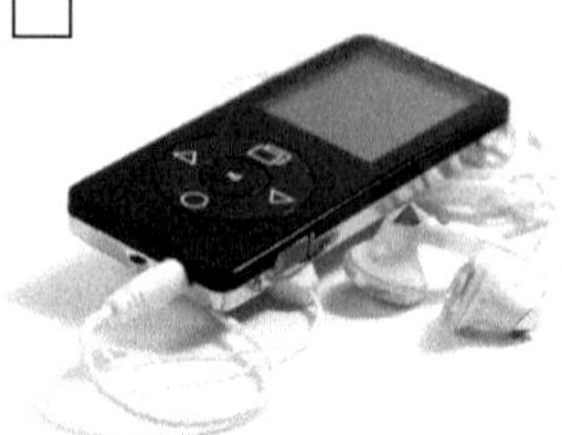

D ☐

E ☐

F ☐

3 ▶75 Listen again and complete the sentences with the correct information.

1 Mark's going to ________ .
2 He's staying there for ________ .
3 It's Rafa's ________ .
4 Mark's flight is leaving at ________ .
5 Mark's taking a couple of ________ .
6 The month is ________ .
7 Gemma thinks Mark needs to take ________ .
8 On Monday, there's ________ .

4 Rewrite these informal forms in formal language.

Example:
1 sorta = *sort of*
2 kinda = ________
3 dunno = ________
4 yeah = ________
5 ya = ________
6 gonna = ________
7 stuff = ________
8 What d'ya mean? = ________

5 Rewrite the informal sentences in a formal way.

1 That's sorta far to go for four days.
____
2 What d'ya mean?
____
3 I think it's kinda cold there now.
____
4 I dunno.
____
5 So, when d'ya leave?
____

6 ▶76 Complete the sentences from the conversation with the correct words. Then listen and check your answers.

1 ________ , Mark! What are you so happy about?
2 ________ , but it's a special occasion.
3 Do you have your passport and ________ ?
4 I ________ . I think it's ________ cold there right now.

7 Decide if these sentences are correct (*C*) or incorrect (*I*).

1 Mark's happy because he passed his math test. ____
2 Right now it's hot and sunny in the USA. ____
3 Mark needs to get up early tomorrow morning. ____
4 Gemma thinks Mark's planning to take the wrong clothes. ____
5 Mark's ready for the test on Monday. ____
6 Mark's an organized person. ____

VOCABULARY 2

Adjectives for describing objects

1 Complete the sentences with the correct adjectives.

1 This T-shirt is comfortable when it's hot because it's made of c *o t t o n*.
2 Samira lives in a very big house. In fact it's e_______.
3 My jewelry box isn't round. It's s_____.
4 This toy is worth a lot of money. It's very v_______.
5 These new lawn chairs are just made of p______, but they're very comfortable.
6 There is a lot of red, green, and blue in the poster. It's c_______.
7 Helen's new dog is very small. It's t___.
8 I love your necklace – it's such an u______ design.

2 Look at the pictures. Then write the vowels (a, e, i, o, u) to complete each adjective.

1 v *a* l *u* *a* b l *e*

2 _ s _ f _ l

3 _ n t _ q _ _

4 _ l d - f _ s h _ _ n _ d

5 s p _ c _ _ l

6 c _ l _ r f _ l

3 Complete the sentences with the adjectives in parentheses in the correct order.

1 My friends have a(n) *amazing wooden* (wooden / amazing) table in their living room.
2 The actress lives in a(n) __________ (white / old) house on the edge of our town.
3 Katy bought a __________ (silver / tiny) phone.
4 We're having a meal in a __________ (traditional / small) restaurant.
5 You can't wear that __________ (old / cotton) T-shirt!
6 In the picture my mom's wearing a __________ (long / pink) skirt.

WORDS & BEYOND

4 a Match the words in Column A to the definitions in Column B.

Column A	Column B
secondhand	a child's toy that looks like a small person or baby
doll	exactly the same as something else
wooden	the paper/plastic that covers a new product before it's opened or used
identical	made out of wood
packaging	used / not new

b Complete the text with the words in the box.

doll identical packaging secondhand wooden

My favorite present was a beautiful (1) __________ that my grandma gave me for my seventh birthday. It wasn't new – my grandma bought it at a (2) __________ store in the town where she lives. It's actually very old and is (3) __________, not plastic like the ones today are. What makes it really special is that it's (4) __________ to one that my grandma had as a child when she was young. I remember how excited I was when I saw the brand name on the (5) __________ and found it inside. I named her Ella, after my grandma. I still have her too!

5 Complete the sentences with the words in the box.

ceremony diving stuff turned

1 My birthday was yesterday. I __________ 17.
2 It was a small __________ – just close friends and family, but it was the perfect wedding day for my sister.
3 Moving out of Mom and Dad's is going to take forever – I've collected so much __________ in my room over the years.
4 Would I like to go __________ with you off the coast of Northern Australia? You bet!

GRAMMAR 2 Past tenses review

»» Talk about past actions

1 › Complete the grammar tables.

Simple past

Affirmative		
I/You/He/She/It/(1) ____________/They		enjoyed the party.
Negative		
I/You/He/She/It/We/They	(2) ____________	have a good time at the festival.
***Yes/No* questions**		
(3) ____________	I/you/he/she/it/we/they	go out last weekend?

Past progressive

Affirmative		
I/He/She	was	dancing all night.
We/You/They	(4) ____________	celebrating her birthday.
Negative		
I/He/She	(5) ____________	wearing a coat.
We/You/They	weren't	eating in class.
***Yes/No* questions and short answers**		
Was I/he/she	playing loud music?	Yes, I/he/she was. No, I/he/she (6) ____________ .
(7) ____________ we/you/they	talking to a lot of people?	Yes, we/you/they were. No, we/you/they weren't.
***Wh-* questions**		
What (8) ____________ they doing?	They were listening to the radio.	
Where was he (9) ____________ ?	He was going to school.	

2 › Choose the correct option to complete the sentences.

1 When I woke up this morning, it *was poured* / *was pouring*.
2 Mandy and I *prepared* / *were preparing* sandwiches for the party when I dropped the cheese on the floor.
3 We took a taxi because we *didn't want* / *weren't wanting* to be late to the party.
4 While I *waited* / *was waiting* for the band to start, I talked to Tom.
5 When I *found* / *was finding* Helen, she was talking to some friends.
6 Every time I saw Michael, he *danced* / *was dancing*.

3 »› Complete the phone call with the correct form of the verb in parentheses.

A: Hi. I (1) *called* (call) earlier. (2) *Were* you *watching* (watch) TV?
B: No, I (3) ____________ (not watch) TV! I (4) ____________ (work) on the project, and I (5) ____________ (listen) to some music at the same time.
A: (6) ____________ you ____________ (get) my email about asking Jane to help with the project?
B: No, I didn't. When (7) ____________ you ____________ (send) it?
A: I (8) ____________ (send) it this afternoon.
B: No. My internet connection (9) ____________ (not work) this afternoon. It's OK now. I'll check. But I think that's a good idea.
A: While I (10) ____________ (work) on the project I (11) ____________ (notice) a couple of mistakes. I (12) ____________ (not change) anything, but we can talk about them tomorrow.
B: That's cool. See you tomorrow!

4 »»› Complete the email with the correct form of the verbs in the box.

be buy come dance fall hurt listen shop speak

Hi Luz,
I'm having a great time in Mexico! I'm glad I (1) ____________ to your advice and (2) ____________ a Spanish phrasebook. I definitely need to practice my Spanish since I can't understand anybody! While I (3) ____________ at the market yesterday, I (4) ____________ to one of the store clerks in Spanish, and she didn't understand me at all! Fortunately Rosalia was there to help!
Rosalia's quinceañera last night (5) ____________ amazing. About 60 people (6) ____________ . Unfortunately while I (7) ____________ I (8) ____________ down and (9) ____________ my leg! That was the end of my dancing.
I'm coming home tomorrow, and I have a present for you. 🙂
See you soon,
Kelly

Make and react to invitations

1 ▶77 **Look at the pictures and listen to four short conversations. Match the conversations (1–4) to the pictures.**

A ☐

B ☐

C ☐

D ☐

2 ▶77 **Choose the correct word(s) to complete the conversations. Then listen again and check your answers.**

1 **Dan:** Hi! Pete and I are going to the movies tonight. Would you like to come?
Jim: I'm sorry, (1) ***but I can't come*** / ***I'm free***. I'm going to a party with Rachel.
Dan: (2) ***Great!*** / ***That's too bad***. Another time!

2 **Lea:** Hi, Mac. I'm having a barbecue on the beach for our class.
Mac: (3) ***Sorry.*** / ***Great!*** When is it?
Lea: It's on Saturday afternoon. Can you come?
Mac: (4) ***I'm sorry, I can't.*** / ***Sure, I'd love to.*** I'm free that afternoon.

3 **Ann:** Jane and I are going on a day trip to New York next Saturday. Would you like to come with us?
Lori: (5) ***That sounds fantastic.*** / ***I'm sorry.*** I'd love to. Thanks for inviting me.

4 **Ron:** Hi, Sam. I'm inviting some people out for pizza tonight. Are you free?
Sam: Sorry. (6) ***I'd love to come, but I can't.*** / ***I'd love to.*** I'm going to a concert with my brother.

3 Decide if the phrases are used to accept (*A*) or refuse (*R*) invitations.

1 I'd love to come, but I can't. ______
2 Sure. That sounds great. ______
3 Yes, I'd love to. Thanks for inviting me. ______
4 I'm sorry, but I can't come. ______

4 ▶78 **Number the sentences in order to make a conversation. Then listen and check your answers.**

Carla: We're thinking of having it after school tomorrow at four o'clock. Can you come then? ☐
Lucas: That sounds like fun. I'd love to. When is it? ☐
Carla: Fantastic! Meet at my house on Wednesday at four o'clock. Don't be late! ☐
Lucas: Sure, Wednesday sounds great. ☐
Carla: That's OK. We can have it on Wednesday. Are you free then? ☐
Lucas: Oh, sorry. I'd love to, but I have to babysit my little brother tomorrow afternoon. ☐
Carla: Hi, Lucas. I'm trying to organize a surprise birthday party for Tina. Would you like to come? [1]

5 a PRONOUNCE **Circle the words with the /e/ sound. Underline the words with the /eɪ/ sound.**

age baby date friend get
net paint then twenty

b ▶79 **Listen and check your answers.**

c Write two more words with the /e/ sound and two with the /eɪ/ sound.

/e/ ______ ______
/eɪ/ ______ ______

WRITING

Make a writing plan

1 Complete the tips with the words in the box.

REMEMBER HOW TO ...

make a writing plan

a heading   notes   questions

- Write (1) __________ for the text summarizing its content.
- Write (2) __________ about the details you want to include.
- Answer your questions and make (3) __________ .

2 A writer is preparing to write about a special day. Add the questions (a–c) to her Writing Plan for this paragraph.

a What happened? Who was there? What did I do?
b What, where, and when was it?
c Why was it special? What do I remember about it?

Writing Plan

1 What my special day was: __________

2 Details about the day: __________

3 Why it was special for me: __________

3 Read *A special day*. Did the writer follow the writing plan?

4 Read the story again. Underline the introduction. Put parentheses around the main body. Circle the conclusion.

A special day

A really special day for me was my brother's wedding last summer. Ana, my new sister-in-law, wanted her wedding to be memorable, and it was! They got married at her grandparents' ranch. The wedding reception was in the barn. It was decorated in a cowboy theme. Each table had a cowboy hat filled with orange and yellow flowers. Outside they had four enormous grills to cook the barbecue beef dinner for 200 guests. They even had horses to ride. After dinner, the country-western band started playing. They taught us how to line dance. I stayed on the dance floor all night! My best memory is how Ana surprised everyone when she walked in wearing orange cowboy boots under her elegant white wedding dress. The whole day was fantastic, but best of all, now I have a very special sister-in-law.

5 **Now think about your own special day. Complete the *Writing Plan* below with your own questions. Use Exercise 2 to help you.**

WRITING PLAN

1 Introduction: ☐

....

....

2 Main body: ☐

....

....

3 Conclusion: ☐

....

....

WRITE AND CHECK

6 **Write about your special day. Then review your writing and check (✓) 1–3 in the *Writing plan*.**

Collaborate to organize a group activity

1 **Read the conversation between Carol and her friends. What event are they organizing? What things do they need to organize?**

Carol: So guys, Ms. Talbot asked me to get a group of us to organize the end-of-year party. I've decided we can have it at the new Spanish restaurant. OK? We need to find out who is coming, first of all. And we need to call the restaurant to reserve a table and tell them what menu we'd like. I thought it would be nice if we brought some decorations like balloons too. Oh, yes, and we need to think about music – the restaurant has a sound system, but we need to bring our own music.
Paco: I have a great idea for music.
Carol: I just told you about the music!
Paco: I thought we could get a Spanish band to play.
Carol: Sorry, Paco, but it's easier if we just bring recorded music. Now, there are two different menus. We can choose the menu with an appetizer and a main course, or the one with a main course and dessert.
Andy: How do we decide?
Carol: I don't like desserts, so let's go with the one with an appetizer.
Paco: OK, I guess. Is that it?
Carol: Pretty much. So if the rest of you can choose some of the tasks to organize, that'd be great. It doesn't matter which ones you choose.
Andy: OK.
Paco: What about you?
Carol: I'm the organizer, so I don't really have time to take on any of the big tasks.

2 **Which sentences say how the group worked together? Check (✓) them.**

1 a Everyone's ideas were listened to. ☐
  b One person gave most of the ideas. ☐
2 a Everybody was given a specific job. ☐
  b Most people didn't have a specific job. ☐
3 a The group voted on decisions. ☐
  b One person made all the decisions. ☐
4 a Everyone was given an equal share of the work. ☐
  b There was not an equal share of the work. ☐

3 **Write some advice for the group on how to work together better.**

....

....

....

....

1 Number the life stages in order from youngest to oldest.

1	child	1	senior	3	young adult	2
2	teenager		baby		parent	
3	senior		baby		college student	
4	young adult		teenager		middle-aged person	
5	adult		teenager		child	

2 Read the clues and complete the crossword. The answers are all words from this unit.

Across

1 Together your mom and dad are called your ________ .
2 You do this at the stage in your life when you finish work.
3 A king wears this on his head.
4 A birthday party or wedding is an example of this.
5 This is a toy that looks like a small person or baby.
6 You vote in this to choose someone.

Down

7 This is a series of actions often done as part of a celebration.
8 You need this document before you can drive a car.
9 When you get married, you have a wedding ________ .
10 You study at a college or a ________ after you graduate from high school.
11 This is another word for the work you do. It's your ________ .

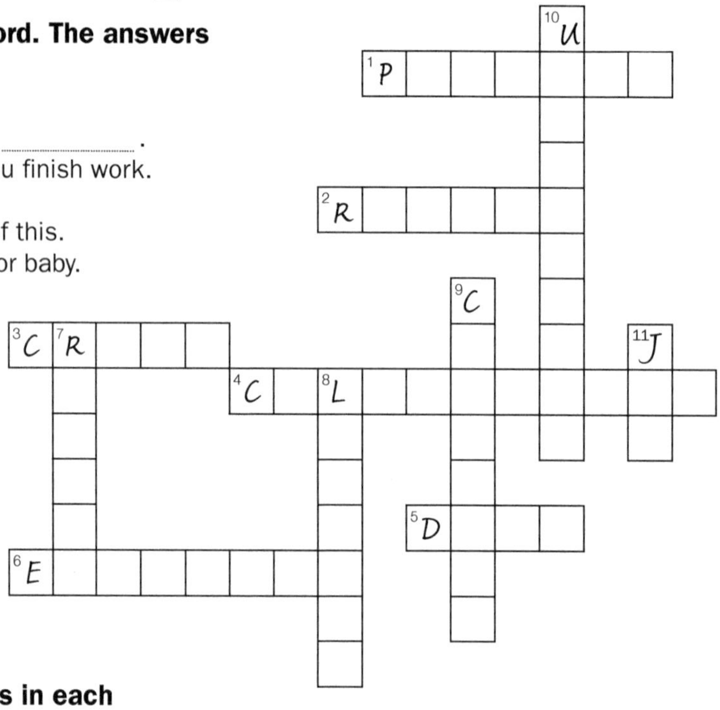

3 Complete the adjectives to describe items in each category. Then find your answers in the word search.

opinion: u _ _ _ _ l, v _ _ _ _ _ _ e, u _ _ _ _ _ l, o _ _ -f _ _ _ _ _ _ _ d, t _ _ _ _ _ _ _ _ _ l

size: e _ _ _ _ _ _ s, t _ _ _

shape: s _ _ _ _ e

age: a _ _ _ _ _ e

color: c _ _ _ _ _ _ l

material: w o o d e n, c _ _ _ _ n

R	R	S	R	E	N	J	U	S	E	P	F	T	I
W	O	O	D	E	N	O	R	M	O	U	S	R	V
A	F	J	T	T	V	E	O	V	I	C	E	A	O
E	S	C	U	N	R	W	L	E	P	Q	C	D	L
X	R	O	S	S	E	A	D	A	A	C	O	I	A
R	O	T	E	M	U	S	F	L	N	C	N	T	Y
D	E	T	F	S	T	A	A	G	T	O	D	I	L
V	U	O	U	T	M	C	S	A	I	L	H	O	Z
C	N	N	L	N	I	Y	H	T	Q	O	A	N	H
T	U	E	O	T	C	D	I	W	U	R	N	A	V
X	S	S	N	E	O	D	O	N	X	F	S	L	T
E	U	E	S	C	A	L	N	S	Q	U	A	R	E
T	A	C	F	R	S	T	E	A	I	L	D	R	B
I	L	J	T	I	N	Y	D	E	S	L	R	L	I

ALL ABOUT ME

1 Think of your favorite object, for example, your phone. Describe it using some of the adjectives you learned in this unit. ________

2 Think of a celebration that you went to last year. What was it like? Was there a ceremony?

____

3 What life stage are you at now? ________

1 Choose the correct option to complete the sentences.

A: Hi! Alex told me that (1) ***you shared* / *you're sharing*** an apartment with your sister right now. (2) ***How does it go?* / *How's it going?***
B: It's amazing. Naomi and I always (3) ***get* / *are getting*** along well, and we (4) ***don't argue* / *are not arguing***, so everything is fine.
A: I bet you miss your mom's cooking!
B: Well, Naomi's a good cook too. She (5) ***cooks* / *is cooking*** excellent pasta!
A: Sounds good. What's the apartment like? Is it big, modern ... ?
B: Well, listen – what (6) ***do you do* / *are you doing*** right now?
A: (7) ***I just watch* / *I'm just watching*** a show on TV. Why?
B: (8) ***Do you want* / *Are you wanting*** to come over and see the apartment? It's a little messy because (9) ***we decorate* / *we're decorating*** right now. But we can hang out.
A: Thanks. That's a great idea. I'd love to.

2 Complete the text with the correct present form of the verb in parentheses.

My name is James and I (1) ________ (look) for an Italian e-friend. I'm studying Italian at school, and right now I (2) ________ (prepare) to take my final exams. I really (3) ________ (need) to practice my Italian! OK – so I (4) ________ (study) Italian conversation this year – and it's a lot of fun! I'd like to write regularly to someone in Italy who also enjoys art and literature and would like to practice English.

3 Complete the text with the correct past form of the verbs in the box.

carry come cut fall get happen invite need run start

A day from my childhood that I remember is my fifth birthday party. I remember it for several reasons! My mom (1) ________ 10 of my friends over to our house and I was very excited. I (2) ________ dressed in my good clothes, and I (3) ________ around the house when something terrible (4) ________ . I (5) ________ down in the kitchen and (6) ________ my leg so badly that I (7) ________ to go to the hospital. While my dad (8) ________ me to the car, my friends (9) ________ , and that's when I (10) ________ crying. No party, no presents! A terrible day!

4 Decide if these sentences are correct (*C*) or incorrect (*I*). Rewrite the incorrect sentences.

1 While I was waiting for the movie to start, I was buying some popcorn. ____
____
2 I'm sorry, Mrs. Rivers, but I'm not understanding what we have to do for homework. ____
____
3 When she arrived at the party, she was the only girl there. ____
____
4 Right now we celebrate our soccer team's victory. ____
____
5 We were late for the wedding, so we took a taxi. ____
____
6 I was walking really slowly so I missed the last train home. ____
____

UNIT 2

PACK YOUR BAGS

VOCABULARY 1 >>> Travel items

1 Read the clues and complete the crossword.

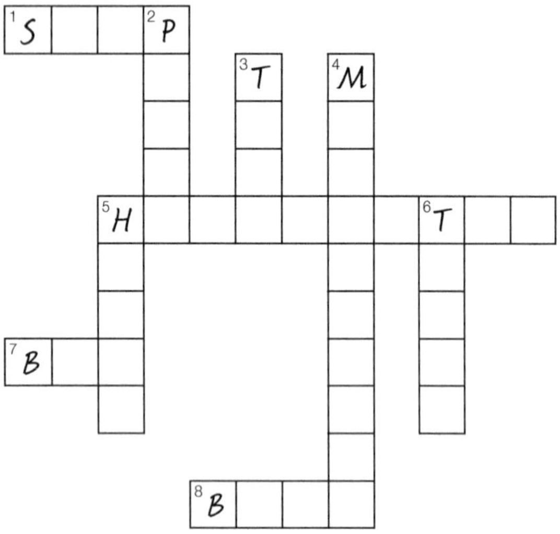

Across
1 This is a very large boat.
5 This machine flies in the air but has no wings.
7 This travels on the road. You can take it to work, but you need to buy a ticket first.
8 It has two wheels but no engine. You can ride it.

Down
2 Many people fly on one of these to go on vacation.
3 You pay someone to drive you in this.
4 This machine has only two wheels.
5 This is an animal that you can travel on or race on.
6 This is a large road vehicle that carries things, not people.

2 Complete each sentence (1–6) with the verbs in the box.

drive (x2) fly ride (x2) sail

1 In New York a quick way to get around is to .... on the subway.
2 My dad's job is to .... planes between New York and London.
3 It must be hard to .... a bus since they're very big.
4 In my country you can .... a car when you're 17.
5 If you go to Brazil, there are boats that .... down the Amazon.
6 A lot of young children want to learn to .... a bicycle.

3 Write the name of each item under the picture.

1 *hairbrush*

2 ....

3 ....

4 ....

5 ....

6 ....

7 ....

8 ....

9 ....

10 ....

11 ....

4 Choose the correct option to complete the sentences.

1 You cut things with ***a hairbrush / scissors / shampoo***.
2 You put money in a ***visa / wallet / boarding pass***.
3 You wash your hair with ***shampoo / a hairbrush / a toothbrush***.
4 When you go on vacation you put your clothes in a ***sleeping bag / suitcase / wallet***.
5 You brush your teeth with ***a toothbrush / a hairbrush / shampoo***.
6 When your hair is messy you use ***a hairbrush / toothpaste / a boarding pass***.

5 Match the sentence parts.

1 At the airport they gave me ....
2 I need a new picture for my ....
3 When we went to Spain the airport lost our ....
4 To go to some countries you need a special ....
5 When I go camping I always take a ....
6 On the long walk I took some food and water in my ....

a sleeping bag.
b backpack.
c a boarding pass.
d passport.
e visa.
f luggage.

6 a Write the items from Exercise 3 that you need for each vacation. You can use the same item more than once.

Flying to a different country	Staying at a hotel	Going camping

b Add one more item to each column.

Identify the purpose of a text

1 Complete the tips with the correct words.

REMEMBER HOW TO ...

identify the purpose of a text

- Use the (1) h___d___gs, (2) l___ut, (3) p___r__s, and (4) w__b___ks to identify the type of text.
- Read the (5) b___nn___g of the text and decide who the readers might be.
- Identify the writer and the writer's (6) g___ – is it to give information, entertain, or persuade?

2 Look at the headings, pictures, and layout of the texts but don't read them yet. Match the texts to the correct text type (1–3).

Text A ___ Text B ___ Text C ___

1 a recommendation on an organization's website
2 a student blog on a school website
3 advice for a special-interest website

3 Now read the texts in Exercise 2 and write the goal of each text: *instruct*, *persuade*, or *inform*.

Text A: ___ Text B: ___ Text C: ___

4 Read the texts carefully and decide if these statements are correct (*C*) or incorrect (*I*).

1 Text A is for people who like camping. ___
2 Text B is for a particular reader. ___
3 Text C is for people who know a lot about China. ___
4 Text C is for people interested in other countries. ___
5 Text B is for people interested in all types of volunteer work. ___

5 Read the three texts again. Which texts do the following:

1 give sensible advice? ___
2 give facts and figures? ___ ___
3 describe a trip to another country? ___
4 give some surprising information? ___
5 give a specific time of year to do an activity? ___

A

Hikers' World

NEIL'S TOP TIPS:
This week, hikers, we're looking at packing for a trek. Follow these tips to make sure your backpack is comfortable:

1) Only take what you really need. Remember it'll be hot out there, and you need to be able to carry everything.
2) Take cotton clothes – cotton is cool, dries quickly, and is light to carry.
3) Pack items in the order that you use them. This means your sleeping bag should be at the bottom.
4) Make sure liquids such as shampoo and toothpaste are placed in a plastic bag – in case they spill inside your backpack.

B

Volunteer Latin America ★★★★★

Volunteer Review: *Mariela Hernandez Garcia, 15*
See other reviews (5)
If you love tamarin monkeys like I do, this is exactly the program for you. The program places volunteers at different centers that work to protect the tamarin monkeys. I can't recommend this enough – not only do you get to work closely with these beautiful animals, but you learn a lot about their environment, as well as work with amazing people. If you're looking for something to do this summer, I really advise you to try this!

C

My trip to the Great Wall of China

Lucy Chivers, Junior

I've just come back from a trip to China. I saw the Great Wall of China, and it was just fantastic. For those who don't know, the Great Wall runs for over 21,000 kilometers and was built around 206 BC. Like many people, you probably think it's all one continuous wall, but actually it's a lot of separate wall segments built over hundreds of years. And one last thing – I bet you'll be surprised to know that the Great Wall can't be seen from the moon, despite what many people think!

MOVE BEYOND

Go online and find information about another international adventure trip for young people. Prepare a short speech. Decide first whether you want your talk to instruct, inform, or persuade your classmates.

GRAMMAR 1 Present perfect

Talk about how long something has happened

1 Complete the grammar table.

Affirmative			
I/You/We/They	(1) ______ ('ve)	planned a vacation.	
He/She	has (2) (______)	read a brochure.	
Negative			
I/You/We/They	have not (haven't)	traveled outside the USA.	
He/She	has not (hasn't)	bought a guidebook.	
***Yes/No* questions and short answers**			
Have	you	called Eric?	Yes, I (3) ______ . No, I haven't.
Has	the teacher	graded your essay?	Yes, she has. No, she (4) ______ .
***Wh-* questions**			
What	have	you packed?	(5) ______ packed jeans, T-shirts, and a sweater.
(6) ______	has	Chris been?	He's been to the bank.

2 When do you use the present perfect? Complete the sentences with the words in the box.

already/just/yet ever/never exact time

- To talk about past experiences in your life, often with the words (1) ______ .
- To talk about past actions when you don't know the (2) ______ .
- To talk about recent events with the words (3) ______ .

3 a Read the email and underline the present perfect tense.

Hi! I've just arrived in Miami and I'm sending a message from the airport. I had a great flight. It only took three hours, and we watched a good movie. I've never watched a movie on a plane before :) Anyway, I'm waiting for Rocio, but she's late – as usual. She hasn't called since last night, so I hope she hasn't forgotten. I've been here for 15 minutes, and I've already bought you a little present! I sent you an email from the airport in Boston. Have you received it yet? Oh, I think I can see Rocio! Bye for now.

b Find two time expressions in the email used with *for* and *since*.

______

______

4 a Complete the table with past participles.

Base verb	Past participle
be	
wait	waited
travel	
buy	
read	
write	
speak	
catch	
do	
make	

b Circle the irregular verbs in the table in Exercise 4a.

5 › Choose the correct option to complete the sentences.

1 I've known Maria (for) / *since* six months.
2 I've played soccer *for* / *since* I was five.
3 Hannah has been in Paraguay *for* / *since* two weeks.
4 The boys haven't seen their cousin *for* / *since* last November.
5 Dave has been in the hospital *for* / *since* a long time.
6 Penny has been in her bedroom *for* / *since* she came home from school.

6 › Put the words in order to make sentences.

1 never / I've / in an expensive hotel / stayed / .
....
2 swum / Have / you / yet / in the ocean / ?
....
3 unpacked / just / his suitcase / He's / .
....
4 already / I've / in the pool / three times / been / .
....
5 traveled / they / ever / Have / to Europe / ?
....
6 hasn't / plane / taken off / yet / Our / .
....

7 ›› Complete the sentences with the words in the box.

already ever for ~~just~~ never yet

1 I've *just* talked to Mark. He called in the last few minutes.
2 Have you .... finished your homework? You only started it at 5:00 p.m., and it's 5:10 p.m. now.
3 I've .... been to Patagonia. I'd love to go.
4 I'm sorry, I haven't emailed Sarah .... , but I'll do it now.
5 Has Danny .... gotten more than 50 percent on a math test? I don't think so!
6 We've been here .... two hours. Where is she?

8 ›› Use the words to make sentences or questions with the present perfect.

1 I / not / call / Paul for two weeks.
I haven't called Paul for two weeks.
2 you / speak / to Kenny about the party?
....
3 We / buy tickets / for the concert on Wednesday.
....
4 Sally / just / get her grades.
....
5 Which of these books / you / read?
....
6 The teacher / not / give / us any homework!
....
7 Where / you / be / until now?
....
8 We / just / win / the World Cup!
....

9 ›› Complete the postcard with the present perfect form of the words in the box.

~~be~~ do eat go make speak

Hi, everyone!

We're having a fantastic time on vacation. (1) We *'ve been* here for one week. We (2) .... some amazing food and I (3) .... a little Spanish! Let's see! Dan (4) .... in the ocean yet and Iliana (5) .... friends with some Costa Ricans!
(6) What .... you .... for vacation?

See you soon!

Ben

10 ››› Answer with the present perfect and the word in parentheses.

1 Have you left the station yet?
Yes, I've just left. (just)
2 Have you checked the guidebook?
.... (already)
3 Have you ever been to China?
No, ... (never)
4 Has your sister gotten her results?
No, ... (yet)
5 How long have you had a pet dog?
.... (for / five years)
6 How long have you lived in California?
.... (since / 2005)

11 ››› For each sentence, write what the person says. Use a verb from the box in the present perfect.

arrive change eat fail ~~lose~~ spend

1 Harry can't find his passport.
Harry: "*I've lost my passport* ."
2 Bev offers to buy James and Davina lunch, but they had breakfast half an hour ago.
James and Davina: "We ...."
3 Caroline is waiting for a taxi. She hears the noise of a car outside.
Caroline: "The taxi ...."
4 The weather was good all day. Now it's raining.
Helen: "The weather ...."
5 Gary bought a lot of things yesterday. Now he has no money.
Gary: "I ...."
6 Brett took his driving test this morning. Now he looks sad.
Brett: "I ...."

LISTENING

Listen for the information you need

1 Complete the tips with the phrases in the box.

REMEMBER HOW TO ...

listen for the information you need

listen for the main ideas
listen for specific information

- First (1) ________ .
- Don't worry if you can't understand everything.
- Listen for words you know. They can help you understand important ideas.
- Then (2) ________ .
- Decide what you want to know.
- Think about the words you might hear.

2 a 80 Listen to Janie's voice messages (1–3) and match them to pictures A–C.

A ☐

B ☐

C ☐

b Now choose the correct option.

1 Message 1 is ***positive*** / ***negative***.
2 Message 2 is ***positive*** / ***negative***.
3 Message 3 is ***positive*** / ***negative***.

3 80 Listen again and complete the notes.

Message 1

1 Time now: ________
2 Final destination: ________
3 Location now: ________
4 Length of time in traffic jam: ________

Message 2

1 Time now: ________
2 Location now: ________
3 Reason for delay: ________
4 Length of time to wait: ________

Message 3

1 Time now: ________
2 Current method of transportation:
____
3 Estimated time of arrival: ________

4 Use the information from Exercise 3 to complete Janie's blog post.

Janie's Blog Home New posts Contact

Well, we're here now, and the festival is fantastic! Our trip wasn't good, though. To start with, we got stuck for (1) ________ in a traffic jam on the (2) ________ because a bus broke down. Then there was a delay at the airport because of the (3) ________ . They said we would have to wait for (4) ________ hours, but then the flight got canceled! We decided to go by (5) ________ instead and took a cruise ship to the Bahamas. We sailed all (6) ________ and finally arrived early the next morning.

1 Complete the boarding pass with the noun form of the word in parentheses.

GO BEYOND AIRLINES

FLIGHT X133 LOS ANGELES TO BUENOS AIRES

Name: Alvaro Castro
(1) *seat* (sit) number: 43G
(2) ______ (depart) time: 7:45 a.m.
(3) ______ (arrive) time: 11:30
(4) ______ (reserve) number: 335U829YX
(5) ______ (distant): 6,250 miles
(6) ______ (fly) time: 15 hours 45 minutes
If you have a (7) ______ (connect), please go straight to the gate.

2 Complete the sentences with the answers from Exercise 1.

1 Alvaro took a direct ______ from Los Angeles to Buenos Aires.
2 On some flights you have to pay extra to make a seat ______ .
3 The ______ between Los Angeles and Buenos Aires is 6,250 miles.
4 The ______ time of our flight is 7:45 a.m., so we should leave soon.
5 The plane was late, so Alvaro missed his ______ and had to wait for the next available flight.
6 Let me know your ______ time, and I can pick you up at the airport.

3 Read the clues and complete the crossword.

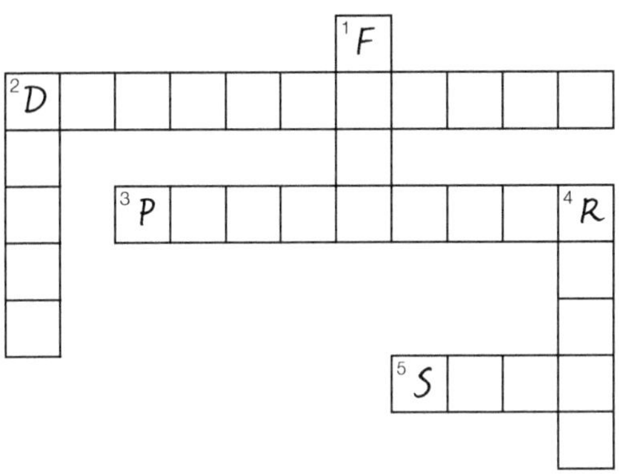

Across
2 This is the place you want to get to at the end of a trip.
3 This is the name for a person who is traveling.
5 You sit in this on an airplane.

Down
1 This is the money you pay to travel.
2 This happens when your flight or ship leaves or arrives late.
4 This is the planned direction of your trip.

WORDS & BEYOND

4 Match the words in Column A to the definitions in Column B.

Column A	Column B
line	the act of traveling from one place to another
trip	missing home when you're in another place
voyage	when you go somewhere and come back again
journey	the people who work on a plane or ship
passport control	to begin to fly a plane in the air at the beginning of a flight
gate	a part of an airport where you get on or off a plane
homesick	the act of showing your ticket and giving your luggage to the staff at the airport
check in	to guide a plane safely back to the ground at the end of a flight
crew	the area where your documents are checked
customs	a group of people politely waiting to do something
take off	the place where your luggage is sometimes searched
land	a long journey, usually by ship

5 Complete the sentences (1–8) with words and phrases from Column A of Exercise 4.

1 When I got on the plane, the flight ______ was very friendly and offered me something to drink.
2 The ______ to check in for the flight was so long it went out the door.
3 Because of the storm, their plane couldn't ______ and the passengers had to wait inside the airport.
4 Sunny felt ______ because she was missing her family so much.
5 A: What ______ does our flight leave from?
B: Gate 43, I think.
6 We're going on a school ______ to San Francisco next week.
7 We were late getting out of the airport because ______ decided to search our suitcase.
8 Lola's plane is due to ______ at 3:00 p.m., so we should be at the airport no later than 3:15 p.m. to pick her up.

GRAMMAR 2 The future

Talk about events in the future

1 Match the sentences (1–5) to the forms of the future tenses (a–e).

1 The train leaves at 9:57 a.m.
2 Donna and I will probably go backpacking in the summer.
3 Sam's going to visit his uncle in Missouri in July.
4 If we don't hurry through passport control, we're likely to miss our flight.
5 Diane's coming to the airport to pick us up later.

a *going to*
b present progressive
c *be* + *likely to* + base verb
d simple present
e *will/won't* + base verb

2 Choose the correct verb form to complete the sentences.

1 The Dallas flight ***lands*** / ***is going to land*** at 9:45 p.m.
2 ***You're likely*** / ***You'll definitely*** see me at the station.
3 ***We're meeting*** / ***We'll meet*** Tom at 4:15 p.m. I've already arranged it with him.
4 The train ***is being*** / ***is likely to be*** late this afternoon because of an accident.
5 ***You'll get*** / ***You're getting*** excellent grades, I'm sure!
6 ***I'm going to ask*** / ***I'm asking*** Mike to play tennis later.

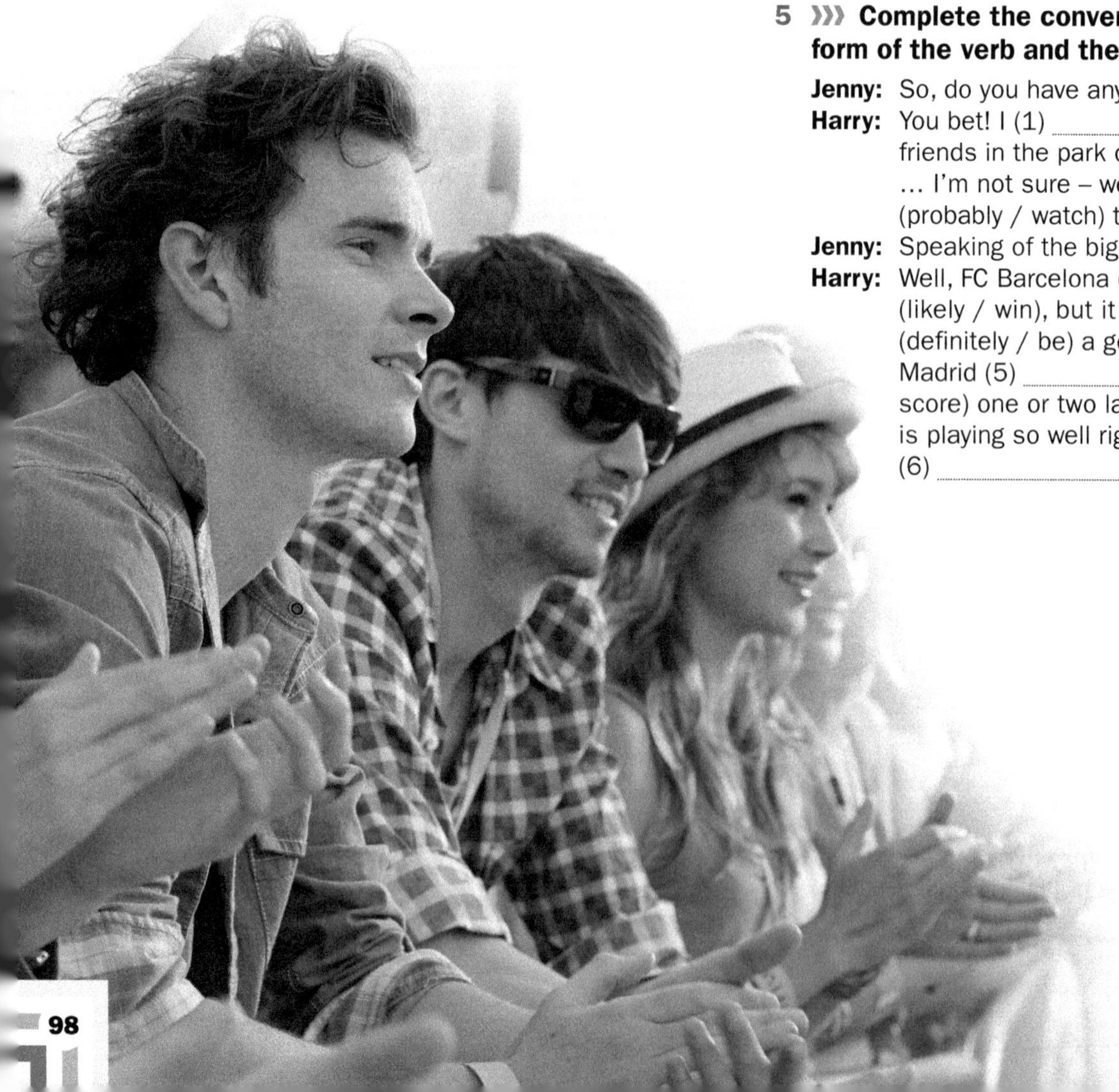

3 Complete the questions with the correct future form of the words in parentheses.

1 What time ________ (your plane / leave) in the morning?
2 How ________ (you / get) to the airport?
3 ________ (you / eat) at the hotel before you leave?
4 ________ (you / need) help with your suitcases in the morning?
5 ________ (you / likely / recommend) the hotel to your friends?
6 ________ (anybody / meet) you when you land at the airport?

4 Complete the text with the correct future form of the verb in parentheses.

I'm so happy that it's Friday! I (1) ________ (have) a quiet weekend because I'm really tired. I (2) ________ (play) volleyball tomorrow morning. But then I (3) ________ (relax) in front of the TV all afternoon! My favorite game show (4) ________ (be) on at 3.30 p.m., so I (5) ________ (definitely watch) that. My cousin and her family (6) ________ (likely come) over on Sunday for lunch, so I (7) ________ (probably go) for a walk in the park with them in the afternoon. My first class on Monday (8) ________ (start) at 8:00 a.m., so it's an early night for me on Sunday.

5 Complete the conversation with the correct form of the verb and the word in parentheses.

Jenny: So, do you have any plans for the weekend?
Harry: You bet! I (1) ________ (meet) some friends in the park on Saturday morning. Then … I'm not sure – we (2) ________ (probably / watch) the big game.
Jenny: Speaking of the big game – any predictions?
Harry: Well, FC Barcelona (3) ________ (likely / win), but it (4) ________ (definitely / be) a good game. I think Real Madrid (5) ________ (probably / score) one or two late goals. FC Barcelona is playing so well right now that they (6) ________ (not likely / lose).

SPEAKING 2

Check in at the airport

1 Put the words in order to make phrases you can use to check that you understand something.

1 hear / I / Sorry, / that / didn't / .

....

2 that, / repeat / you / please / Could / ?

....

3 say / please / you / again / that / Can / ?

....

4 understand / I / Sorry, / don't / .

....

2 What places in an airport do these pictures show? Complete the pictures with the words in the box.

Arrivals Check-in Customs Departures ~~Gates 1–29~~ Passport control

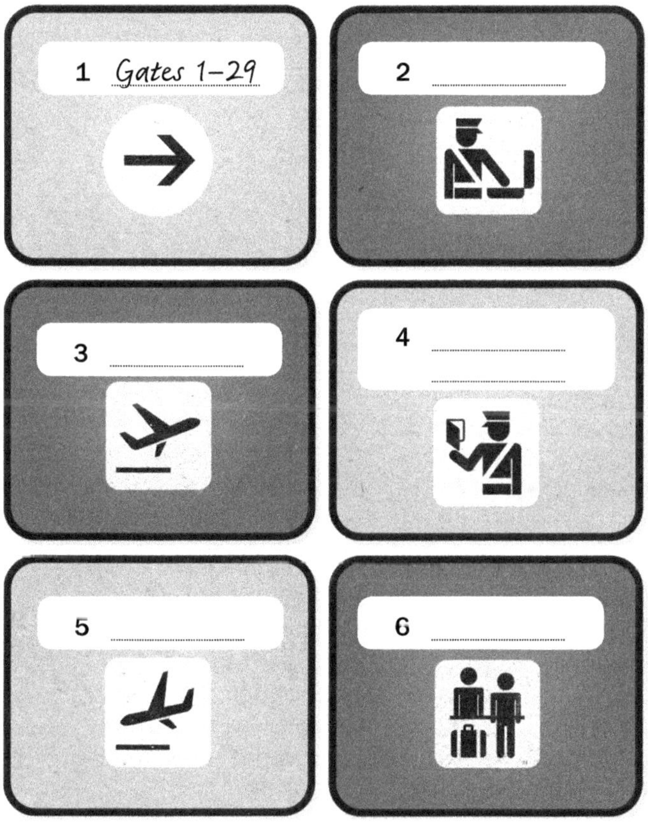

3 ▶81 Listen to three conversations about different places in an airport. Which two places in Exercise 2 are not mentioned?

....

....

4 ▶81 Listen again. Write the phrase from Exercise 1 that you hear in each conversation.

Conversation 1: ....

Conversation 2: ....

Conversation 3: ....

5 Read the conversation at the check-in desk and complete it with the phrases in the box.

a good flight are you checking boarding pass Can I have Gate 15 gate number is it Here you are I'd like to check in I have your carry-on bag

A: (1) .... for the 10:20 flight to Seattle, please.
B: (2) .... your passport, please?
A: Yes. (3) ....
B: Thank you. How many bags (4) .... ?
A: (5) .... two suitcases.
B: That's fine. Do you have any sharp objects in (6) .... ?
A: No, I don't.
B: Good. Here's your (7) .... You can go straight to Departures now.
A: Which (8) .... ?
B: It's (9) .... Have (10) .... !

6 ▶82 PRONOUNCE Listen and write the words with the sounds /b/ and /p/ in the correct column. Then listen again and check your answers.

Words with /b/	Words with /p/

WRITING

Use correct verb tenses

1 Read the tips for using correct verb tenses.

REMEMBER HOW TO …

use correct verb tenses

- Decide if the action is past, present, or future.
- Look at the rules for past, present, and future tenses in Units 1 and 2.
- Use the correct tense with the correct time words (*yesterday, tomorrow, right now, for two years, always*).

2 Match the uses (1–8) to the sentences (a–h).

1 To talk about habits and routines ______
2 To talk about future arrangements ______
3 To say something was in progress in the past ______
4 To make predictions about the future ______
5 To talk about experiences from the past to the present ______
6 To talk about things that are happening now ______
7 To talk about actions that happened at a particular time in the past ______
8 To talk about actions that happened at an unspecified time in the past ______

a We went to a restaurant last night.
b I'm sitting by the swimming pool.
c We're having dinner with another family tonight.
d My dad goes jogging on the beach every day.
e We've been here for three days.
f I was swimming in the ocean this morning when I saw a huge fish.
g I've been to Italy.
h I think the trip to the mountains tomorrow will be very interesting.

3 Complete the blog below with the time expressions in the box.

at 4:15 p.m. every day every summer for 10 years next year right now seven days ago since then tonight yesterday

4 Write an example from the blog of each of the following tenses.

1 Simple present: ______
2 Present progressive: ______
3 Present perfect: ______
4 Past progressive: ______
5 Simple past: ______
6 Present progressive for future arrangements: ______
7 Future *will*: ______

MY BLOG

We're really enjoying our trip to Quebec. (1) ______ we're staying in a cottage near the mountains, and it's beautiful. Marianne's parents have had this cottage (2) ______ , and they come here (3) ______ . Marianne and I go walking and climbing (4) ______ , and the views are amazing. (5) ______ we were walking near Lake Champlain when I saw an enormous fish jump out of the water! Marianne said it was Champ, the lake's monster. I arrived here (6) ______ , and I think I've walked about a hundred kilometers (7) ______ ! I really like her mom and dad too. (8) ______ they're taking us into the local town to have dinner. I'm looking forward to it. But I'm not looking forward to leaving! I'm taking the plane on Thursday (9) ______ , and I'll be really sad to go. It's been a wonderful vacation. I'll definitely come back again (10) ______ if Marianne's parents invite me.

5 **You're going to write a vacation postcard. Use the *Writing plan* to help you prepare notes in your notebook.**

WRITING PLAN

1 **Say where you are** ☐

Which city are you in? Why did you decide to go there? How did you get there? What was your trip like? Who are you with?

2 **Describe the place** ☐

Where are you staying? What can you see from your room? What's the public transportation like?

3 **Describe your activities and plans** ☐

What have you visited? What did you do yesterday? What have you eaten? What are you going to visit tomorrow?

4 **Say when you'll write next** ☐

WRITE AND CHECK

6 **Write your answer. Then check your writing and check (✓) the stages in the *Writing plan*.**

Respect other people's personal space

1 **Read the email. Where was Kate? What was she trying to do?**

Hey Sam,
I hope you're well. We're having a fantastic time in Chicago, but it's very stressful! We were at Union Station yesterday, and we were in line for tickets. I couldn't believe how crowded it was. There were so many people in line, and everyone was pushing. There was one woman who was so close to me that her face was right next to mine, and she was standing on my feet. She didn't seem to mind at all, but I was really uncomfortable. I couldn't really move without losing my place in line, and I didn't know where to look or what to do. In the end, we decided to leave and come back later to get our tickets. I just hope it's less busy then! I'll send some pictures of our trip later.
Kate

2 **Read the email again. What was Kate's problem?** ____________

3 **Look at the advice for protecting your personal space. Check (✓) the tips that you would give to Kate.**

1 Ignore the other person. ☐
2 Move back. ☐
3 Shout at the other person. ☐
4 Ask the other person to move back politely. ☐
5 Stare at the other person until they move away. ☐

1 Complete the compound nouns. Use the clues to help you.

1 sl_______ bag
2 f_______ date
3 c_______-o_______ bags
4 sh_______ object
5 c_______ student
6 p_______ control
7 b_______ pass
8 dr_______ license

Clues

1 You use it at night when you're camping.
2 Not the second or third date but the ...
3 These are bags you can carry onto a plane.
4 This might be dangerous.
5 This is what you are after high school.
6 This is a place in the airport.
7 You need it to get on a plane.
8 You need it to use a car.

2 Find the one that doesn't match.

1 adult / senior / passenger / child
2 toothbrush / visa / passport / boarding pass
3 subway / ferry / train / route
4 enormous / unusual / homesick / valuable
5 journey / fare / voyage / trip
6 shampoo / hairbrush / backpack / toothpaste
7 arrivals / check-in / gate / suitcase
8 vote / land / take off / delay

3 Read the clues and complete the crossword.

Across

3 Someone who is between 13 and 19 years old.
5 T-shirts are usually made out of this material.
7 An adjective that describes a T-shirt that is red, blue, green, and yellow.
9 This is what you make when you want to reserve a hotel room.
11 You use these to cut things.
12 Someone who has just been born.

Down

1 Furniture that is very old.
2 You might miss this if your flight is late.
4 Your passport and visa are examples of these.
6 This is another name for a short journey.
8 This is the opposite of arrival.
10 You use this to pay for things.

4 Complete the sentences with the words in the box.

destination	middle-aged	old-fashioned	route	seat	square	trip	useful

1 This gadget is really _______ – it's a screwdriver, hammer, and scissors all in one.
2 Picture frames are usually _______ or rectangular.
3 He's very _______ – he doesn't like using technology.
4 I would say that Tom's at least 40 – he's definitely _______ .
5 I hope I'm not sitting next to anyone on the flight – it's a long _______ and I need to sleep.
6 When we reach our _______ , we need to check the time of the next train.
7 I've bought a really cheap ticket to Miami, but unfortunately it's not the quickest _______ .
8 If we both reserve a _______ on the plane, then we'll definitely be able to sit together.

ALL ABOUT ME

1 Think of a vacation you went on in the past. Where did you go? What did you pack?

____

2 What do you think is the most important thing to pack when you go on vacation? What can you do with it? _______

3 Where are you going to go on your next vacation? What will you do there?

____

1 Choose the correct option to complete the sentences.

1 I'm sorry, I can't go swimming with you today because ***I work*** / ***I'm working*** on my school project. ***I'll definitely be able to*** / ***I'm being able to*** go tomorrow instead.
2 The teacher ***doesn't want*** / ***isn't wanting*** to give us homework tonight because he ***doesn't have*** / ***isn't having*** a lot of free time for grading right now.
3 My mom ***has worked*** / ***works*** at the airport for five years. She ***loves*** / ***has loved*** her job.
4 Where ***do you go*** / ***are you going***? ***Are you likely to be*** / ***Are you being*** back for lunch?
5 They ***build*** / ***are building*** a new train station, so Dad ***drives*** / ***is driving*** to work for a few weeks.
6 ***Have you seen*** / ***Do you see*** Magda this morning? I think she might be sick. She didn't feel well while we ***were listening*** / ***listen*** to the band last night.

2 Use the prompts to complete the conversation.

A: (1) How long have you been home ? (How long / you / be / home)
B: (2) ________ . (I / just get back)
(3) ________ . (My / plane / land / 11:30 this morning)
A: (4) ________ ? (you / have / wonderful time / China)
B: (5) ________ . (I / never enjoy / trip / so much) It was amazing.
A: (6) ________ (I / see / some pictures / Great Wall / yesterday) and I
(7) ________ ! (think about / you)
B: (8) ________ (While / I / walk / along Great Wall) I texted you.
A: (9) ________ . (My / phone / not work / last Thursday/ so) I didn't get it.

3 Complete the second sentence so it means the same as the first. Use the word given. You should write between two and five words.

1 Dad became a teacher seven years ago.
been
Dad ________ seven years.
2 I regularly go jogging.
day
I ________ .
3 It will probably rain this afternoon.
likely
It ________ this afternoon.
4 I saw Grant a few minutes ago.
just
I ________ Grant.
5 My phone rang in the middle of dinner.
while
My phone rang ________ dinner.
6 I've known Tom for six months.
ago
I ________ .

4 Complete the sentences with the correct form of the verbs in the box.

arrive board drink exit find land ~~leave~~ miss ~~take~~ wait

1 Someone ***has*** / ***will*** left a large suitcase near Gate 7. Please pick it up or security ***will*** / ***have*** take it away.
2 Attention passengers who ***are*** / ***have*** ________ for delayed flight 209. We are happy to announce the plane ***did*** / ***has*** ________ and boarding will begin in 15 minutes.
3 Ladies and gentlemen, we ***have*** / ***are just*** ________ a cell phone in the departure lounge café. If you lost your cell phone while you ***have*** / ***were*** ________ a cup of coffee this morning, please see the agent at Gate 17.
4 Flight 691 ***is*** / ***has*** ________ . If you are meeting passengers from this flight, please wait outside Customs, where they ***are*** / ***will*** ________ shortly.
5 Attention passengers on flight 576 to Houston. If you ***have not*** / ***will not*** ________ yet, please go to the gate immediately, or you ***will*** / ***have*** ________ your flight.

MY MUSIC

VOCABULARY 1 »» Music words

1 Label the pictures with the words in the box.

conductor drums flute guitar musician opera orchestra singer trumpet violin

1 ....

2 ....

3 ....

4 ....

5 ....

6 ....

7 ....

8 ....

9 ....

10 ....

2 Look at each set of words and find the one that does not match. Say why it's different.

1 (rock) / concert hall / venue
Rock is different because it's a type of music.
2 classical / performance / pop
....
3 jazz / keyboard / piano
....
4 brass band / orchestra / hip hop
....
5 folk / audience / reggae
....
6 guitar / drums / musician
....
7 conductor / singer / venue
....
8 opera / violin / trumpet
....

3 Choose the correct word to complete the sentences.

1 Adriana loves classical music and would like to be ***a conductor / an audience*** when she's older.
2 Do you have tickets for ***the concert / the venue*** on Friday?
3 My brother has just joined ***a brass band / a band.*** He plays the drums and his friends play the guitar and piano.
4 At the end of the concert, the entire ***audience / performance*** stood up and clapped for about 10 minutes.
5 Gabriel is only 15 and already a talented ***singer / musician.*** He can play the drums, guitar, violin, and flute.
6 My parents love opera. They can't stand modern music like ***hip hop / classical***.

4 a Complete the email with words from Exercises 1–3.

Hi Joanna,

I had an amazing time last night at the rock (1) .... ! It's too bad you couldn't come. It was at the Mayflower Theater, which is an enormous (2) .... It can hold up to a thousand people. It was pretty full last night since the band is really popular. Everyone wanted to see the girl who plays the (3) .... because she's tiny, but she can hit them really hard! It was so loud! The (4) .... absolutely loved them, and at the end of the (5) .... everyone shouted and clapped until they came back and played more songs. I think the (6) .... was pretty tired. You could hardly hear his voice by the end. I really admire (7) ....s who can play their instruments like that. I'd love to be in a (8) .... , but I need to learn to play an instrument first!

See you,

Alberto

b What kind of music do you like? Did you like the same kind of music three years ago?

....
....
....

READING

Understand new words

1 Complete the tips with the words in the box.

REMEMBER HOW TO …

understand new words

after   before   mean   part   similar

- Identify the (1) __________ of speech (verb, noun, adjective, adverb).
- Is there a (2) __________ word in your language? Does its meaning help you?
- Look at the words and sentences (3) __________ and (4) __________ the new word.
- Guess what the new word might (5) __________ and check your idea in the sentence.

2 Complete the table with the words in the box.

audience   beautifully   classical   conductor   fantastic   listen   sing   well

Noun	Verb	Adjective	Adverb

3 Look at the picture and scan the text, then answer the questions.

1 Is it a popular event?

____

2 Is the text an ad, a review, or part of an email?

____

4 Read the text again and complete the information.

Name of show: __________

Day of week: __________

Country where the event took place in 2014:

____

Country that won in 2014: __________

A EUROPEAN PARTY!

So, what were you doing on Saturday night? Were you out with your friends or were you one of the millions who stayed in to watch the Eurovision Song Contest?

The Eurovision Song Contest is an **annual** event where singers from different European countries compete to win the title of best song in Europe. Each year it takes place in the country that won the previous year. This year it was Denmark's turn to **host** the contest.

There is a huge **range** of performances. There are bands and individual singers; pop, rock, folk, and even opera. Some singers just stand and sing under a single **spotlight**, while others choose to have a lot of lights. One year a singer stood on a box while another man was **upside down** in it. He looked very uncomfortable!

There were a few songs of a really high **standard** that deserved to win. There were a couple that were terrible – but that's part of the joy of the Eurovision Song Contest. Most singers gave a great performance, although one or two walked onto the stage very **nervously**. They didn't look confident at all.

It was no surprise that Austria won in 2014, and although a lot of people **moaned** about the results the next day, for me it was the obvious winner. It was a fantastic contest!

5 Look at the words in bold in the text. Decide what part of speech (for example, noun or verb) they are and add them to the table in Exercise 2.

6 Choose the best meanings for the words in bold in the text in Exercise 3.

1 annual
  a yearly   b every summer

2 host
  a to travel overseas   b to receive guests and hold an event in a particular place

3 range
  a number   b variety

4 spotlight
  a stage   b a single bright light

5 upside down
  a with his back to us   b with his feet above his head

6 standard
  a level   b sound

7 nervously
  a in a worried way   b in a confused way

8 moan
  a complain   b celebrate

MOVE BEYOND

Go online and find out three more facts about the Eurovision Song Contest. Is there a similar contest in your country?

____

____

____

GRAMMAR 1 Verbs followed by gerunds or infinitives

Talk about things you enjoy doing

1 Complete the grammar tables with the correct form of the verb in parentheses.

	Verb	Infinitive
I	want	(1) ________ (go) to the festival.
He	's learning	(2) ________ (play) the guitar.
They	're planning	(3) ________ (buy) the tickets.
Questions		
Are you	hoping	(4) ________ (become) a musician?
Have they	decided	(5) ________ (go) swimming?

	Verb	Gerund
I	don't mind	(6) ________ (perform) on stage.
She	hates	(7) ________ (listen) to reggae music.
Questions		
Can you	imagine	(8) ________ (be) famous?
Do they	enjoy	(9) ________ (watch) live concerts?

2 Match the rules (1–2) to the correct sentences (a–e). Which can be matched to both rules?

1 verb followed by gerund ___ ___ ___
2 verb followed by infinitive ___ ___ ___

a He wanted to go home.
b He loves sailing. He loves to sail on the weekends.
c I enjoy studying English.
d He decided to go to college.
e I don't mind helping Dad wash the car.

3 Look at these verbs and their gerund form. Write each one next to the correct spelling rule.

become/becoming create/creating ~~drum/drumming~~ hope/hoping plan/planning sit/sitting stop/stopping swim/swimming take/taking write/writing

1 Double the consonant and add *-ing* *drum / drumming,* ________

____

2 Remove the "e" and add *-ing* ________

____

4 Complete the diagram with the verbs in the box. Some verbs can be followed by the gerund or an infinitive. Write these verbs in the middle section.

decide don't mind enjoy forget hate hope imagine inspire learn ~~like~~ love plan practice prefer want would like

Verbs followed by infinitive | *like* | Verbs followed by gerund

5 a Mark the underlined forms correct (✓) or incorrect (✗).

Why do I enjoy (1) to be ☐ in a band? Well, I always wanted (2) playing ☐ the guitar. So, when I was about 10, I got a guitar for my birthday, and I decided (3) to practice ☐ as much as possible to become a really good player. I didn't mind (4) practicing ☐. I mean, I never found it boring because I loved what I was doing. First, I learned (5) playing ☐ classical music, but I soon discovered I really wanted (6) playing ☐ rock music instead. I went to my first rock concert when I was 15 – a U2 concert. It was really inspiring (7) to see ☐ them play. I never forgot (8) to see ☐ the Edge perform. He's an amazing guitarist. I hoped (9) being ☐ like him some day, but I never thought I would get the chance – and now look at me! I would like (10) meeting ☐ him some time and say thank you for inspiring me to become a rock star!

b Now rewrite the incorrect sentences correctly.

(1) Why do I enjoy being in a band?

____

____

____

____

____

____

6 › Choose the correct option to complete the sentences.

1 I've often imagined ***moving*** / ***to move*** to Costa Rica. It must be very hot and sunny there.
2 The teacher has decided ***teaching*** / ***to teach*** us some English songs in class next week.
3 I need to practice ***playing*** / ***to play*** my violin before the concert.
4 I want ***to go*** / ***going*** shopping with my sisters on Saturday.
5 I don't mind ***to travel*** / ***traveling*** by train. Do you?
6 I hope ***to get*** / ***getting*** into a music school next September.

7 › Complete the text with the correct form of the verb *to be*.

I like (1) *being* a child, but I think I would also like (2) ______ an adult. I can't stand (3) ______ told what to do all the time. I want (4) ______ my own boss, make my own decisions, and enjoy (5) ______ able to do what I want, when I want. Then I can decide (6) ______ a rock star and no one can tell me that it's a silly idea. Once, I went to a Coldplay concert. The singer was amazing. It inspired me (7) ______ a singer too. I hope (8) ______ very successful. I want my band (9) ______ famous. I would like (10) ______ rich too, but we'll see! I sometimes imagine (11) ______ on the front cover of all the magazines and I think, "Wow! That sounds amazing." Mom says I can be anything I want, but she also says, "Don't forget (12) ______ a child while you're young. That's just as amazing as being a rock star." I guess she's right!

8 ›› Complete the message with the correct form of the verbs in the box.

come join listen make see watch win write

Hi, Jacob – it's Julia. We're planning (1) ______ the Eurovision Song Contest on TV on Saturday. Do you want (2) ______ us? I haven't asked Betti because I know she hates (3) ______ to any kind of pop songs! But Alex and Jorge have decided (4) ______ over. I don't mind (5) ______ some sandwiches. I know that our entry, Margit Hellat, is really hoping (6) ______ this year – especially after she didn't get any votes last time! Maybe this year's contest will inspire some good young musicians (7) ______ a really good song for us next year. Hope (8) ______ you later – about 7:30?

9 ›› Use the prompts to complete the conversations.

1
A: This is a lot of work. I can't do it on my own.
B: I ______ (not / mind / help / you).
2
A: Can you translate this song from Spanish?
B: You should ______ (learn / speak / Spanish) yourself!
3
A: Do you still play the drums?
B: No, I ______ (decide / learn / the guitar) instead.
4
A: What time are you going to the concert on Friday?
B: I ______ (not / plan / go) until 9:00 p.m.

10 ›› Complete the sentences with the correct form of the verb in parentheses.

1 The British singer Adele inspired me ______ (start) singing too.
2 I didn't enjoy ______ (watch) the World Cup Final because I felt really nervous.
3 I can't stand ______ (go) to large venues because I hate crowds.
4 I hoped ______ (get) tickets for Bruno Mars's concert, but they were sold out.
5 The audience didn't mind ______ (wait) for the band because they were so popular.
6 The band decided ______ (not record) an album this year.

11 ››› Complete the second sentence so it means the same as the first. Use the word given.

1 I don't think I wrote down the assignment. **forget**
I ______ the assignment.
2 I like listening to jazz, but I like folk more. **prefer**
I ______ rather than jazz.
3 I can finish the typing for you. **mind**
I ______ the typing for you.
4 I hate listening to heavy metal music. **not stand**
I ______ heavy metal music.

12 ››› Complete the sentences with the verbs in the box and the gerund or infinitive of the verb in parentheses.

decide enjoy ~~forget~~ hope

1 Don't *forget to send* (send) an email to Suzy about band practice.
2 I ______ (see) you again soon. Please stay in touch.
3 I ______ (swim) when I was five, and now I compete professionally.
4 Have you ______ (buy) a new tablet computer or not?

LISTENING

Transfer spoken information to a table

1 Complete the tips with the words in the box.

REMEMBER HOW TO …

transfer spoken information to a table

decide listen read write

- (1) ______ all the information in the table.
- (2) ______ what information you need.
- (3) ______ for the information you need and (4) ______ notes in the table.

2 You're going to listen to an interview with two teenagers talking about music. Look at the first column in the table. Think about what the interviewer will ask and complete his questions with your ideas.

The interviewer asks …	Elisa	Ricardo
(1) What ______ do you play?	pop and (5) ______	(10) ______ music and love songs
(2) What ______ do you play?	(6) ______	(11) ______
When did you start playing?	(7) ______	(12) ______
(3) Who ______ ?	the music teacher	(13) ______
(4) How many ______ ?	(8) ______	one
What do you like about playing music?	(9) ______	(14) ______

3 (83) Listen to the interview. Complete the interviewer's questions with what you hear.

4 (83) Listen to the interview again. Complete the table with Elisa's answers.

5 (84) Listen to the interview with Ricardo and complete the table with his answers.

6 (84) Complete Ricardo's sentences from the interview. Then listen again and check your answers.

1 I play mostly ______ .
2 As for instruments, ______ .
3 I sing ______ .
4 In fact, last month I ______ .
5 People often ask me ______ .

7 What three questions would you like to ask your favorite band?

______
______
______
______
______

Adverbs of degree

1 Write each adverb under the correct picture to describe how happy the woman is.

extremely	fairly
incredibly	pretty
really	totally
very	

1 ______ 3 ______ 5 ______
2 ______ 4 ______ 6 ______
7 ______

2 Choose the correct option to complete the sentences.

1 The biology homework Mr. Davies gave us was ***totally*** / ***incredibly*** difficult.
2 You know Tom's never had an accident. He drives ***a lot*** / ***really*** carefully.
3 This concert is ***a little*** / ***a lot*** boring. I want to fall asleep!
4 This CD is ***totally*** / ***extremely*** amazing! I've listened to it five times today.
5 He's ***an extremely*** / ***a pretty*** good player. He did well, but he wasn't the best.
6 We took the train to the festival; it was ***really*** / ***a lot*** quick.
7 The movie was ***fairly*** / ***extremely*** funny. The entire audience was laughing the whole time.
8 Tomas practiced hard for his piano recital, so on the day he was only ***a little*** / ***very*** nervous.
9 Daniela didn't feel well yesterday, but today she's feeling ***fairly*** / ***a lot*** better.
10 The band was ***totally*** / ***a little*** focused on playing and didn't talk to the crowd once.

3 Circle the adverb that can replace the adverb in bold in the sentences.

1 The opera was **incredibly** long. It went on for over four hours.
a little / ***extremely*** / ***fairly***
2 Susana has worked **very** hard for her audition, and I really hope it goes well.
incredibly / ***pretty*** / ***a little***
3 Charlie is actually **fairly** shy and doesn't really like going out much.
totally / ***really*** / ***a little***
4 Come on! We're **extremely** late for the party!
really / ***a little*** / ***pretty***
5 I'm **pretty** tired, so I think I'll stay in tonight.
a little / ***incredibly*** / ***extremely***
6 I don't like listening to heavy metal music because it's **really** loud.
incredibly / ***a little*** / ***very***

WORDS & BEYOND

4 Complete the text with the words in the box.

audition confidence convey criteria focused gesture stage talent

As I stood on the side of the (1) ______, waiting for a(n) (2) ______ from someone telling me that it was my turn to (3) ______, I began to doubt myself. Was I good enough to do this? Did I have the (4) ______ to be myself and (5) ______ to the judges how much this meant to me? I was full of fear. I knew I had some (6) ______, but would it be enough to get the part? What were the (7) ______? Was I what the judges were looking for? Then, slowly, a sense of calm came over me. I was (8) ______ now. This was my big chance, and I had to go for it. They gestured for me to come forward. "Here we go," I thought. "Take your chance – you can do this."

GRAMMAR 2 Comparative adverbs

Compare how people do things

1 Complete the sentences with the correct comparative or superlative adverbs in the box.

better carefully fast harder more beautifully the most beautifully the quickest worse

Comparative adverbs

One-syllable adverbs

1 *Amy studies ______ than Lisa.*

Two or more syllable adverbs

2 *Larissa sang ______ than Claudia.*

Superlative adverbs

One-syllable adverbs

3 *Lisa does math ______ of all the students.*

Two or more syllable adverbs

4 *Dave paints ______ of all the students in art class.*

As … as adverb comparison

… (*not*) verb + *as* + adverb + *as* …

5 *Larry runs as ______ as Mike.*

6 *My dad doesn't drive as ______ as my mom.*

Irregular forms

7 *Lisa isn't good at English. She does ______ in English than in math.*

8 *Amy is good at English. She does ______ than Lisa.*

2 Complete the table.

Adverb	Comparative	Superlative
fast	faster	(1) ______
hard	(2) ______	the hardest
creatively	more creatively	(3) ______
badly	(4) ______	the worst
high	higher	(5) ______
early	earlier	(6) ______
powerfully	(7) ______	the most powerfully
well	(8) ______	the best
confidently	more confidently	(9) ______
far	(10) ______	the farthest

3 Find and correct the mistakes.

1 The audience shouted most loudly for Anna than for Mark.
The audience shouted more loudly for Anna than for Mark.

2 Kevin swam the more fast in the competition.

______

3 I didn't do as good in math this year as I did last year.

______

4 My friend paints more beautifully as many professional artists.

______

5 Greta danced more better than the other dancers in the audition.

______

6 Freddy sings the most badly in the whole school!

______

4 Complete the blog post with the correct comparative form of the adverb in parentheses.

And the winner is …

Today we had our school end-of-year celebration, and for the first time we decided to have an informal awards night to celebrate all of our hard work this year. It was so much fun. Valeria won the award for scoring (1) ______ (high) than anyone else in the class exams. Felipe works (2) ______ (hard) in our class, so he won best student award. A lot of people won awards for playing music. Luciana won best singer. She sings (3) ______ (beautifully) than anyone I've ever heard. Catalina and Jorge both won the award for best musician. They both play their instruments (4) ______ (well) each other so we couldn't decide between them. Violeta won the best sportsperson award. This year she ran (5) ______ (fast) and swam (6) ______ (well) than anyone else. And what about me? Well, I didn't do (7) ______ (well) the others, but I did win one award – most helpful student of the year, and I guess I'm happy with that!

5 Put the words in order to make comparative and superlative sentences.

1 as / Can / you / Max / creatively / paint / as / ?

______

2 need / You / to learn / neatly / more / to write / .

______

3 the / Oliver / performed / audition, / At / the / confidently / most / .

______

4 run / Isabel / as / fast / only / 13 / as Nicola / can't / she's / because / .

______

SPEAKING

Present other people's opinions

1 Read the two parts of the conversation. Match each part to the correct picture.

A

B

1

Amita: Hey, Malike, how was your trip to Bali with your family?

Malike: Oh, we had a really fantastic time. On the last day we saw this traditional Balinese dancing. My mom said they danced more gracefully than any ballet dancer she's seen.

Amita: Really? Why are they so good?

Malike: A (1) .... say it's because they learn to dance with their hands when they're very young. Because they hear music from such an early age, they have this totally amazing sense of rhythm.

Amita: What was (2) .... ?

Malike: I (3) .... the dancing was great, but I really loved the costumes. They were so colorful and beautiful. Some (4) .... they look a little strange, but I (5) .... what other people think. I loved them.

2

Amita: So, tell me more about this dancing. What kind of music do they dance to?

Malike: They dance to the gamelan.

Amita: Gamelan? What's that?

Malike: It's a kind of traditional band with instruments like drums, strings, and flutes. My brother thought they were cool, but my dad hated it because it was too noisy!

Amita: And what (6) .... you? What did (7) .... ?

Malike: Well, I don't really (8) .... I was so busy watching the dancers, I don't really remember what the music was like.

2 85 Read the conversation again. Try to complete the words and phrases (1–8) in the blanks. Then listen and check your answers.

3 Find and write phrases from Exercise 1 in the correct circle below.

Asking for an opinion

Giving an opinion

Presenting other people's opinions

4 a PRONOUNCE Write the words with the sounds /ɔ/ and /ɑ/ in the correct column.

~~audience~~ audition caught ~~concert~~ confidence costume modern opera song thought

/ɔ/	/ɑ/
audience	*concert*

b 86 Listen and check your answers.

c Add two more words to each column.

WRITING

Link contrasting ideas

1 Complete the tips with the words in the box.

REMEMBER HOW TO …

link contrasting ideas

although   but   even though   however

- Use (1) ______ to join two parts of a sentence.
- Use (2) ______ and (3) ______ at the beginning of a two-part sentence.
- Use (4) ______ at the beginning, the middle, or the end of a contrasting sentence.

2 Choose the correct option to complete the sentences.

1 ***Although*** / ***However***, I enjoyed playing the violin, I wasn't very good at it.
2 I liked all the bands at the festival, ***but*** / ***although*** it rained all the time so it wasn't much fun.
3 I auditioned for the orchestra. ***Even though*** / ***However***, they didn't choose me.
4 The concert hall was enormous, ***even though*** / ***but*** the audience was very small.
5 When I was young my mom played a lot of rock music. ***Even though*** / ***However,*** she preferred folk.
6 ***Even though*** / ***But*** she isn't a very good singer, her last album was very successful.

3 Complete the article with the correct linking words (for example, *although* or *but*). There may be more than one correct answer.

MY MUSIC PROFILE

Big Beat Dan, reggae musician

Music has always been a big part of my life. When I was a child, my mom played a lot of reggae and jazz. (1) ______ we were poor, my parents saved up for me to take guitar lessons, and later I taught myself the drums. At 18 my parents wanted me to get a job. (2) ______ , I formed a band instead. We became famous, and now we play in huge venues all around the world.

(3) ______ I play music for a living, it's still a very personal thing. I couldn't live without it. It just makes me feel incredibly happy and alive.

I tour a lot. (4) ______ , I don't get homesick because my family often comes with me. My friends and family don't really see me as a celebrity, (5) ______ just as little Dan Gooding from Hope Town. (6) ______ I'm famous, no one in my town treats me differently, and I respect that.

4 Decide if these sentences are correct (*C*) or incorrect (*I*). Rewrite the incorrect sentences using the same linking word.

1 The composer Beethoven was deaf, he wrote some amazing classical music although. *I*
Although the composer Beethoven was deaf, he wrote some amazing classical music.
2 Even though Chantal had problems with her back, she wanted to be a ballet dancer. ______
______
3 However I'd like to be a singer, I get nervous in front of an audience. ______
______
4 My boyfriend can't sing, but he can play the drums. ______
______
5 Although I had a lot of homework, I went to the concert. ______
______
6 But the band is very famous in Europe, no one has heard of them in the USA. ______
______

5 **You're going to write your own music profile. Look at the *Writing plan* and make notes.**

WRITING PLAN

1 **Make notes about music in your life.**
When did you start listening to music? Do you play an instrument or sing? Have you been to any concerts or festivals? ☐

2 **Give your own opinion about music.**
Is it a personal thing or something that you share with other people? How do you feel about music in your life? What are your favorite bands? ☐

3 **Include the opinions of others.**
Do other people think you're musical? Do your friends like your music? ☐

4 **Write contrasting sentences about yourself and music using your notes.** ☐

WRITE AND CHECK

6 **Write your profile. Then check (✓) the stages in the *Writing plan*.**

Stay on task and avoid distractions

1 **Read the conversation. What is Dan doing?**

Dan: Hi, Luca! What are you up to?
Luca: Oh, hi, Dan. I just finished my homework, so I'm going to play my keyboard a little.
Dan: Oh, cool. I finished my homework too. I'm painting my room white. I've painted one wall, but I don't have any more white paint. Do you have any?
Luca: Sure. I'll bring it over to your house. I'm not busy.
Dan: No, that's OK. I'll come and pick it up. I'm bored anyway. Painting's so boring! I'm hungry too.
Luca: No problem. I have snacks at my house.
Dan: Why don't we just make some lunch? I'll stop at the supermarket on my way.
Luca: Great. And when you get here, I'll play you the new song I wrote for the band.
Dan: Hey, I'll bring my guitar then, and we can practice. I need to be home by six because we're having an early dinner.
Luca: No problem. See you in a few minutes.

2 **Read the conversation again. Dan was painting his room. Did he stay on task? What did he do right? What did he do wrong?**

3 **What advice would you give Dan?**

GET ORGANIZED

1 Read the clues and complete the crossword.

Across

5 This is a way of behaving that has been followed for a long time.
6 You need this to travel to some countries but not all.
7 This is the name for a large band that has a conductor.
10 This is another word for "very large."
11 The official part of getting married is called this.

Down

1 This is a word to describe something that is worth a lot of money or is very useful.
2 This is a series of actions done regularly, usually as part of a celebration.
3 Something that is, for example, red, blue, and green can be described as this.
4 This is someone who travels on a plane or train.
8 This is an instrument that you sometimes hit with a stick.
9 This is the traditional music of a particular region or people.

2 Use the clues to find the nouns in the word spiral. The letters giving the end of one word and the beginning of the next have been given.

Clues

1 This is last part of the airport that you go through after passport control.
2 You use these to cut your hair, for example.
3 You use this to wash your hair.
4 This is a performance where people sing.
5 This is someone who is older than 18.
6 This is a kind of brass instrument.
7 You take this when you travel somewhere and return home.
8 You need this when traveling to foreign countries. It has your picture in it.
9 You use this to brush your teeth.
10 This has spinning blades, and you fly in it.
11 This is the way you go between two places.
12 This is when you vote to choose someone.

ALL ABOUT ME

1 **Would you like to go to a festival or other international music event?** ____________________

2 **Where would you like to go?** ____________________

3 **Is it something you'd like to do now or at a different stage in your life?** ____________________
____

1 Put the words in order to make questions.

1 **Q:** to / you / music / listen / Where / do / to / like / ? ______
A: In my room.
2 **Q:** concert / going / the / television / you / on / Are / watch / to / ? ______
A: No, I have to work tonight.
3 **Q:** saw / I / were / going / Where / you / this / you / when / morning / ? ______
A: To my tennis lesson.
4 **Q:** an / ever / learned / play / you / Have / instrument / to / how / ? ______
A: Yes – the flute when I was eight.
5 **Q:** music / you / have / rock / long / liked / How / ? ______
A: Since I was about 10.

2 Choose the correct option to complete the sentences.

1 Yesterday, we ***decided*** / ***have decided*** to get our tickets online.
2 I don't usually like that band, so I don't think I will enjoy ***to listen*** / ***listening*** to the new album.
3 I ***don't*** / ***didn't*** mind waiting while you have your piano lesson.
4 Is the band planning ***to play*** / ***playing*** in our town on their tour?
5 Can you imagine ***to be*** / ***being*** so close to the stage? It'll be amazing!
6 Would you like ***to borrow*** / ***borrowing*** my music magazine?

3 Complete the sentences with the correct form of the word in parentheses.

1 Sorry! My phone call took a little ______ (long) than I expected.
2 Do you think it's a lot ______ (hard) to perform in front of a big audience?
3 The judges chose the winner ______ (quick) than they did last year.
4 Jack doesn't play the guitar ______ (well) as Peter.
5 We all sang badly in the performance, but I was the ______ (bad).
6 The last song in the concert was the ______ (good). It's my favorite!

4 Match the sentence parts.

1 Adam is going to
2 It's likely to
3 I don't think I'll
4 Sara was inspired to
5 I'd like to
6 I hope to

a rain this afternoon, so take an umbrella.
b join the school orchestra after she heard them practice.
c play soccer on Saturday if it doesn't rain.
d visit his uncle in Malaysia next summer.
e learn to play the piano, but I can't read music.
f be able to go to the festival this weekend, unfortunately.

5 Complete the second sentence so it means the same as the first. Use the word(s) given.

1 Kyle and Susie both speak English fluently.
as
Susie ______ .
2 Nick is diving better than everyone in the competition.
best
Nick ______ .
3 I've arranged to meet Matthew after school today.
am
I ______ .
4 Helena started playing the drums six years ago.
has
Helena ______ .
5 This is my first visit to Paris.
been
I ______ before.
6 It'd be good for us to take a vacation in Maine this summer.
would like
We ______ .

4 VERY IMPORTANT PEOPLE

UNIT

VOCABULARY 1 >>> People and relationships

1 Match the adjectives in Column A to the definitions in Column B.

Column A	Column B
ambitious	looking happy and positive
generous	having a strong wish to be rich or successful
sensitive	not polite; a person who says or does things that might upset or anger other people
creative	not afraid of danger or difficult things
competitive	not saying unkind or rude things
cheerful	being aware of and responding to other people's feelings
brave	willing to be more kind, helpful, or giving (with money, for example) than most people
polite	describes a person who can think of a lot of new ideas
rude	wanting to win in whatever you do

2 Complete the sentences with adjectives from Exercise 1. You will not use all the words.

1 My uncle's really ________ ; whenever we go out for pizza, he pays for everyone.
2 Sarah's very ________ . She can easily detect when other people are feeling sad.
3 I enjoy writing stories and painting pictures. I'm ________ .
4 My brothers both want to become successful and earn a lot of money. They're ________ .
5 Makiko's the most ________ person I know. She always wants to get the best grades in class.
6 My dad's a very ________ person. He's always happy and smiling.

3 Complete the sentences with the words in the box.

acquaintance classmates enemies guest neighbor relative

1 Maria and Megan don't like each other at all. They're definitely ________ and not friends!
2 Jude is Sasha's ________ . They live next door to each other.
3 Jack and I go to the same school. We're ________ , so we have the same teacher.
4 Tyler is my ________ . He's my mom's youngest cousin.
5 Lupita is our ________ . She's staying with us for a few days.
6 I don't know Leon that well. He's more of a(n) ________ than a friend.

4 a Read the conversations. Write the words in the box under each conversation to describe the relationship between the people.

close friends old friends online friends teammates

1 Hey, Sophie! I haven't seen you for such a long time!
I know. It's been about five years. How are you?
____
2 See you at the game tonight, Filippo.
Sorry, I've hurt my foot. I can't play.
____
3 Hey, Jim, what's up? I'm bored.
Not much. Just surfing some websites. Want to chat?
____
4 Hey, Laura, I really need to talk to you. You're the only one who'll understand.
Of course. I'm always here for you.
____

b Write sentences about people in your life who match the relationships in Exercise 4a.

Example: *Charlotte is a close friend.*
____
____

5 Read about the people that Belen knows. Label the pictures with their names.

A

____

B

____

C
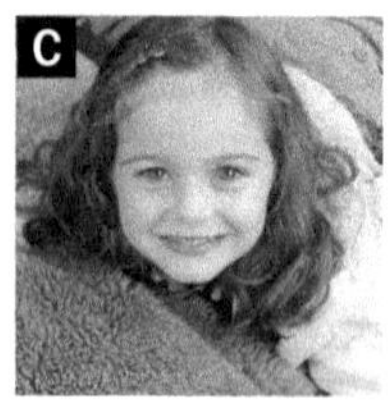
____

D

____

E

____

1 My neighbor, Mrs. Mendoza, is very kind. She's pretty old, and she has gray hair.
2 My little cousin Lucia's only six, so she's pretty short and she has these beautiful big eyes. She's very funny. She makes everyone laugh a lot.
3 Emma's my best friend, and she's 16 like me. She has long straight hair. She's fairly shy until she gets to know you.
4 David's my classmate and the most popular boy in school. He has short hair, and he's really smart.
5 My older sister Rita has short straight hair. She's not a very cheerful person. In fact, she's pretty bad-tempered!

Recognize examples

1 Complete the tips with the words in the box.

REMEMBER HOW TO …

recognize examples

first for example for instance
headings like such as

- Look at the words after (1) ______ and (2) ______ in the middle of sentences.
- Look at the words after (3) ______ and (4) ______ at the beginning of sentences.
- Look under (5) ______ . The (6) ______ sentence is sometimes an example.

2 Put the words in order to make sentences.

1 very / I'm / shy / people / with / I / acquaintances / don't / know, / such as / .

______

2 is / generous. / My neighbor / last week / really / For example, / MP3 player / me / he / lent / his / .

______

3 My cousins / share / such as / a lot of things, / clothes and books / .

______

4 are / very / different. / Diego and I / For instance, / soccer / I / love / he / but / tennis / prefers / .

______

3 Match the sentence parts.

1 She's the person I turn to if I have a problem. For example, ___
2 He always does things to make people laugh, such as ___
3 We do a lot of things together, like ___
4 I'll do anything to try and beat him. For instance, ___

a going to the movies and swimming.
b when I was having issues at school, I emailed her first for advice.
c I didn't tell him about a test we had at school last week so I could get a better grade.
d telling jokes and funny stories.

4 Read the article and answer the questions.

Friends forever

Do you have a friend or relative that you have a close relationship with?
We asked students from around the world to share their experiences.

1 Close but in different countries *Julieta and Mia*
I live thousands of miles away from my cousin Julieta, but we're really close friends. She's the person I turn to if I have a problem. For example, when I was having issues at school, I emailed her first for advice. We don't see each other very often, but we email all the time.

2 A very special aunt *Vi and Stefania*
Vi's my mom's younger sister. She's only 10 years older than me, so she's more like a sister than an aunt. She's a really kind and generous person, and we do a lot of things together, like going to the movies and swimming.

3 Competitive teammates *Rodrigo and Bruno*
Rodrigo and I play on the same team, but we're always trying to do better than each other! He's my closest friend, but I'll do anything to try and beat him. For instance, I didn't tell him about a test we had at school last week so I could get a better grade. It was a little mean, but he's really smart, so he didn't mind.

4 An acquaintance who became a friend *Alex and Adrian*
Alex was a friend of a friend, but we've become close friends over time. He's probably the most cheerful person I know, and he always does things to make people laugh, such as telling jokes and funny stories.

1 Which two people don't see each other very often?
______
2 Who is very intelligent?
______
3 Which person is more like a sister?
______
4 Who is a very funny person?
______
5 Who has a mainly online relationship?
______
6 Who was someone else's friend first?
______

MOVE BEYOND

Go online and read about someone famous talking about his or her family. What are the person's relationships with the different members of their family like?

______

______

GRAMMAR 1 First conditional with *if/unless*

Talk about possible situations in the future

1 Choose the correct option to complete the grammar table.

First conditional

Condition clause	Result clause
If + (1) ***present*** / ***future*** tense ...	... (2) ***present*** / ***will, may, might*** + base verb.
If I see Jane, If she doesn't get here soon,	I'll tell her about the party. I might call her.
Unless + (3) ***present*** / ***future*** tense ...	... (4) ***present*** / ***will, may, might*** + base verb.
Unless I invite Angie,	she'll be angry with me.

2 Decide if these statements are correct (*C*) or incorrect (*I*).

1 We use the first conditional to talk about a present situation. ......
2 We can use *unless* with an affirmative verb in the *if* clause to mean *if not*. ......
3 In a first conditional sentence the *if* clause describes the result of a situation. ......
4 The *if* clause can come first or second in the sentence. ......
5 We use a comma after the *if* clause when the *if* clause comes first. ......

3 Read the conversation and answer the questions.

Marco: If we wait any longer, we'll be late for the movie.
Enrique: I know, but Greta will be annoyed if we leave without her.
Marco: If you always wait for her, she'll never learn to be on time.
Enrique: I know, but my parents will be angry if we don't wait for her. If we leave now, Dad will have to take her.
Marco: OK. But I'll go by myself unless she's here in five minutes.
Enrique: That's fine. I'm sure she'll be here.

1 Why is Marco worried?
....
2 Who are they waiting for?
....
3 What two things might happen if they don't wait?
....
4 Does Marco think it's a good idea to wait?
....
5 What is he going to do?
....

4 Check (✓) the correct sentences.

1 ☐ **A** If it rains later, we won't have the barbecue.
☐ **B** If it will rain later, we won't have the barbecue.

2 ☐ **A** Dad will help us with the cooking unless he's busy.
☐ **B** Dad won't help us with the cooking unless he's busy.

3 ☐ **A** Unless everyone comes, we'll have too much food.
☐ **B** If everyone comes, we'll have too much food.

4 ☐ **A** If we cook a lot of burgers, there'll be enough for everyone.
☐ **B** If we will cook a lot of burgers, there is enough for everyone.

5 ☐ **A** Unless you give me some money, I'll buy some soda.
☐ **B** I'll buy some soda if you give me some money.

5 › Put the words in order to make sentences.

1 my / If / sister / me / doesn't wake / happy / up / be / tomorrow, / early / I'll / .
If my sister doesn't wake me up early tomorrow, I'll be happy.

2 meet / after / unless / school / We'll / class / our / late / finishes / .

3 morning / has / tennis / Harry / this / practice / rains / unless / it / .

4 don't / you / want / If / go / shopping, / to / I'll / myself / go / by / .

5 If / the / your / key, / let / neighbor / in / forget / you / will / you / .

6 will / My / give / brother / us / a / there's / ride / unless / a / his / with / problem / car / .

6 ›› Choose the correct verb so the second sentence has the same meaning as the first.

1 If Dave doesn't call me, I'll be upset.
Unless Dave ***calls*** / ***doesn't call*** me, I'll be upset.

2 We'll be late if the train doesn't come soon.
We'll be late unless the train ***comes*** / ***doesn't come*** soon.

3 If I get good grades, I'll go to college.
Unless I ***get*** / ***don't get*** good grades, I'll go to college.

4 Chloe will get her driver's license if she doesn't make some silly mistakes.
Chloe will get her driver's license unless she ***makes*** / ***doesn't make*** some silly mistakes.

5 The teacher will get angry if they talk during the test.
The teacher will get angry unless they ***talk*** / ***don't talk*** during the test.

6 I'll buy some new jeans online if I don't find any at the mall tomorrow.
I'll buy some new jeans online unless I ***find*** / ***don't find*** some at the mall tomorrow.

7 ›› Match the sentence beginnings (1–6) with the endings (a–f). Add commas where necessary.

1 If I get home early ____
2 Unless I can earn some more money ____
3 I'll wear my new dress ____
4 If we win this game ____
5 My cousin will give me some advice ____
6 Jonas won't talk to me again ____

a if I go to Georgia's party.
b we'll be in the finals of the competition.
c unless I apologize.
d I'll take the dog for a walk.
e I won't be able to go to Lisbon.
f if I ask her for help.

8 ››› Use the prompts to make questions and answers using the first conditional.

1 What / you / do / if / she / say / no?
What will you do if she says no?
If / she / say / no / I / probably cry.
If she says no, I'll probably cry.

2 What / you / do / if / you / miss / the train?

If / I / miss / the train / I / catch the bus.

3 Who / you / invite / to play soccer / if / Tom / not / come?

If / Tom / not / come / I / invite / Mark.

4 Where / Dave and Mike / stay / if / they / go / to Tokyo?

If / Dave and Mike / go / to Tokyo / they / stay / with Yuko.

5 If / Beatriz / visit / you / where / you / take / her?

If / Beatriz / visit / us / we / take / her / to the theme park.

9 ››› Complete the messages with the correct form of the verbs in the box.

be explain get invite not accept not be not go not understand respect talk

12:30

Ruby: Hey, Max. I've got a problem. I promised Helena that I'd watch her at the swim meet on Saturday, but Veronica just invited me to spend the weekend with her family at their beach house. If I (1) ____ to the swim competition, Helena (2) ____ upset and she might never (3) ____ to me again.

Max: But if you (4) ____ Veronica's invitation, she (5) ____ hurt and may never (6) ____ you again.

Ruby: That's what I'm afraid of!

Max: LOL! But Veronica's cool. If you (7) ____ to her about your promise to Helena, she (8) ____ you for being a good friend.

Ruby: You're right. I need to be honest with her. If she (9) ____ the importance of a promise, she (10) ____ a good friend to me either.

LISTENING

Use stress and intonation to help you understand

1 Complete the tips with the words in the box.

REMEMBER HOW TO …

use stress and intonation to help you understand

down	feelings	important	stressed	up

- People stress the most (1) ______ words when they speak. Listen for (2) ______ words.
- When people express strong (3) ______, their voices go (4) ______ and (5) ______ more. Listen for these changes.

2 a ▶87 Listen to parts of a conversation. Write down the words Maria stresses.

1 ______, ______
2 ______, ______
3 ______, ______
4 ______, ______

b ▶87 Listen again. Practice saying Maria's sentences.

3 ▶88 Read the conversation and underline the words that you think are stressed and important. Then listen and check your answers.

Bea: You look stressed.
Selma: I'm not stressed. I'm tired.
Bea: Why's that?
Selma: Pete called me. And not in the afternoon, but late at night.
Bea: Did he have a problem?
Selma: Yes, he needed help with homework.
Bea: Math homework or English homework?
Selma: Both!
Bea: But why is he calling anyone so late? I'd be kind of mad!

4 ▶89 Listen to the conversation and choose the correct answer.

Karen and Steve are talking about:
a someone they both met a long time ago.
b someone they know with a special ability.
c someone they know who went to a soccer game.

5 ▶89 Listen again and decide if these statements are correct (*C*) or incorrect (*I*).

1 Brad is Karen's friend. ______
2 Karen can't remember people's faces. ______
3 Karen is impressed by Anna's special ability. ______
4 Anna can remember everything she's ever read. ______
5 Steve would like to be like Anna. ______
6 People like Anna sometimes help the police. ______

6 ▶90 Listen and underline the stressed word in the sentence. Then match each sentence (1–3) to the correct meaning (a–c).

1 I'm so angry. ______
2 I'm so angry. ______
3 I'm so angry. ______

a I'm very, very angry.
b I'm the person who is angry.
c I'm feeling angry, not sad or afraid.

7 ▶91 Listen and underline the stressed word in the sentence. Then match each sentence (1–3) to the correct meaning (a–c).

1 John can remember everything. ______
2 John can remember everything. ______
3 John can remember everything. ______

a John will remember all the things, not just some.
b John is definitely able to remember.
c John is the person with a good memory.

VOCABULARY 2

Extreme adjectives

1 Write the vowels to complete the adjectives (1–10). Then match them to the correct meaning (a–j).

1 a m a z i n g ___d___ a very hard to believe
2 t___rr___f___ ___d ______ b very angry
3 f___r___ ___ ___s ______ c very big
4 sh___ck___d ______ d very good or surprising
5 ___nc___ ___nt ______ e very scared
6 ___xh___ ___st___d ______ f very interesting
7 h___g___ ______ g very tired
8 ___wf___l ______ h very surprised (negative)
9 ___nb___l___ ___v___bl___ ______ i very old
10 f___sc___n___t___ng ______ j very bad

2 Complete the email with adjectives from Exercise 1.

Hi Michelle,

The concert was really (1) ______, but I missed the train and my dad was (2) ______ because he had to come and pick me up! We didn't get home until midnight, so this morning I was (3) ______ because I didn't get much sleep. Mom gave me a(n) (4) ______ breakfast, but I wasn't hungry at all. And because I didn't sleep much I had a(n) (5) ______ headache. Not good! The worst thing was we had an English test. We were all (6) ______ because we weren't expecting one! I couldn't remember anything.

Hope your day was better!

Candice

WORDS & BEYOND

3 Complete the sentences with an adjective that describes a person's character.

1 Jake told me this morning that he wants to be a successful businessman before his 20th birthday. Our child is very *a*______!
2 Thank you for lending me the money. You're very *g*______.
3 I'm pretty *s*______. I cry a lot when I watch a sad movie.
4 I'm no good at thinking of new ideas, but my sister is really *c*______.
5 Mike is *c*______ when he plays tennis. He always wants to win, so it's hard to have fun when you play with him.
6 Ada is a *c*______ person. She has a smile on her face every time I see her.
7 Cruz is really *b*______. He ran after the man who tried to rob him, even though the man was twice his size.
8 He isn't *p*______. He never says please and thank you.
9 You're so *r*______. That really hurt my feelings.

4 Find the answers to Exercise 3 in the word search.

C	B	T	V	G	O	R	N	I	C	T	S	O	I	W	G
N	R	H	A	A	F	E	D	E	W	E	V	E	H	C	J
E	A	E	E	X	F	E	A	M	B	I	T	I	O	U	S
E	V	E	A	A	V	P	S	O	F	E	F	S	S	L	E
T	E	P	A	T	I	E	N	T	V	N	G	D	S	N	N
R	Y	I	P	A	I	E	F	I	V	R	T	T	T	H	S
R	H	F	P	O	E	V	T	L	J	R	T	S	I	Z	I
E	N	O	G	P	L	I	E	C	T	E	U	E	C	E	T
D	I	A	L	A	T	I	A	P	A	O	W	N	P	N	I
L	O	T	E	E	R	S	T	L	R	T	T	U	O	E	V
D	N	S	P	N	N	C	H	E	E	R	F	U	L	I	E
S	S	M	C	P	E	E	N	D	V	R	V	T	I	D	P
C	O	N	F	I	D	E	N	T	R	D	H	S	T	I	D
C	P	S	V	U	G	K	M	D	O	I	E	P	E	E	Z
D	L	L	R	Q	O	F	X	S	E	C	A	A	Z	L	N
C	R	E	A	T	I	V	E	W	T	L	C	T	F	E	A

GRAMMAR 2 Second conditional

Talk about imaginary situations in the present and future

1 › Complete the grammar table with the words in the box.

simple past (x2)   would (x2)

Second conditional

Condition clause: statements	Result clause
If + subject + (1) ________	subject + (2) ________ , *might*, *could* + base verb
If I were you, If I had more time, If he exercised more often,	I would tell him. I'd come and visit you. he might be healthier.
Condition clause: questions	**Result clause**
If + subject + (3) ________	(4) ________ + subject + base verb
If you had the money, If your mom knew,	would you buy a house? (Yes, I would. No, I wouldn't.) what might she say?

2 › Choose the correct option to complete the rules for the second conditional.

1 We use the second conditional to talk about ***a real / an imaginary*** situation in the present or future.
2 The *if* clause uses the ***simple present / simple past***.
3 The result clause uses ***would / will*** and the base form of the verb.
4 You ***can / can't*** use *might* and *could* in the result clause.
5 The *if* clause can come ***first only / first or second***.

3 › Complete the second conditional sentences with the correct form of the verb in parentheses.

1 If I ________ (have) enough money, I ________ (buy) the latest smartphone.
2 If I ________ (change) schools, I ________ (miss) my friends.
3 My friend ________ (be) upset if I never ________ (call) her.
4 If I ________ (be) older, I ________ (drive) a car.
5 I ________ (understand) my friend Elia better if I ________ (speak) Spanish.
6 My sister ________ (move) to Australia if she ________ (have) the chance.

4 ›› Use the words to make questions in the second conditional.

1 What / you / do / if / you / get lost / overseas?
____
2 What / you / do / if / you / lost your homework?
____
3 Where / you / go / if / you / can travel / anywhere?
____
4 How / you / feel / if / you / can (not) / answer / any questions on a test?
____

5 ›› Match each picture to the question it answers in Exercise 4. Then write an answer to each question.

A 2

tell the teacher
If I lost my homework, I'd tell the teacher.

B ___

feel stressed
____
____

C ___

ask for directions
____
____

D ___

see the pyramids
____
____

6 ››› Complete the blog with the correct second conditional form of the verbs in the box.

can go   can take (x2)   fly (x2)   have (x2)
let   start   stop   visit (x2)

So, my friend Zara has just left on a trip around the world. I'm so jealous! If I (1) ________ anywhere in the world, I think I (2) ________ Asia first. If I (3) ________ in Bangkok, I (4) ________ the train down to the south, to Surat Thani. If I (5) ________ in Surat Thani, I (6) ________ my online friend, Somchai. Then, if I (7) ________ enough money, I (8) ________ by plane to Japan and stay with my friend Suki in Kyoto. After that, if I (9) ________ time, I (10) ________ a ship from Japan to Hawaii to visit my cousin Kayo. I've always wanted to go on a trip across the ocean. Then, if Kayo's parents (11) ________ her come with me, we (12) ________ to the west coast of the USA to see our Aunt Lia, who lives in San Francisco. After that, I'd probably have to fly back for school!

Make and react to requests

1 Complete the phrases with the words in the box. More than one answer is possible.

can could do help would

1 .... I borrow your phone?
2 .... you give me a ride, please?
3 Would you .... me with this problem, please?
4 .... you mind if I leave early today?
5 .... you mind if I opened the window?

2 Check (✓) the replies that are positive and (✗) the replies that are negative.

1 OK. ☐
2 All right. ☐
3 Sorry, I can't. ☐
4 Sure. ☐
5 Of course. ☐
6 I'm afraid ... ☐
7 No, go ahead. ☐
8 Not at all. ☐

3 Circle the requests and responses in Exercises 1 and 2 that are formal, and underline the ones that are informal.

4 ▶92 Choose the correct option to complete the sentences. Then listen and check your answers.

1 **A:** Excuse me. We're here on vacation. (1) ***Would*** / ***Do*** you take a picture of us, please?
B: Of (2) ***right*** / ***course*** ... Smile!

2 **A:** We don't have a menu on our table. Would you mind if we (3) ***borrow*** / ***borrowed*** yours for a moment?
B: (4) ***Not*** / ***Go*** at all. Here you are.

3 **A:** I'm going out tonight. (5) ***Could*** / ***Do*** you mind doing the laundry?
B: Sorry, (6) ***I'm afraid I can't*** / ***go ahead.*** I'm going out too.

4 **A:** I have to go to the library. I won't be long. (7) ***Can you*** / ***Would you mind*** tell Mom that I'll be back in time for dinner?
B: (8) ***Not*** / ***All*** right.

5 **A:** You have some great ideas for your essay. (9) ***Would*** / ***Do*** you mind if I use some of them?
B: Sorry, but you should think of your own.

5 a Put the words in order to make requests.

a it / Would / me / for / check / you / ?
....

b I / call / you / Do / if / mind / phone / Debbie / to / borrow / your / ?
....

c a / ask / I / you / favor / Can / ?
....

d fix / Can / that / you / ?
....

e too / look / that / you / Could / at / ?
....

b ▶93 Read the conversation and insert the requests from Exercise 5a in the correct place. Then listen and check your answers.

Sara: Ron, what are you doing here?
Ron: It's Marty's computer. He's having problems with it.
Sara: (1) ......
Ron: OK. Go ahead.
Sara: It's my laptop. (2) ...... I can't get online.
Ron: OK. No problem.
Sara: Thanks, Ron. You're a star! Oh, another thing – I dropped my hair dryer, and it won't work now. (3) ....
Ron: Sure. I'll do that after the laptop.
Sara: Thank you so much! What would we do without you?
Ron: That's what friends are for!
Sara: Oh, one final thing. I can't get a signal on my new phone. (4) ....
Ron: Sorry, I'm afraid I'm no good with phones.
Sara: That's OK. (5) ....
Ron: Not at all. Here you are!

6 How many requests have you made today? What did you ask for?

....

....

7 ▶94 PRONOUNCE Underline the words you think are stressed in the sentences. Then listen and check your answers, and practice saying them.

1 **A:** If you fixed my phone, what would it cost?
B: If I fixed your phone, I'd do it for free.

2 **A:** If you had to go on stage, how would you feel?
B: If I had to go on stage, I'd feel confident.

3 **A:** If your teacher made a mistake, what would you do?
B: If my teacher made a mistake, I'd point it out.

WRITING

Use a dictionary

1 Complete the tips (1–5) with the correct phrases (a–e).

REMEMBER HOW TO ...

use a dictionary

- Use a bilingual dictionary (1) ____
- Look for the correct part of speech: (2) ____
- Make sure you choose the correct translation or (3) ____
- Read the phonetic transcription (4) ____
- Use a monolingual dictionary (5) ____

a noun, verb, adjective, adverb.
b to translate words.
c to see how you pronounce words.
d definition if there is more than one.
e to see definitions in English.

2 a Read the poem and match the underlined words to the dictionary definitions.

What's on your mind?
You ask because I'm quiet.
Should I tell you the truth?
Or should I just hide it?
Friends should be <u>frank</u> (3)
Isn't that what they say?

But I don't want to hurt you
It isn't my way.
If I told you, you'd cry
And I couldn't <u>bear</u> (____) that
So, I think I'll just <u>lie</u> (____)
And not <u>relay</u> (____) to you
that I'm leaving today.

Definition /laɪ/
1a Verb: to be in a position in which your body is flat on a surface such as the floor or bed; *I need to lie down because I have a headache.*
1b Verb: to deliberately say something that is not true; *My parents get angry if I lie to them about anything.*
1c Noun: something that you say or write that is not true and that you know is not true; *You must never tell a lie to a good friend.*

Definition /beə(r)/
2a Noun: a large wild animal with thick fur; *We watched a documentary about bears in North America.*
2b Verb: to support the weight of something; *The table couldn't bear the weight of my dad, and it collapsed.*
2c Verb: *can't bear* not accept or do something because it makes you very unhappy; *I can't bear watching TV shows about endangered animals.*

Definition /fræŋk/
3 Adjective: honest about the situation or your opinions, even if this offends people; *To be frank, I think you've made a very big mistake.*

Definition /rɪˈleɪ/
4 Verb: to communicate information, news, or a message to someone; *Rose immediately relayed the news to her boss.*

b Which words in the poem would you look up in a bilingual dictionary and which ones would you check in a monolingual dictionary? Why? ____

3 a Find a word in the box that rhymes with each word (1–8).

afford	choose	lend	pretty	train	ship	sight	~~sky~~

1 fly *sky* *why*
2 city ____ ____
3 cruise ____ ____
4 bored ____ ____
5 flight ____ ____
6 trip ____ ____
7 friend ____ ____
8 plane ____ ____

b Add another word to each pair of words.

4 You're going to write a poem about an imaginary trip. Read the poem below and answer the questions.

If...

If I could go anywhere
I'd travel the world
I'd take all my friends
And my relatives too
We'd see cities and sights
Different cultures and people
We'd eat wonderful food
And take a lot of pictures
And when we came home
We'd feel happy and relaxed
As we shared amazing memories
With wonderful people

1 Is the poem simple or complicated? ____
2 Do all the words rhyme? ____
3 Is there punctuation (periods, question marks) in the poem? ____
4 Is it a real situation? ____
5 Who would the writer take? ____
6 What would they see? ____
7 What would they do? ____
8 How would they feel at the end? ____

5 **Make a plan for your poem. Use the *Writing plan* to help you prepare and make notes to answer the questions.**

WRITING PLAN

1 **Choose a situation** ☐

What is the imaginary situation?

2 **Include details** ☐

Where would you go? How would you go there? What would you see or do? Who would you go with? How would you feel?

3 **Choose a title** ☐

Should it be one of the lines? Could it be a single word?

4 **Include new words** ☐

Experiment and find words you didn't know before. Check their definition in a dictionary. Check the pronunciation of the words.

WRITE AND CHECK

6 **Write your poem. Then check (✓) the stages in the *Writing plan*.**

Decide what's important to you

1 **Read the conversation. What decision does Ella have to make? What does she decide?**

Carrie: What's the problem? You look stressed.
Ella: I have to make a decision about what I'm going to do during next week's vacation.
Carrie: It's a vacation. You shouldn't stress!
Ella: I know! My oldest friend Sam wants me to go to the beach with her and her family for the week. And my mom and dad want us all to spend the weekend in Seattle. They want to take me to this new art exhibition.
Carrie: What do you want to do?
Ella: Well, it'd be nice to go to the beach with Sam and her family since we haven't seen each other in a long time, but my mom and dad might be upset if I don't go with them.
Carrie: Can't you do both?
Ella: Yeah, but I also have a big soccer game on the Monday when we get back, and if I'm gone for the whole week, I'll miss practice.
Carrie: I see what you mean. Well, maybe you should stay home and go to practice, and then go away with your parents for a couple of days.
Ella: I guess so.

2 **Read the conversation again and answer the questions.**

1 Do you think Ella made the right decision for her? ……
2 What are the benefits of Ella …
   a going away with Sam? ……
   b going away with her parents? ……
   c staying home to practice? ……
3 What do you think is most important to Ella?
4 What do you think she should do?

3 **Number these things in order of importance for you (most important = *1* and least important = 6).**

	On school nights	On the weekends
1 spending time watching television or surfing the internet	☐	☐
2 spending time with friends	☐	☐
3 spending time doing hobbies and other fun activities	☐	☐
4 spending time doing homework and studying	☐	☐
5 spending time with family	☐	☐
6 helping mom/dad do household chores, such as washing the dishes	☐	☐

1 Match the headings (1–5) to the circles (A–E). Then choose the one that doesn't match in each circle.

1 adjectives to describe objects
2 people
3 places in an airport
4 instruments
5 extreme adjectives

A 2
toddler conductor connection acquaintance enemy neighbor senior

B ______
violin flute trumpet drum heavy metal keyboard guitar

C ______
terrified traditional exhausted furious amazing incredible ancient

D ______
check-in customs gate passport control departure lounge stage

E ______
square enormous wooden plastic patient round tiny

2 Complete the blog with the words in the box.

acquaintances celebrations distracting focused friend friendships homesick huge miss online reminds stuff

24 AUGUST COMMENTS

What do you like about social networking sites? I love them because I can have a (1) ______ number of (2) ______ friends! And I can develop real (3) ______ with people who were once just (4) ______ . I even arranged to go to a movie with a (5) ______ of a friend on my site! My page (6) ______ me about so many things – birthdays, (7) ______ , all kinds of (8) ______ I would usually forget. And when I'm away and a little (9) ______ I can immediately get in touch with everyone I (10) ______ . My dad's not too crazy about social networking sites. He says they're (11) ______ for people when they should be (12) ______ on other things. I just know I'd be lost without mine.

3 Read the clues and complete the crossword.

Across
4 Something that is worth a lot of money is ______ .
8 When you're older and stop working, you ______ .
10 You put things in this when you take a trip.
11 People who have no sense of this can't dance.
12 You make this when you reserve a ticket or a vacation.

Down
1 You keep your money in this.
2 This is a place where events are held.
3 This is the name for a group of people politely waiting to do something.
5 We use these to cut things with.
6 These are people you're at school with and who have the same teacher.
7 A person who is traveling, for example on a plane or train, is a ______ .
9 You have to do one of these if you want to get a part in a play.

ALL ABOUT ME

1 How many close friends do you have? ______

2 How long have you known your oldest friend? ______

3 When were you last exhausted and why? ______

1 Choose the correct option to complete the sentences.

1 If Billy ***invites*** / ***invited*** / ***will invite*** me to his birthday party, I'll go.
2 I ***won't get*** / ***will get*** / ***might get*** a part in the play unless I do very well in the audition.
3 If the plane leaves on time, we ***land*** / ***will land*** / ***would land*** at 6:30.
4 What would your teacher say if you ***are*** / ***were*** / ***will be*** late for school?
5 If I ***tell*** / ***told*** / ***will tell*** Sarah that I didn't like her new skirt, she'd never talk to me again!
6 If all my classmates ***will agree*** / ***agreed*** / ***agree***, we'll have an end-of-year camping trip.

2 Complete the advice column with the correct form of the verb in parentheses.

Q: I have a problem. My sister has taken my leather jacket, and she refuses to give it back. If I (1) ________ (take) it back when she's not looking, she'll get really angry. And if I tell my parents, they (2) ________ (be) furious and she'll cry. My friends gave me the jacket for my birthday, and they'll be upset unless I (3) ________ (wear) it tonight when we go out. Help! What would you do if you (4) ________ (be) me?

A: If I were you, I (5) ________ (explain) to your sister exactly why you need the jacket tonight. If she (6) ________ (not understand) and won't give it back, then tell your parents! I (7) ________ (not worry) about her feelings if she won't give it back. If she (8) ________ (care) about you, she wouldn't take things like that.

3 Complete the online chat with the correct form of the verb in parentheses.

James: Hi! How long (1) ________ (you / be) a member of this online group?

Al: I (2) ________ (join) about three months ago. I enjoy (3) ________ (chat) with people from different countries.

James: Yeah. I decided (4) ________ (join) because I want (5) ________ (practice) speaking English.

Al: (6) ________ (you / have) a lot of online friends?

James: Yes. I chat regularly with about 10 people, but they all speak English (7) ________ (confident) than I do.

Al: You speak English a lot (8) ________ (good) than I do!

James: Oh, no. I have to go now. My mom (9) ________ (call) me for dinner. Do you think (10) ________ (you / be) online later?

Al: Yes. Unless my dad (11) ________ (want) me to help in the yard, I'll be online around 7.

James: Let's chat then. Bye!

4 Complete the second sentence so it means the same as the first. Use the word given.

1 We will have the party outside unless it rains.
if
We won't *have the party outside if it rains*.

2 Jas is a neater writer than Mason.
writes
Jas ________.

3 My plan is to travel overseas after my exams.
hope
I ________.

4 When the band was on stage, many people in the audience left.
playing
While ________.

5 We'll probably be late, so let's meet inside the restaurant.
likely
We're ________.

6 Rock music is OK, but I prefer heavy metal.
mind
I ________.

FIVE SENSES

VOCABULARY 1 >>> The senses and sense verbs

1 Label the picture with the words in the box.

back face foot hand knee
leg neck shoulder toe

2 Label the pictures with the senses in the box. Then write the part of the body associated with the sense.

hearing smell taste ~~touch~~

A

touch
hand

B

……
……

C

……
……

D

……
……

3 a Choose a sense for each situation and write it in the table.

hearing sight smell taste touch

Situation	Sense	Sense verb
1 a warm bath	touch	feel
2 sweetness of lemonade		
3 cooking dinner		
4 a painting in an exhibition		
5 the radio		
6 a terrible noise		
7 when someone calls your name		
8 holding a cat		
9 watching the sunset		

b Now choose a sense verb for each situation above and write it in the table. There may be more than one sense verb for each situation.

feel hear listen look see
smell taste touch watch

c Add another situation for each sense.

1 touch ……
2 smell ……
3 sight ……
4 hearing ……
5 taste ……

4 Choose the correct option to complete the sentences.

1 If I stay in tonight, I'll probably just ***see*** / ***watch*** TV.
2 Ugh! That food has too much salt it in. It ***tastes*** / ***feels*** awful.
3 That ***sounds*** / ***listens*** like a good party that my neighbors are having!
4 What are you cooking for dinner? It ***smells*** / ***feels*** amazing.
5 If you stopped talking, you'd be able to ***hear*** / ***listen*** the teacher.
6 The water ***feels*** / ***tastes*** too cold, so I'm not going swimming in the ocean today.
7 Where's Emily? I can't ***watch*** / ***see*** her anywhere.
8 If you can't find your homework, ***watch*** / ***look*** on the kitchen table. I think it might be there.
9 Please ***hear*** / ***listen***, everyone. I have something important to tell you all.

Use pictures to help you understand

1 Complete the tips with the words in the box.

REMEMBER HOW TO ...

use pictures to help you understand

before connection style visuals when

- (1) __________ you read, look at any pictures or other (2) __________ .
- Think about the (3) __________ between the pictures, the title, the topic, and the (4) __________ of text (news story, manual).
- Look at the visuals (5) __________ you read. They can help you understand new words.

2 a Look at the pictures and answer the questions.

1 Where do you think the text comes from?
   a a magazine
   b a recipe book
   c a history book
2 What do you think the text is about?
   a food that's good for us
   b different tastes of food
3 What information do you think it includes? Check (✓) one or more.
   a recipes for different foods ☐
   b biological information about our body and taste ☐
   c examples of foods that have the different tastes ☐
   d recommendations on how much food we should eat ☐
   e information about a new discovery ☐

b Now read the text quickly to check your answers.

3 Read the text in more detail and decide if the sentences are correct (*C*) or incorrect (*I*).

1 There are only four tastes: sweet, salty, sour, and bitter. ____
2 Tastes can only be recognized on certain parts of the tongue. ____
3 If you put a potato chip on the end of your tongue, you'll be able to taste that it's salty. ____
4 Umami was only discovered recently. ____
5 Food with an umami taste is not as healthy as food with a salty taste. ____
6 Scientists hope to use umami food in a medical setting. ____

4 Choose the correct meaning for these words from the text.

1 detect
   a recognize   b look for
2 tip
   a advice   b end
3 appetite
   a desire to eat   b illness

MOVE BEYOND

Go online and find a recipe for a traditional meal in your country that has an umami ingredient in it.

____

____

THE FOUR TASTES
and their new fifth friend

How many different tastes are there? Most people would say four: sweet, sour, salty, and bitter. Most people love sweet foods, such as cookies and cake, and salty foods, like cheese, are popular too. Less popular are sour foods, like lemons. A lot of people don't like bitter foods, such as coffee.

Many people don't know that our tongue has different areas that can detect each taste. If you put food of a different taste on a different part of the tongue, you can't really taste it. For example, we can only taste bitter food at the back of our tongue, so if you put the tip of your tongue into a cup of coffee, it won't taste bitter. We can only taste sweet and salty foods in a particular part of the tongue.

Another thing that many people don't know is that there is actually a fifth taste, called *umami*. This was discovered by scientists as far back as 1908, but it has only recently been accepted as an official taste. It's a hard taste to describe, but it's the salty, sweet taste that you find in cooked mushrooms and Parmesan cheese. The good thing is that it tastes good, but you only need a little of it to make your food taste great. That's why it's healthier than sweet and salty foods. Scientists hope to use it to make food tastier for people with poor appetites, such as hospital patients.

That's great news for umami fans. It's not just tasty, but healthy!

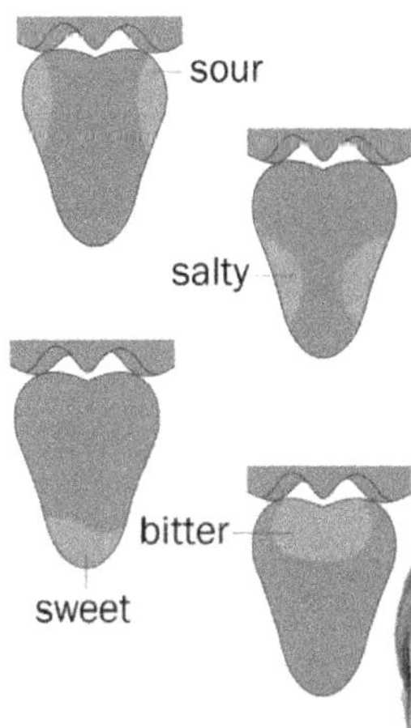

GRAMMAR 1 Passives (past, present, and future)

Use the past, present, and future passives to talk about senses

1 Complete the grammar table.

Simple present passive		
Affirmative	subject + *am/is/*(1) ________ + past participle	Many perfumes are produced in France.
Negative	subject + *'m not/*(2) ________ */aren't* + past participle	My favorite perfume isn't produced in France.
Question form	*Am/Is/Are* + (3) ________ + past participle *Where* + *am/is/are* + subject + past participle	Is it produced in France? Where is it produced?
Simple past passive		
Affirmative	subject + (4) ________ */were* + past participle	The wallet was found on the train.
Negative	subject + *wasn't/*(5) ________ + past participle	The wallet wasn't found by a cleaner.
Question form	*Was/Were* + subject + past participle *Where/Who* + *was/were* + subject + past participle	Was the wallet found on the train? When was the wallet found?
Future passive		
Affirmative	subject + (6) ________ *be* + past participle	The winner will be chosen this evening.
Negative	subject + (7) ________ *be* + past participle	The winner won't be given a lot of money.
Question form	*Will* + subject + (8) ________ + past participle *Where/When* + *will* + subject + *be* + past participle	Will the winner be interviewed on television tomorrow? When will the winner be interviewed?

2 a Read examples 1–3. Then answer questions a–c.

1 The train was delayed.
2 More than $1 billion is spent on processed foods each year in the USA.
3 The bank on Denver Street was robbed last night.

a Do we know who did the actions? ________
b Is the action or the person (or people) who did the action more important? ________
c Is the person (or people) who did the action very obvious? ________

b Choose the correct option to complete the uses. Use your answers to Exercise 2a to help you.

We use the passive when …
1 we ***know*** / ***don't know*** who or what did the action.
2 the person who did the action is ***more important*** / ***not as important as*** the action.
3 the person, people, or thing who did the action is ***very obvious*** / ***not very obvious***.

3 Decide if these sentences are active (*A*) or passive (*P*).

1 This email was sent on September 4th. ____
2 We weren't told about the schedule changes. ____
3 Jasmine likes traveling overseas. ____
4 The meal will be cooked by a famous chef. ____
5 The tickets won't arrive before Friday. ____
6 This jewelry is made by artists in Morocco. ____
7 My sister made her own wedding dress! ____
8 Who directed the movie? ____

4 Underline the passive forms in the text.

What a fantastic day! After the Hollywood Boulevard trip we were taken to a new art exhibition at the Getty Center. It was opened by a famous movie star last week, and the theme is color. A lot of famous paintings in the world were brought together by the curators of the gallery. It's magical. The colors are fantastic. When you come next month, I want you to visit it! The exhibition guide is written in five languages, so you won't have any problems! One painting was damaged during its trip here, but it will be repaired by the time you get here. A week after your visit all the paintings will be sent back to their owners in different countries, so we're lucky to see them. The center is beautiful, too. It was built in 1954, and it's known for its parks and panoramic views of Los Angeles.

5 Complete the table with the passive forms you underlined in Exercise 4.

Present passive	Simple past passive	Future passive

6 › Put the words in order to complete the passive sentences.

1 thrown / is / these / away / days / .
Too much food ______
2 is / bought / in / supermarkets / .
Most food ______
3 delivered / was / one / after / I / ordered / hour / it / .
The pizza ______
4 will / in / be / people's / grown / gardens / .
In the future, more vegetables ______
5 were / by / We / told / the manager
______ that the restaurant was closing.
6 are / small / by / companies / made / .
Some of the best products ______

7 › Choose the correct options to complete the text.

A famous sushi restaurant in London (1) ***was made*** / ***made*** history today when their new flying tray service (2) ***was launched*** / ***launched***. That's right! When you order one of its famous sushi burgers, it (3) ***isn't delivered*** / ***doesn't deliver*** by a person, but by a flying tray known as the iTray.

The tray, which has propellers like a plane, (4) ***fits*** / ***is fitted*** with a flat top that can carry a plate of food. It (5) ***is controlled*** / ***controls*** by a computer app and (6) ***is traveled*** / ***travels*** up to 15 miles per hour. It (7) ***designed*** / ***was designed*** to create an interesting dining experience for customers, says the company. Right now the iTray is only available in certain branches of the restaurant, but the company hopes it (8) ***will take off*** / ***will be taken off*** – literally – next year!

8 ›› Complete the email with the correct passive form of the verbs in the box.

built deliver give (x2) not cook open serve take

Hey Yadira,

Have you read about the restaurant that delivers your food on a flying tray? It's going to completely change the way that food (1) ______ . I have to say I'm not sure about it. I prefer it when food (2) ______ to your table by a real person. My mom says that when she was a child, you were lucky if you (3) ______ to a restaurant at all!

Anyway, I had a great birthday. We went to this amazing Korean barbecue restaurant in Los Angeles. Have you been to one? The food (4) ______ in the kitchen – you cook it yourself at the table! You (5) ______ a barbecue grill by the waiter, although sometimes the barbecue (6) ______ into the table, and then you (7) ______ a plate of raw meat and you put it on the barbecue. It's so cool! Apparently, a new Korean barbecue restaurant (8) ______ by a famous Korean chef next year. We should definitely go when I visit.

Selma

9 ››› Rewrite the active sentences in the passive.

1 People first made this delicious sauce in Vietnam.
This delicious sauce was first made in Vietnam.
2 Then David Tran, an immigrant, produced the sauce in Los Angeles in the 1980s.
______
3 He mixed it in buckets at home and drove it to customers in his van.
______
4 He named the hot sauce Sriracha.
______
5 Today, people of all nationalities in the USA love the sauce.
______
6 Famous chefs and chain restaurants use the sauce for many meals.
______
7 David Tran's company sells more than $60 million of Sriracha each year.
______
8 David won't share the sauce's recipe with anyone.
______

Follow a conversation

1 Complete the tips with the correct phrases in the box.

REMEMBER HOW TO ...

follow a conversation

an important point contrasting information examples

- *Basically, ...* and *The thing is, ...* introduce (1) ________ .
- *For example, ...* and *For instance, ...* introduce (2) ________ .
- *Although, Even though,* and *However* add (3) ________ .

2 a Complete the sentences with a correct phrase from the box. Check capitalization!

although basically even though for example the thing is

1 ________ I don't usually like wearing yellow, this jacket looks good on me.
2 There are times when I don't really want to go out. ________ , when I've had a long day at school.
3 I couldn't download the music I wanted. ________ , I need a special program and we don't have it.
4 Tom's waiting outside for me ________ I told him to meet me in the classroom.
5 It isn't hard to check your messages on a cell phone. ________ , you need to go to voicemail and it's all there.

b ▶95 Listen and check your answers. What other phrase could you use in each sentence?

c Complete these sentences with your own ideas.

1 I like ball games. For instance, I sometimes play ....
2 Even though my grandmother lives far away, ...
3 I don't know if I can go on vacation this year. The thing is ....

3 ▶96 Listen to the radio interview. What is the main topic of the interview?

a an unusual problem
b interesting colors
c a scientific experiment

4 a ▶96 Listen again and decide if these statements are correct (*C*) or incorrect (*I*).

1 Everyone agrees that Stella has a problem. ____
2 Synesthesia is an easy problem to understand. ____
3 An example of synesthesia is seeing colors when you hear different words. ____
4 When people with synesthesia hear music, they see one particular color. ____
5 For some people, seeing colors all the time can be hard. ____
6 The interviewer thinks she might have synesthesia. ____

b Do words or sounds have colors for you?

____

____

5 a Complete the text using words or phrases from the *Remember how to* box.

(1) ________ most people today think of pink for girls and blue for boys, you might be surprised to learn that this is a fairly new idea. Sure, it would be really weird to see a three-year-old boy dressed in bright pink today. (2) ________ , in Victorian times, that wouldn't have been so strange at all! Back then, (3) ________ , parents dressed their children in colors like pinks, blues, and whites. (4) ________ it sounds strange now, boys in Victorian times wore dresses too – just like the girls! (5) ________ things have changed a lot since then.

b ▶97 Now listen and check your answers.

VOCABULARY 2

Color idioms

1 Write the correct colors to complete the phrases.

1 once in a ______ moon
2 see ______
3 get the ______ light
4 as ______ as night
5 out of the ______
6 tell a ______ lie
7 as ______ as a sheet
8 be in the ______
9 ______ and ______
10 feel ______

2 Match the comments (1–10) to the idioms (a–j).

1 "I couldn't see anything in the cave." ___
2 "My cousin and I went for ice cream, but she spent the whole time texting her friends." ___
3 "I have spent WAY too much money on clothes this month." ___
4 "I never get good grades on tests. Well – very rarely." ___
5 "It isn't clear who caused the accident." ___
6 "Great news! The teacher says we're allowed to organize an end-of-year celebration." ___
7 "All my friends are going to the concert, but I can't go. I feel SO depressed." ___
8 "My best friend just told me she's moving to a new school. I didn't know, so it was a total shock." ___
9 "Maybe I didn't tell the complete truth when I said I liked your haircut. I just didn't want to upset you." ___
10 "I felt very scared." ___

a It happens once in a blue moon.
b I saw red.
c It isn't black and white.
d We have the green light.
e It came out of the blue.
f I'm in the red.
g I told a white lie.
h I'm feeling blue.
i I turned as white as a sheet.
j It was as black as night.

3 Find an idiom from Exercise 2 (a–j) to match each picture (A–E).

A

B

C

D

E

WORDS & BEYOND

4 Complete the text with the words in the box.

ban complaints pale pharmacist potato chips tongues

I read a really strange story in the newspaper this week. People were eating bags of Smokey Blue (1) ______ and getting sick. Their skin color got (2) ______ and their (3) ______ were turning green. There were a lot of (4) ______ emailed to the company that makes Smokey Blue. A lot of people said there should be a (5) ______ on selling them. My friend, who works as a (6) ______, said a lot of people were going to the drugstore to get medicine.

GRAMMAR 2 *(In order) to ... , so that ...*

Talk about the purpose of doing things

1 Complete the grammar table with the correct option.

Action	Linking words	Reason
I'm saving up a lot of money	in order to	(1) buy a skateboard / I can buy a skateboard.
I'm saving up a lot of money	so that	(2) buy a skateboard / I can buy a skateboard.
I learned to play the drums	to	(3) play in a band / I could play in a band.
I learned to play the drums	so	(4) play in a band / I could play in a band.

2 Choose the correct option to complete the sentences.

1 I listen to music ***to*** / ***so that*** relax when I'm stressed.
2 The painter Van Gogh went to the south of France ***in order*** / ***so that*** he could paint beautifully bright pictures of the countryside.
3 I often speak to my old friends online ***so that*** / ***in order to*** we don't lose touch.
4 The city organized a concert ***in order to*** /***so that*** celebrate the musician's music.
5 Athletes follow a strict diet ***in order to*** /***so that*** maximize their energy levels.
6 I had a big breakfast this morning ***in order to*** / ***so that*** I didn't feel hungry during my history test.

3 Match sentence parts.

1 Jack took a summer job ____
2 Some guests made reservations early ____
3 Mom always has coffee in the morning ____
4 Dad is going to leave home later today ____
5 We'll be sent directions ____
6 I'm setting my alarm clock tonight ____

a so that I don't oversleep.
b in order to get the best room in the hotel.
c so that he could earn some money.
d so that we know the best route.
e to wake up quickly.
f to avoid the traffic.

4 Complete the article with (*in order*) *to* or *so that*. You will need to use each phrase more than once.

Australian Jessica Watson had a very different childhood from most other children. When she was a child, her family decided to live on a boat for five years. (1) ____ become well educated, she and her brothers and sisters were taught by their mother.

From the age of 12, Jessica wanted to sail around the world by herself. (2) ____ do this, no one would be able to help her on the trip, except by radio. Surprisingly, her parents supported her, and when she was 16, they started to help her prepare. (3) ____ she could get experience, she worked on other boats.

She set off from Sydney on October 18, 2009. Her boat, *Ella's Pink Lady*, was able to sail itself, (4) ____ Jessica could sleep at night. (5) ____ keep the boat in good condition, she had to do all the repairs herself. Jessica expected the trip to take eight months and to travel 23,000 miles.

(6) ____ it could be recognized as an official round-the-world voyage, she had to cross the equator and travel 21,600 miles.

Jessica arrived back in Australia seven months later. When she arrived, her parents were waiting for her in the harbor (7) ____ they could welcome her home. Her voyage was not recognized as an official record, but it was still an amazing thing to do.

5 Rewrite the sentences using the words in parentheses.

1 We met at the café to have a good talk. (**so that**)
____.
2 I organized a party so that we could celebrate Javier's birthday. (**in order to**)
____.
3 I studied hard so that I would do well on the test. (**in order to**)
____.
4 We took one small piece of luggage in order to check in more quickly. (**so that**)
____.
5 I'm taking an online English course so that I can improve my listening and grammar skills. (**to**)
____.

Ask for help with words at the pharmacy

1 Put the words in order to make phrases you can use to ask for help when you don't understand something in English.

1 in / sure / say / how / not / it / I'm / English / to / .

2 that / mean / Does / ... ?

3 something / I / for / need / ...

4 thing / right / this / the / Is / for / ... ?

5 it's / called / know / what / don't / I / .

6 difference / the / What's / between / ... ?

7 understand / means / what / don't / this / I / .

8 that / need / I / of / some / ...

9 for / It's / ...

2 Complete the table with the phrases from Exercise 1.

Explaining what you need	Asking for help

3 98 Complete the excerpts with words from some of the phrases from Exercise 1. Then listen and check your answers.

1

A: Good morning. I (1) ________ for my skin. I sat in the sun too long. I'm not sure (2) ________ in English.

B: You mean you got sunburned?

A: Yes. (3) ________ my problem? I don't know (4) ________ .

B: That's sunscreen. It protects you from the sun. You need this one if you're already sunburned.

A: Thank you very much for your help.

2

A: Hello. I want to buy some insect repellent. (5) ________ between this one and this one?

B: This one is a liquid that you put on your skin, but this one's a spray.

A: It says "For external use only." I don't understand (6) ________ . My English isn't very good.

B: It means you can put it on your skin, but you can't eat it.

A: (7) ________ your skin?

B: That's right.

A: OK, I'll take the spray.

4 99 Number the sentences in order to make a conversation. Then listen and check your answers.

A: Good morning. What can I get you? ☐
B: Here, please. ☐
A: Is that for here or to go? ☐
B: Yes, please, a chocolate one. And some eggs for breakfast, please. What's the difference between sunny-side up and eggs over easy? ☐
A: You mean cookies? ☐
B: OK, thank you. Then I'd like the eggs over easy, please. ☐
A: Sunny-side up means the eggs are cooked only on one side. Eggs over easy are cooked on both sides. ☐
B: I'm sorry, I don't understand what that means. ☐
A: Do you want to eat and drink here in the café or take it with you? ☐
B: I'd like a cup of coffee and one of those ... I'm not sure how to say it in English. ☐

5 a PRONOUNCE Circle the consonant combinations in each word in the box. Then complete the table with the words.

attend fact ~~grass~~ help pink
school ~~sound~~ speak street throat

Beginning of word	End of word
*gr*ass	*sound*

b 100 Listen to each group of words and repeat them.

6 What do you do when you don't understand a word or some information in English?

WRITING

Link similar ideas

1 Complete the tips with the words in the box.

REMEMBER HOW TO ...

link similar ideas

after and as well end true

- Use (1) __________ to join two parts of a sentence.
- Use *also*, *too*, and (2) __________ to add another fact.
- Use *also* (3) __________ *be* and *can*, but before other verbs.
- Use *too* and *as well* at the (4) __________ of a sentence.
- Use *not only* + *but also* to say that two things are (5) __________ .

2 Choose the correct option to complete the sentences.

1 My friend's house has a big yard with a tennis court ***also*** / ***and*** a swimming pool!
2 She not only has two dogs, but she ***also*** / ***too*** has two horses.
3 She has a big bedroom with two beds. She has her own bathroom ***also*** / ***too***.
4 She lives there not only with her parents and brother but ***as well*** / ***also*** with her grandparents.
5 From her bedroom window she can see the forest. She can ***as well*** / ***also*** see a river.
6 Her parents have an apartment in England. They have another small house in France ***and*** / ***as well***.

3 Read about different kinds of vacations. Join the sentences using the words in parentheses.

1 We always go camping. I love sitting outside listening to the birds singing. (**and**)
We always go camping, and I love sitting outside listening to the birds singing.

2 I like to go sightseeing. I like to visit the places that local people go to. (**not only ... but also**)
____

3 We usually go the park. We go to see our relatives in the city. (**as well**)
____

4 My cousins always come on vacation with us. My aunt and uncle sometimes come with us. (**too**)
____

5 My friends and I rent a small house in the mountains. We go walking every day in the fresh air. (**and**)
____

6 I stay at home for my vacation. I do nothing for a week. It's so relaxing! (**not only ... but also**)
____

4 Read about someone's favorite kind of vacation and complete the sentences with the correct linking words.

MY FAVORITE KIND OF VACATION

HOME FORUMS REGISTER LOG IN

A
I think everyone has a favorite kind of vacation, and it depends on what they like to do. For me, my favorite kind of vacation is one where I can get away from everybody (1) __________ totally relax.

B
I usually go to this small place in the mountains and rent a small house. (2) __________ does it have no phone, but it (3) __________ has no phone signal, so I can't use my cell phone. I love it because I can be by myself and I don't need to talk to anyone. I can go walking, and I can (4) __________ go swimming in a small lake nearby.

C
This kind of vacation makes me feel calm and relaxed, and it makes me feel less stressed (5) __________ . Not having to talk to anyone for a week is great.

D
I love this kind of vacation because I always connect with nature again and come home with more energy (6) __________ . For me, that is exactly what vacations are for!

5 Match the headings (1–4) to the paragraphs (A–D) in Exercise 4.

1 How it makes me feel ____
2 Why I love this kind of vacation ____
3 My favorite kind of vacation ____
4 Where I go and what I do ____

6 **You're going to write about your favorite kind of vacation. Use the *Writing plan* to help you prepare.**

WRITING PLAN

1 **Describe the kind of vacation you like** ☐
Do you like a city or country vacation? Do you like an active or a relaxing vacation? Where do you like to go?

2 **List where you go and what you do** ☐
What things do you do while on vacation? What places do you like to visit? Who do you go with?

3 **Give examples of how you feel** ☐
How do you feel while on vacation? How do you feel when you return?

4 **Explain why you like this vacation** ☐

5 **Connect your ideas with linking words** ☐

WRITE AND CHECK

7 **Write about your favorite kind of vacation. Check (✓) the stages in the *Writing plan*.**

Recognize nonverbal communication

1 **Read the conversation between Gina and Kara. Where was Gina? Who was she talking to?**

Gina: Hey, Kara – you know, Mendi, the new international student?
Kara: Yes, I met her last week at the basketball game. She was so interesting. I love meeting people from other countries.
Gina: But don't you think she's a little strange?
Kara: No, why do you say that? What's strange about her?
Gina: Well, I was talking to her the other day, and she had her arms folded the whole time. I don't know why that made me a little uncomfortable, but it did.
Kara: Maybe she was cold. Was that the only thing you thought was strange?
Gina: I found myself backing away because she was standing so close to me. Every time I took a step back, she took a step forward.
Kara: Well, maybe people in her country are used to crowds, so they stand closer together than we do. Don't you remember when we talked about personal space in class and how it's different for everyone?
Gina: Oh, yeah. I didn't even think of that. The other thing she did was to keep her eyes down. She never once looked at me. I thought she was just really shy, but maybe it's a cultural difference.
Kara: I'm sure that's what it was.

2 **Check (✓) the body language that Mendi showed.**

1 She touched things a lot while she was talking. ☐
2 She stood close to Gina. ☐
3 She had her arms folded. ☐
4 She kept her eyes down while they were talking. ☐
5 She moved her head to one side while they were talking. ☐
6 She mirrored Gina's body language. ☐

3 **What advice would you give Mendi about her nonverbal communication?**

....
....
....
....
....

1 Write the words in the box in the correct column in the table.

back blond eyes face good-looking hair hearing knee nose shoulder small smell sound straight tall touch watch wavy

Parts of the body	Appearance	Sense verbs

2 Complete the idioms and phrases.

1 as white as a ______
2 talk behind somebody's ______
3 once in a ______ moon
4 give somebody a ______ time
5 as black as ______
6 have something in ______

3 Complete the adjectives. Then use them to finish the sentences.

1 _ e _ s _ _ i _ e — Des isn't very ______. He probably won't care you if you are upset.
2 c _ m p _ t _ t _ v _ — Harry is a ______ person and doesn't like to lose or be second.
3 _ m b _ t _ _ _ s — My friends aren't very ______ and don't really care what job they get in the future.
4 f _ r _ _ _ s — My dad was ______ when I borrowed his car without permission.
5 b l _ n d — My friend is ______ and has a special dog that leads him around safely.
6 h _ m _ s _ c k — I always get ______ when I'm away from my family for a while.
7 _ n _ r m _ _ s — My uncle brought us a(n) ______ box of chocolates.
8 v _ l _ _ b l _ — This ring isn't very ______, but I really love it.

4 Read the clues and complete the crossword.

1 Very surprised in a negative way.
2 The name given to an older or retired person after middle age.
3 This is another word for "totally" or "incredibly."
4 This is a cream for brushing your teeth.
5 This is a long thin metal instrument that you play by blowing into.
6 This is someone in your family, such as your cousin or aunt.
7 If you can't see something, it's ______.
8 This is a place where you might go to see a concert or festival, for example.
9 This is an informal word for "things."
10 Secret word: ______

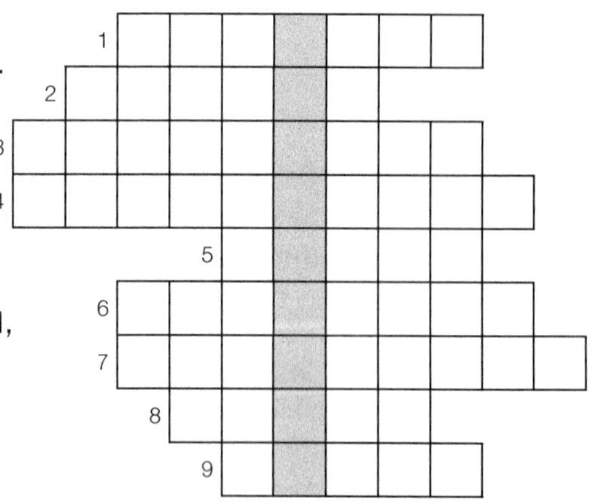

ALL ABOUT ME

1 **Which is your strongest sense?** ______
2 **What part of the body do you use to play your favorite sport?** ______
3 **When did you last tell a white lie?** ______

1 Complete the text with the correct passive or active form of the verb in parentheses.

Smoothies are not a new creation. They (1) ______ (invent) in the 1970s and (2) ______ (make) using a mix of fresh fruit, ice, and sometimes other things like yogurt. Many people (3) ______ (drink) them when they first came out, and today they (4) ______ (be) as popular as ever. People (5) ______ (think) they're a healthy choice, but it (6) ______ (claim) by health scientists that they're not actually that healthy, mainly because they can be very high in sugar. No one knows if they (7) ______ (continue) to be popular and if many (8) ______ (sell) in the future.

2 Rewrite the parts of the sentences in italics using the word given.

1 I watched the documentary *because I wanted to learn* more about memory.
so
______

2 Sam gets better grades than his brother because he *does a lot of hard work*.
harder
______

3 I took an extra English class this semester *because I want* to communicate with people during my trip to the USA.
order
______

4 Janice is a *louder talker* than anyone I know!
loudly
______

3 Put the words in order to make sentences.

1 with / more / can / glasses / see / clearly / I / new / these / .
______

2 I / to / go / the / new / pizza / was / wanted / place, / closed / but / it / .
______

3 spare / Sam / streaming / enjoys / time / music / new / in / his / .
______

4 in / must / class / more / You / carefully / listen / .
______

5 I / books / was / to / because / start / writing / of / my / love / of / inspired / .
______

6 anyone / Ben / family / than / Spanish / our / better / in / speaks / .
______

4 Match the sentence beginnings (1–6) with the endings (a–f).

1 If I played the guitar better,	___	a he'll be very upset.
2 It would surprise me	___	b I would be in the band.
3 I wouldn't stay in the USA for more than a week	___	c unless my friend comes over.
4 I'll finish the project tonight	___	d if Kenny failed the audition.
5 If Nick doesn't win the talent show,	___	e I'll watch it again next week.
6 If I like the TV show,	___	f unless I had a lot of money.

5 Complete the second sentence so it means the same as the first. Use the word given. You should write between two and five words.

1 She probably won't come to the party next week. **not likely**
She's *not likely to* come to the party next week.

2 We hope to go on vacation to Bermuda this summer, but we're not sure yet. **plan**
We ______ to Bermuda this summer.

3 I really want to take some dancing lessons. **like**
I ______ learn to dance.

4 You didn't remember to send Pablo a card for his birthday. **forget**
You ______ Pablo a birthday card.

5 There are worse players than Jennifer on the team. **better**
Jennifer's ______ some of the players on the team.

6 Unless you agree to come, I'm not going either. **If**
______ come, I'll go too.

BEFORE YOU READ

Cowardly Lion

Scarecrow

Tin Man

Wicked Witch

1 a How much do you remember? Choose the correct word to complete the sentences.

1 Dorothy ***was*** / ***wasn't*** sleeping when the Wicked Witch first saw her.
2 The witch thought Dorothy and her three friends ***would*** / ***would not*** make good slaves.
3 The Scarecrow and the Tin Man ***saw*** / ***didn't see*** the wolves coming.
4 The Tin Man swung his ***axe*** / ***hammer*** when the wolf ran up to him.
5 There were ***14*** / ***40*** wolves.
6 The Wicked Witch was very ***afraid*** / ***angry*** when she saw Dorothy and her friends.

b What other things do you remember? Complete the sentences about each character below.

1 The Wicked Witch of the West ....
2 The wolves ....
3 The Tin Man ....
4 Dorothy ....

WHILE YOU READ

2 Read the excerpt from *The Wizard of Oz* and check your answers to Exercise 1. Did you forget any important information?

The Wicked Witch of the West had only one eye, but she could see everything. She saw Dorothy first. The girl was fast asleep with her friends all around her. The Wicked Witch was very angry, and she blew on her silver whistle. Almost at once, a pack of wolves ran toward her. The animals had long legs, red eyes, and sharp teeth.

"Go and tear those strangers to pieces!" the Wicked Witch told the Leader of the wolves.

"Don't you want to use them for slaves?" the Leader of the wolves asked.

"No, they are no use to me," the Wicked Witch replied. "One is made of tin and one of straw. The girl and the lion won't be able to work for me. Tear them to pieces."

"We will!" the Leader said and the wolves all ran toward the strangers.

The Scarecrow and the Tin Man saw the wolves coming.

"Leave this to me," the Tin Man said, and he raised his axe. As the Leader ran up, the Tin Man swung his axe. The wolf's head was cut from its body.

There were forty wolves. The Tin Man raised his axe forty times. Forty heads were cut off, and all the wolves were dead. Then the Tin Man sat down and smiled.

"That was a good fight," he said to the Scarecrow.

When Dorothy woke up in the morning, she saw the wolves' heads and bodies all around her. At first, she was afraid, but then the Tin Man told the girl everything.

"Thank you for saving my life," she replied. Then she hugged him.

3 Look at the story again and find the things the characters *think*, *feel*, and *know*.

1 How did Dorothy feel when she saw the heads and bodies of the dead wolves all around her? ....

2 At first the crows were afraid of the Scarecrow. What did they think he was? ....

3 What did the Tin Man feel when the bees stung him? ....

4 How did the Wicked Witch feel every time she learned the strangers were not dead? ....

5 What did the Wicked Witch think the Winkies would do with the spears? ....

6 What two things did the Scarecrow know about bee stings that helped him save everyone?

....

AFTER YOU READ

4 Match the words in the box to the definitions.

axe (line 21) hugged (line 33) pack (line 5)
strangers (line 8) straw (line 13) whistle (line 5)

1 a thing that makes a high sound when you blow into it ....
2 a group of dogs or wolves ....
3 dried stalks/pieces of grass ....
4 people you do not know ....
5 a tool for chopping wood ....
6 put your arms around another person ....

5 a ▶101 Listen to Alan and Sofia talking about *The Wizard of Oz*. Complete the sentences with the correct name(s) and the verb in parentheses.

1 .... (like) the action in the story.
2 .... (think) the Scarecrow had a smart idea.
3 .... (can) imagine feeling the straw on her skin.
4 .... (not want) to think about the wolves' teeth.
5 .... (wonder) how they will protect themselves from the Witch's magic.
6 .... (want) to read the next chapter.

b Do you agree with Alan and Sofia? Write sentences.

I like the start of the story.

....

....

6 Complete the *Reading report*.

Book title	
Genre	Author
Summary (max 200 words)	
Verdict (What you like and don't like about the extract. Think about the characters and the story.)	
Did you find the extract easy (0) or difficult (5) to read?	0 1 2 3 4 5
Would you like to read the rest of the book? no (0) yes (5)	0 1 2 3 4 5
Would you recommend the book to a friend? no (0) yes (5)	0 1 2 3 4 5

EXTEND

7 Do one of the tasks.

Task A
Dorothy kept a journal about her trip through Oz. Write the journal entry describing the day the bees attacked. Describe the Scarecrow's plan and how they did it. Describe what she smelled, heard, and felt while she was under the straw.

Task B
The Cowardly Lion was always afraid. Write a description of the attack that the Cowardly Lion thought was the scariest. Describe in detail what the Lion saw and heard during the scariest attack.

EXTRA READING *The Call of the Wild*

BEFORE YOU READ

1 How much do you remember? Decide if these sentences are correct (*C*) or incorrect (*I*).

1 The Americans loaded their sled very efficiently. ____
2 Hal promised his sister he would be good to the dogs. ____
3 Hal had no experience driving a sled. ____
4 The dogs stopped when the sled fell over. ____
5 To make the load lighter, Mercedes took things they needed out of the sled. ____
6 The new dogs had experience pulling sleds. ____

WHILE YOU READ

2 Read the excerpt from *The Call of the Wild* and check your answers to Exercise 1. Then correct the sentences that are incorrect.

When Buck arrived with the other dogs at the Americans' camp, he could see at once that these people were not well organized. The tent was badly put up, the plates were unwashed, and there were things lying everywhere. As well as Charles and Hal, there was also a young woman. Her name was Mercedes and she was Charles's wife and Hal's sister.

Buck watched these people, feeling worried, as they took down the tent and put their things on the sled. They worked slowly, but not sensibly or carefully. When the men put a big bag at the front of the sled, Mercedes told them to put it at the back. Then, after they had moved it and put other things on top, she said that she needed it again.

Three men from another tent came out to watch, smiling at each other and laughing.

"Do you think it will move?" one of the men asked.

"Why wouldn't it?" said Charles, annoyed.

"I was just asking," the man said quickly. "You have a big load there. It looks very heavy."

Charles turned his back and got the sled ready, then Hal took out his whip. "Mush!" he called to the dogs. "Let's go!"

The dogs pushed against the harness for a few moments, then stopped. They couldn't move the sled.

"Lazy animals! I'll teach them," shouted Hal, getting ready to hit them with his whip.

"No, Hal, don't!" cried Mercedes, pulling the whip from him. "Poor darlings! You must promise you'll be good to them, or I won't come."

"You know nothing about dogs," said her brother. "You have to whip them to make them work. You ask anyone. Ask one of those men." Mercedes looked up at the men, who were still watching.

"They're weak as water, if you want to know," said one of the men. "They need a rest."

"Rest! Huh!" said Hal, and his whip fell on the dogs. They pushed against the harness with all their strength, but they couldn't move the sled.

"I don't care what happens to you," said the man. "But to help those poor dogs, I'll tell you that you should break out that sled. It's frozen in the snow, and you need to push it out."

Hal did what the man said, and this time Buck and his team were able to pull the sled forward. They moved ahead, trying as hard as they could with the whip coming down on them. But they hadn't gone far when the road turned and went around a bend into Skagway's main street. With such a heavy load, it would be difficult even for an experienced driver, but Hal was new to driving dogs. The sled fell over, and half the things came off it. The dogs didn't stop. Buck was angry because of the heavy load and the whipping, and he started to run, with the rest of the team following.

"Stop! Stop!" cried Hal, but he fell over and the half-empty sled went over him. People stopped to watch and laugh as the dogs ran on through the town. Things went flying from the sled and lay all over Skagway's main street.

Some kind people caught the dogs, picked everything up, and explained a few things to the Americans. They needed a small load and more dogs, they were told. Charles and Hal listened unhappily, and then began to take things off of the sled. Mercedes cried when things were taken out of her clothes bags and thrown away. She cried about everything and said she wouldn't go with them. Then, at last, she stopped crying and began to throw away all their things, even those things that they really needed.

That evening, Charles and Hal went out and bought six new Outside dogs – dogs that were not from the Northland. Together with Buck and his old team, and Teek and Koona, the two huskies that had been bought on a previous trip, Charles and Hal now had fourteen dogs. But the Outside dogs knew nothing, and they didn't like the harness or the trail, and the old dogs were exhausted. Only the two men were happy – and proud too – because they had never seen another sled with fourteen dogs.

3 Read the story again and then answer the questions. Give reasons for your answers.

1 Why is Buck worried about the new people? What did he see at the camp?

2 What did Hal do to show he was not an experienced driver?

3 With the six new dogs, would the load in the sled have to be heavier or lighter? Why?

AFTER YOU READ

4 What or who do the underlined words refer to?

1 <u>She</u> was Charles' wife and Hal's sister. ....
2 <u>They</u> worked slowly, but not sensibly or carefully. ....
3 Mercedes told <u>them</u> to put <u>it</u> at the back. ....
4 "You must promise you will be good to <u>them</u>, or I won't come." ....
5 "Do you think <u>it</u> will move?" one of the men asked. ....
6 "<u>They're</u> weak as water, if you want to know," said one of them. "<u>They</u> need a rest." ....
7 <u>They</u> needed a small load and more dogs, <u>they</u> were told. ....

5 (▶102) Listen to Alan and Sofia talking about *The Call of the Wild*. Who likes the book more? ....

6 a Match the sentence parts. Then write the name of the person speaking (*Alan* or *Sofia*).

....	1 I liked it because	a are about places I've never been to.
....	2 The story still	b to know what happens next.
....	3 I could	c feels relevant.
....	4 I like stories that	d to get into the story.
....	5 I need more time	e it's an adventure story.
....	6 I want	f identify with all the characters.

b Which of the sentences do you agree with? ....

7 Complete the *Reading report*.

Book title	
Genre	Author
Summary (max 200 words)	
Verdict (What you like and don't like about the extract. Think about the characters and the story.)	
Did you find the extract easy (0) or difficult (5) to read?	0 1 2 3 4 5
Would you like to read the rest of the book? no (0) yes (5)	0 1 2 3 4 5
Would you recommend the book to a friend? no (0) yes (5)	0 1 2 3 4 5

EXTEND

8 Do one of the tasks.

Task A

Write about one day in the life of a service dog (a dog that assists a person with a disability). What kinds of jobs does the dog do? What does the dog like and dislike about his life? How do the dog's master and the other people he might meet while accompanying his master treat the dog?

Task B

Rewrite part of the story from the point of view of Buck. Start your story when Hal took out his whip and said, "Mush. Let's go." Finish the story when the sled falls over and Buck and the other dogs run away. Have Buck tell what is happening and how he feels about everything.

"I felt the whip sting my back as soon as he said, 'Mush. Let's go.'" …

Macmillan Education
4 Crinan Street
London N1 9XW
A division of Springer Nature Limited

Companies and representatives throughout the world

ISBN 978-1-380-00772-8

Go Beyond First published 2015
First edition entitled *Beyond* published 2014

Designed by EMC Design Ltd.
Illustrated by Cyrus Deboo pp. 35, 48; Sally Elford pp. 4 (banner), 24–25 (banner), 26 (banner), 36 (banner), 48 (banner), 58 (banner); Bob Lea pp. 14–15 (main), 58–59 (main); Chris Pavely pp. 22, 23, 32, 40, 41, 45, 50, 51; Zara Picken pp. 14 (bottom left), 18.

Cover design by EMC Design Ltd.
Cover photograph by Getty Images/Lonely Planet Images/Ariadne Van Zandbergen
Picture research by Tessa Hammond and Susannah Jayes

The authors would like to thank all the team at Macmillan for everything they have done to make *Move Beyond* possible. We would like to thank Studio8 Ltd. and John Marshall Media, Inc. for their creative work on the videos, and the actors who bring the material to life. We would also like to thank John Marshall Media, Inc. for the production of the audio material. We would also like to thank all the teachers and other individuals who have contributed to the course whose names appear on this page. Finally, we'd like thank our friends and families for all their support.

The authors and publishers would like to express thanks to all those who contributed to the development and formation of *Go Beyond*. In particular, we would like to thank the following teachers, contacts, and reviewers: Cristina Moisén Antón, Argelia Solis Arriaga, Krzysztof Bartold, Paweł Bienert, Agnieszka Bojanowska, Samuel Gómez Borobia, Ma. Eugenia Fernandez Castro, Jolanta Chojnacka, Elsa Georgina Cruz, Dominika Dąbrowska, Barbara Dawidowska, Galina Dragunova, Monika Drygiel-Kobylińska, Mauricio Duran, Natalia Evdokimenko, Maria Teresa Velazquez Evers, Marciana Loma-Osorio Fontecha, Monika Fromiczew-Drożdzińska, Patricia Garcia, Axel Morales Garcia, Miguel Angel Rodriguez Garcia, Aleksandra Gilewska, Joanna Góra, Ewa Górka, Agata Helwich, Bethsabe Ruiz Herrera, Robert Jadachowski, Patricia Guzman Luis Juan, Anna Kacpura, Ruth Kanter, Regina Kaźmierczuk, Katarzyna Konisiewicz, Maria Koprowska, Bogusława Krajewska, Aldona Krasoń, Joanna Worobiec Kugaj, Joanna Kuligowska, Tadeusz Kur, Maria Kwiatkowska, Josefina Maitret, Claire Manners, Laura Elena Medina, Carmen García Méndez, Iwona Mikucka, Talhia Miranda, Claudia Rangel Miranda, Armando Nieto, Joanna Nowak, Anna Nowakowska, Ewa Nowicka, Anastasia Parshikova, Paloma Carrasco Peñalba, Ma. Del Carmen Fernandez Perez, Joanna Płatos, Maria Teresa Portillo, Juan Jose Gomez Ramirez, Aida Rivera, Gabriela Rubio, Gabriela Bourge Ruiz, Irina Sakharova, Małgorzata Sałaj, Patricia Avila Sanchez, Jessica Galvan Sanchez, Miguel Angel Santiago, Karol Sęk, Barbara Sibilska, Tatiana Sinyavina, Agnieszka Śliwowska, Vlada Songailene, Ángela Siles Suárez, Beata Świątkowska, Ewelina Szmyd-Patuła, Agnieszka Szymaniak, José Luis Vázquez, Irma Velazquez, Małgorzata Walczak, Dariusz Winiarek, Justyna Zdunek, Zofia Żdżarska, Dominika Zięba, Marzena Zieleniewska, Anna Zielińska-Miszczuk, Robert Zielonka.

The authors and publishers would like to thank the following for permission to reproduce their images:

Alamy/AF archive p. 29(cr), Alamy/Amazon-Images p. 6(cmr), Alamy/John Bradshaw p. 12(b), Alamy/Kevin Britland p. 26(f/top), Alamy/BSIP SA p. 48(e), Alamy/J C Clamp p. 8(c), Alamy/Cultura Creative (RF) p. 43, Alamy/Digifoto Gold p. 61(5), Alamy/Findlay p. 26(d), Alamy/fStop p. 29(tl), Alamy/Ian Hooton/SPL p. 37(3), Alamy/Johner Images p. 30(cml), Alamy/Alexander Kaludov p. 53(tr), Alamy/LAMB p. 31, Alamy/Timothy Large/Life Style p. 20, Alamy/Betty LaRue p. 42, Alamy/Jeff Morgan 02 p. 26(c), Alamy/Vladimir Nenov p. 61(tl), Alamy/ONOKY/Photononstop p. 37(4), Alamy/Radius Images pp. 26(f/bottom), 47, Alamy/Christopher Scott p. 16(bcr), Alamy/Nik Taylor p. 18(tcr), Alamy/Tetra Images p. 38;
Corbis p. 7(tr), Corbis/Beateworks/Pieter Estersohn p. 56, Corbis/Rex Butcher/JAI p. 24, Corbis/Julian Calder p. 26(b), Corbis/Hero Images p. 46(3), Corbis/JLP/Jose L. Pelaez p. 30(cr), Corbis/Rob Lewine/Tetra Images p. 46(1), Corbis/Lawrence Manning p. 7(cl), Corbis/Mika p. 39, Corbis/Ocean pp. 5(6), 48(b), Corbis/Wavebreak Media Ltd. p. 36(2), Corbis/Christoph Wilhelm pp. 36–37 (background);
Getty Images pp. 8(a, d), 27, Getty Images/AFP p. 26(e), Getty Images/Alija p. 60(tr), Getty Images/Doug Armand p. 19, Getty Images/Keith Brofsky p. 18(tr), Getty Images/CSA Plastock p. 12(a), Getty Images/elkor p. 46(4), Getty Images/Mitchell Funk pp. 48–49(a), Getty Images/Gamma-Rapho via Getty Images p. 34, Getty Images/Adam Hester p. 46(2), Getty Images/Juanmonino p. 37(5), Getty Images/KidStock pp. 10, 16(cr), Getty Images/Ron Levine p. 36(7), Getty Images/Erin Patrice O'Brien p. 6(br), Getty Images/Roy Ooms p. 37(6), Getty Images/Jose Luis Pelaez, Inc. p. 30(cmr), Getty Images/Joseph O. Holmes/portfolio.streetnine.com p. 54, Getty Images/Hira Punjabi p. 62(a), Getty Images/Andy Ryan p. 60(cr), Getty Images/Kristian Sekulic p. 60(tmr), Getty Images/STOCK4B-RF pp. 37(1), 46(5), Getty Images/Thinkstock Images p. 48(c), Getty Images/Adrian Weinbrecht p. 30(cl), Getty Images/Steve West p. 48(d);
Glow Images/Mike Kemp p. 49(cl);
ITN Source p. 5 (stills, except for still 6);
Masterfile p. 9;
Photoshot/Xinhua p. 6(tr);
Reuters Picture Library/Carlos Garcia Rawlins p. 28;
Alison Smith p. 49(bcr);
Superstock/ABK/BSIP/BSIP p. 53(tl);
Thinkstock/Digital Vision p. 11, Thinkstock/Hemera pp. 12(c), 61(tr), Thinkstock/Istockphoto pp. 8(b), 17, 49(cr), 52, 61(3, 4, 6), Thinkstock/Jupiterimages pp. 37(8), 61(2), Thinkstock/iStock/MonkeyBusiness Images p. 16(br), Thinkstock/Ryan McVay p. 61(1), Thinkstock/Photodisc pp. 5(2), 21.

Commissioned photographs by Studio8 Ltd. pp. 33, 55

The authors and publishers are grateful for permission to reprint the following copyright material:
Material from article "World's youngest conductor? Boy, 14, to direct Venezuelan orchestra" by Virginia Lopez, first published in the Guardian 05/20/2012, reprinted with permission of the publisher, p. 28;
Material used from article "The Manchester Color Wheel: development of a novel way of identifying color choice and its validation in healthy, anxious and depressed individuals" by Helen Carruthers, Julie Morris, Nicholas Tarrier, and Peter Whorwell, published by BioMed Central 02/09/2010, p. 52.

Printed and bound by CPI Group (UK) Ltd, Croydon CR0 4YY

2021 2020 2019
10 9 8 7 6